# WELSH MILITIA AND VOLUNTEER CORPS
## 1757-1908

# WELSH MILITIA AND VOLUNTEER CORPS 1757-1908

## 2:
## THE GLAMORGAN REGIMENTS OF MILITIA

by
BRYN OWEN

PALACE BOOKS

First impression: May 1990

Hardback ISBN 1 871904 01 3

Typesetting by Stiwdio Mei
Printing by W.O. Jones

Published by
PALACE BOOKS
Caernarfon · Gwynedd · Wales

# PROFILE OF THE AUTHOR

Bryn Owen was educated at Dolgellau Grammar School for Boys, Dolgellau, Merionethshire, in which County he was born in 1928.

On leaving school he entered the Royal Navy on a regular engagement and was in due course promoted from the Lower Deck and commissioned as a Gunnery Officer.

In 1975, after his retirement from the service, he became involved with the Welch Regiment Museum, and in 1978 was appointed its Curator.

Bryn, a regular contributor to military and other journals, lives with his wife and son at Radyr, Cardiff, where most of his spare time is devoted to military research and writing. He is a Fellow of the Museums Association and an adviser on military matters to the Council for Museums in Wales.

# PREVIOUSLY PUBLISHED WORK

Glamorgan — Its Gentlemen and Yeomanry, 1797-1980. Starling Press, Risca, Gwent, 1983.
Welsh Militia and Volunteer Corps, 1757-1908. 1 : Anglesey and Caernarfonshire. Palace Books Ltd., Caernarfon, 1989.
Owen Roscomyl and The Welsh Horse. Palace Books Ltd., 1990.

# FOREWORD BY
# SIR CENNYDD TRAHERNE, KG, TD.

'The Glamorgan Regiments of Militia. 1757-1908', Volume 2 in a series by Bryn Owen on the Welsh Militia and Volunteer Corps, is a most absorbing work on the military history of the County, and makes a great contribution to British and County History.

The Author traces the history of Glamorgan's Constitutional Force from early times through to the setting of a new Militia in 1757 under the direction of the Lord Lieutenant of the County. This duty was successfully carried out by successive Lords Lieutenant until 1871, when the Crown took over those duties, transferring them to the Secretary of State for War.

The Lord Lieutenant's duty was to provide a nucleus of Officers and Non-Commissioned Officers in time of peace, and on orders from the Crown, in time of War or Civil Strife, to cause the Regiments to be embodied, and brought up to the required strength by means of the Ballot, the Substitute or Recruiting by Drum or other persuasion.

By such means were recruited Glamorgan's Militia, both of which received the title 'Royal' for their particular distinction. The Force had the added advantage of coming from a County of greatly increasing population and wealth during the Industrial Revolution of the late eighteenth and the whole of the nineteenth centuries.

The Royal Glamorgan Militia infantry played a great part in the French Wars from 1761 to 1816, protecting Britain from Invasion, and through voluntary enlistment providing additional numbers for the Regular Army. In 1881, the Royal Glamorgan Militia became a Battalion of The Welsh Regiment and saw active service in South Africa during the Boer War. It continued to render service until such duties were largely taken over by the Territorial Force following the implementation of Army Reforms in 1908.

I commend this Volume with its significant collection of Illustrations to Historians, and to all who honour the brave in Peace and In War.

Cennydd Traherne, KG, TD.

Lord Lieutenant of Glamorgan, 1952-1985

# AUTHOR'S NOTE

Although the Royal Glamorgan Light Infantry has been in the past the subject of several short articles, this book will be the first to draw under one cover a fairly comprehensive record of the Regiment's services together with that of the later raised Glamorgan Artillery Militia.

I pay tribute here to Captain A.H.U. Tindal, that gallant Officer of the old Welch Regiment, who during his Adjutancy of the 3rd (Militia) Battalion, The Welsh Regiment, laid the foundations for much of what is offered here.

I dedicate this book to my wife, Marion, in this 40th year of our marriage. Without her co-operation, patience and forbearance over the years, the research and work to produce this Volume and others in the series would not have been possible.

The series is also dedicated to the men and women of Wales who gave unstinting and loyal service to their country during the two great wars of the present century, and this volume in particular to those of them who had their roots in the County of Glamorgan.

Bryn Owen,
Radyr,
Cardiff.
March 1st, 1990

# PREFACE

This Volume is the second of a series which will place under hard cover a record of the services of the Militia Regiments and Volunteer Corps of Wales during the 18th and 19th Centuries and the first decade of the present. It is a record which in spite of its close connection with the Social History of the Principality, has to date been very much neglected.

To be prepared in time of Peace for War, is an eminently suitable precaution, and will continue to be necessary for as long as certain men or political factions seek to impose their will or doctrines upon others by means of the bomb or bullet. Past history has shown to our cost the price of complacency, and such military preparation as were allowed, often in the face of considerable opposition, has ensured for the inhabitants of the British Isles a continuation of the freedoms which we all demand and cherish.

The Welsh contribution to that end, in both War and Peace, has been considerable, and has given the Welsh a military record which is 'second to none'. The pages which follow tell of Glamorgan's contribution, and will be of interest, not only to those keen on military history, but also to that large band of local and family historians as an aid to further research.

# ACKNOWLEDGEMENTS

W.Y. Carman, FSA.
J.V. Davies, Esq.
W. Davies, Esq.
Major A.G. Harfield BEM. F.R. Hist.S.
C. Lewis, Esq.
N. Lichfield, Esq.
R. Westlake, Esq.
The Trustees of The Welch Regiment Museum

and to all other persons too numerous to mention who over many years contributed to the preparation of this work.

# CONTENTS

# LIST OF ILLUSTRATIONS

# CAPTAIN A.H.U. TINDAL,
# THE WELSH REGIMENT

Appointed Second Lieutenant in the Royal Scots, 30th January, 1878, he transferred in June of the same year into the 69th (South Lincolnshire) Regiment which in 1881 became 2nd Battalion, The Welsh Regiment. Promoted Captain, 7th October, 1887, he was for a period Adjutant of that Battalion, but moved on in June 1892 to take up an appointment as Adjutant, 3rd (Militia) Battalion, The Welsh Regiment, formerly the Royal Glamorgan Light Infantry Militia, which duties he combined with those of Recruiting Officer for the Cardiff Depot.

During his service with the Militia Battalion he drew up for the first time a basic Record of Service of the old Royal Glamorgan, which notes form the basis for this much expanded story.

In November 1897, he joined the 1st Battalion, The Welsh Regiment from which in 1898 he was seconded for service with the West African Regiment. He was mortally wounded during the attack on the Boer Laager at Kheis, 28th May, 1900, and was later buried at Prieska.

# CHAPTER 1

# THE MILITIA — AN OUTLINE HISTORY

In England, the origins of Militia can be traced back to the Fyrd of Saxon times — a force, whose members, in addition to their civil occupations, trained in the use of weapons for the purpose of both local and national defence. The Fyrd over years developed into the General Levy, which like its predecessor was based on the obligation of able bodied men to render service within the boundaries of their own districts, and in the event of invasion or rebellion, march to any part of the country to serve as directed.

In Wales, the principles of this system were imposed upon the population gradually, and was part of a long period of pacification.

During the reign of Edward VI, influential persons were appointed in each district to 'array' and lead the levy. These Commissioners of Array, were in respect of Militia, the forerunners of the Lords Lieutenant[1], who up until the late 19th Century controlled and administered the Force in each County.

Possibly the earliest record relating to a form of Militia in the County of Glamorgan is that Return of Manpower known as the Great Muster. Initiated by Act 30, Henry VIII of 1539, it records that Glamorgan had available 1,000 Able-bodied Men, only 29 of which were properly armed and accoutred, and which included 7 horsemen[2]. For later years, reference to the contribution made by the County can be found in the Calender of the Council in the Marches for Wales and in locally preserved documents relating to the activities of the landed gentry. The term 'Trained' or 'Train' Bands was used to describe such bodies of men in the 17th Century, but by the reign of Charles 1, they were also referred to as Militia.

It will be remembered that a dispute as to whether King or Parliament should control the Militia was one of the factors which led to bloody Civil War and the execution of a King. The restoration of his son to the throne in 1660, saw a country that was sick of military rule allow the foundations to be laid for only a small Standing Army, and place control of the Militia firmly in the hands of the nation's landed gentry. In 1684, the Duke of Beaufort in his capacity as Lord President of the Council of Wales made a tour of the Principality for the purpose of making a "general visitation of his commands there". Thomas Dinely, a member of his entourage, recorded his progress, and in same, gives an account of the Militia Regiments, then a mixture of both Horse and Foot, which the Duke inspected.

In Glamorgan he was met by a Troop of Horse and one Regiment of Foot commanded by the Earl of Worcester who was assisted by Lord Arthur Somerset. The smartly turned out force wore purple coats lined with red, red stockings, broad buff belts and white sashes.

In 1757, a Militia Act[1] changed entirely the method of raising men for the force, and the liability to provide them became the responsibility of the Counties and their Parishes as opposed to hitherto specially appointed individuals. The chief powers nonetheless remained firmly in the hands of the Lords Lieutenant, with the Militia still being regarded as a counterbalance to the Standing Army and controlled by Parliament rather than by the Crown. The Act confined the Militia to the Infantry role and did much to improve its organisation and quality. Men of appropriate age and fitness were selected by ballot, a quota being set for each County; but sadly, a 'Substitute'[5] system destroyed any possibility of it being representative of universal National Service, and threw the main responsibility for Home Defence onto the shoulders of that section of the population who had not the means to purchase exemption.

The Militia was embodied for Garrison Duty at home during the Seven Years War, the War of the American Revolution and the French Revolutionary War, but undoubtedly the most important and interesting period in the history of the force generally and of its individual regiments is the period 1803-1816, when in addition to Garrison duties at home, the Militia provided an essential and most valuable reserve of trained manpower for the Regular Army. Thousands of Militiamen volunteered for service with the Regiments of the Line, and it is true to say that Wellington's campaign in the Iberian Peninsula would at times have been difficult to pursue successfully, were it not for the reinforcements provided by the Militia Regiments at home. Glamorgan in that respect put up its fair quota of men. and as such was well represented in most of the great land battles of that period.

"A successful War seems to demoralise a national military spirit, and military inactivity is usually the sequence," — so stated B.E. Sergeant in his History of the Monmouthshire Militia[6], and such was the situation for many years following the final defeat of Napoleon at Waterloo. The Militia slid slowly into obscurity, with the laws which ordered its annual training rescinded and the Ballot which maintained it at strength suspended. Such matters were after 1816 submitted annually to Parliament for decision which resulted in some sporadic Militia training between 1818 and 1825, and then not until the year 1831, when a state of civil unrest in the country demanded a short resuscitation. For the next twenty years or so, all that remained to remind the nation of the existence of Militia was the presence in each County Town of a small Permanent Staff who paraded for Church on Sundays. Officers continued to be appointed, but with weapons returned to Ordnance and with no men to train, the regiments were reduced to nothing more than a few names on paper.

The succession of Louis Napoleon to the Presidency of France, French military posturing and fears concerning Russian ambitions in the Middle East led Government, c.1850 to some serious reappraisal of matters relating to home defence. One outcome was the Militia Act of 1852[7] which directed that the

Militia — hitherto a force raised by compulsory Ballot, be in the future raised entirely by voluntary enlistment. The Militia Ballot remained suspended, but with the proviso that it could be reintroduced if voluntary enlistment failed to produce the required numbers.

Some 80,000 men were to be raised for the Force by 1853, the Recruits enlisting for five years during which period they would in the first instance produce themselves for 21 days training annually. The years of decline for Militia ended, as in every County, the Lieutenancy made arrangements for recruiting and a reintroduction of annual training. From that date through to April 1908, the Militia, unless otherwise ordered, trained annually. Some regiments were embodied for Garrison duty during the Crimean War and also during the Indian Mutiny.

In 1871 there commenced a long series of Army Reforms, the most immediate of which was directed at the Militia. An Act[5] transferred all power and control of the force from the hands of the Lords Lieutenant to the Crown, the Force thereafter being paid and clothed according to Regulations fixed by Royal Warrant in the same way as the Regular Army. The culmination of the same series of reforms took place in 1881, when the Militia, the Infantry Regiments in particular, were drawn closer under the wing of the Regular Army by becoming numbered Battalions of the recently established Territorial Line Infantry Regiments.

During the South African (Boer) War of 1899-1902, most Militia Regiments were embodied for short periods of Garrison Duty at home, whilst a selected number proceeded on active service to the front. Their duties, mainly on the lines of communication were vital to the success of that campaign.

The story of the Militia serving under that ancient title ends in 1908 when a reorganisation of the Land Forces of the Crown saw the Militia cease to be raised in the United Kingdom. The implementation of the Territorial and Reserve Forces Act of 1907[9] at that date resulted in the disbandment of many of the old Militia Battalions, and the conversion of those that remained into units of the Army Special Reserve.

The term 'Militia' in its loosest form was used to describe the Supplementary Reserve until 1953. The last of the old Force by that date had long before slipped quietly into obscurity — a sad and unpublicised demise, as the old Constitutional Force was in more ways than one the tap root of our present day home defence system.

## Footnotes

1. Lieutenants of Counties. First appointed 1549
2. Hay. Colonel Jackson, C.B., C.M.G. The Constitutional Force
3. Dineley, T. The Account of the Progress of His Grace, Henry, 1st Duke of Beaufort, Lord President of the Council in Wales and Warden of the Marches, through Wales in 1684
4. Act 30 Geo II. c.25

5. A system whereby a person selected by Ballot to serve in the Militia, and who did not wish to render personal service, was allowed to provide at his own expense a Substitute, ie., a man willing to serve on his behalf. Alternatively, such men could pay a Fine to the Lieutenancy, which money, in full or part, was used to provide a Cash Bounty to draw in a Substitute to make up the required quota.
6. Sargeaunt, B.E. The Royal Monmouthshire Militia. RUSI, London, 1910
7. Act 15 & 16 Victoria. c.50
8. Act 34 & 35 Victoria. c.86. s6.
9. Act Edward VII. c9. 2 August, 1907

# CHAPTER 2

## 1759-1760.
# The Raising of the Glamorgan Regiment of Militia

With the nation's resources of military manpower strained to the limit due to the demands of the Seven Years War, and with French invasion plans thwarted only by the presence of the Royal Navy in the Channel, the need to rapidly augment the strength of the land forces at home become a matter of great urgency. In consequence, the 5th June, 1759, saw the Lord Lieutenant of Glamorgan receive the following instructions.

"The King, having by a most gracious message acquainted his Parliament with His having repeated intelligence of the actual preparations making in the French ports to invade this Kingdom, and of the imminent danger of such invasion being attempted, to that end that His Majesty may (if he shall think proper) cause the Militia, or such part thereof as shall be necessary, to be drawn out and embodied, and to march as occasion shall require. I am commanded to signify the King's pleasure to your Lordship, that you do forthwith transmit to one of His Majesty's Principal Secretaries of State, for His Majesty's information, an account of what progress has been made in the County of Glamorgan in the Execution of the Act of Parliament passed in the thirtieth and thirtyfirst year of His Majesty's reign for the better ordering of the Militia Forces in the several Counties of that part of Great Britain called England, and also an exact Return of the actual state and condition of the Militia of the said County may be in readiness drawn out and embodied if His Majesty shall think proper, and to march as occasion shall require.

I am, etc., etc.,
Pitt."


In pursuance of the Act and the above directive the Lieutenancy made arrangements to raise the statutory Quota by ballot in the Hundreds and Parishes of the County. The Regiment did not assemble for training until the following year, when it was drawn out in two parts for that purpose at Swansea and Cardiff.

The new Militia assembled on or shortly after the 19th January, 1760. The following Gentlemen were commissioned to serve as Officers:

Lt. Colonel Sir Edmund Thomas of Wenvoe Castle
Captain Herbert Mackworth of Gnoll Castle, Neath
Captain Sir Edward Mansell, Bt.
Captain William Bassett of Miskin
Captain Thomas Price

Captain Thomas Williams of Neath
Captain John Lucas of Reynoldstone
Captain Robert Jones of Fonmon Castle
Lt. Edmund Treherne
Lt. George Williams of Aberpergwm
Lt. John Dawkins
Lt. John Richards of Cardiff
Lt. Edward Thomas of Wenvoe Castle
Lt. John Beavan of Neath
Lt. William Seys
Lt. Edward Saunders of Norton
Ensign William Williams
Ensign Elias Jenkins of Swansea
Ensign Sylvanus Watkins
Ensign Rees Price of Llangynwyd
Ensign John Landeg
Ensign John Williams
Ensign Richard Beavan
Ensign ... Mangle
Ensign Lewis Williams of Llansannon
Adjutant Samuel Sabine (late Sergeant, 1st Foot Guards)

On June 20th, the Earl of Plymouth, Lord Lieutenant, reported to the King his progress: "To the King's Most Excellent Majesty, I, The Rt. Hon. Other Lewis Windsor[1], Earl of Plymouth, your Majesty's Lieutenant for the County of Glamorgan do hereby humbly certify and return to your Majesty that in pursuance of the several Acts of Parliament made and passed in the Thirtieth and Thirtyfirst year of your Majesty's reign, three fifths of the Militiamen of the said County of Glamorgan have been chosen, sworn and inrolled, and that three fifths of the Commission Officers of the Militia Forces raised in and for the said County have been appointed."

The regiment was to consist of 7 Companies — six of 50 men each and one Grenadier Company[2] of 60 Grenadiers.

The following Equipment was ordered and issued: 360 Short Muskets[3], 360 Bayonets, 360 Ramrods, Scabbards and tanned leather Slings, 360 Cartouche Boxes[4], 360 Hangers[5] with Brass Hilts, complete with Scabbards and tanned leather Waistbelts, 72 spare ash Ramrods, 14 iron Wiping Rods with Worms[6], 3½ Barrels of Powder for exercise, 3 Hundredweight of Ball[7], 720 Musket Flints, 14 Musket Formers, 3½ Reams of fine Paper for Cartridges, 14 Leather Powder Bags.

Additionally Sergeants would have been issued with Halberds[8] and Long Hangers, complete with Scabbards and tanned leather Waistbelts, The Drummers with Drums, complete with Carriages and Cases, Small Hangers,

Scabbards and leather Waistbelts, and for the Regiment, a Stand of Colours, One King's and one Regimental complete with Oilskin Cases.

On the 30th September, 1760, the following were appointed. Sergeants: Luke Howell, James Thomas, John Morgan, William Lewis, George Rosser, Edward Morgan, John Powell, Joseph Waine, John Williams, Christopher Thomas, John Owen, Thomas Morris, David Williams, John Charles, David Lewis, John Stouthall, and Andrew Strong.

By early January 1761, the regiment complete assembled in Cardiff to await further orders.

### Footnotes:

1. 4th Earl of Plymouth. Born 1731. Died 1771
2. Regiments of the period were divided into Battalion and Flank Companies, which last were known as Light and Grenadier Companies. Usually, the tallest and boldest men formed the Grenadier Company, whilst the Light Company specialised in skirmishing and marksmanship. The remainder of the Corps were allocated to Battalion Companies.
3. Presumably the Light Infantry pattern Musket with 39″ barrel as opposed to the 46″ long barrel of the Long Land pattern Musket.
4. A Leather Cartridge Box containing a wooden base piece slotted to hold a number of paper cartridges.
5. A short Sword with brass hilt and slightly curved blade
6. For Musket riming and cleaning purpose
7. (3 x 112) lbs of Lead Shot for Muskets
8. A Pole Arm — replaced in 1792 by the Spontoon, a somewhat similar Polearm which remained in service until 1830.

# CHAPTER 3

# 1761-1762. The First Embodiment

On the 4th January, 1761, the new regiment embodied for service was assembled in Cardiff under the command of Lord Talbot, and shortly thereafter marched for Bideford, North Devon. On arriving at Bristol that order was countermanded, and the Corps was instead diverted to Topsham Barracks, Exeter, where it remained stationed until May.

By June 1762 the regiment was back in South Wales with four Companies quartered in Swansea and the remainder in Cardiff. The Diary of William Thomas[1] written during that period tells us that two members of the Corps were Court Martialled on the 10th of that month — "Was condemned by Court Martial in Cardiff 2 of ye Militia, viz, John of ye Hendy, Gelligaer, to have 300 lashes for miss duty and going home and there staid without liberty 7 days, he had 150 lashes; and George William Carpenter of Llandaff, 200 lashes for running from duty without liberty, of which he had 100."

The Diarist on the 21st June tells us that the four Swansea Companies having travelled to Cardiff by sea, moved on with the remainder of the regiment to Bristol in boats of Mr Priest's Company, which gentleman having delivered them safely to that town receved 18 guineas for his services.

The conduct of certain members of the Glamorgan Regiment during this period left much to be desired, they having been unwillingly drawn from the more unruly element of the County population. As will be seen, not until the Crimean embodiment was the good name of the regiment to be so badly tarnished. Our Diarist goes on to tell us, "Our Militia is very rude and neglecting duty by drinking and whoreing". That entry dated 17th September, 1762, is followed on the 23rd of the month by a report in the *Gentlemen's Magazine* which tells of an affray between Glamorgan Militiamen and Butchers in St. Nicholas Street, Bristol, which event our Diarist later reports on in greater detail.

"Also she told me of ye Riots in Bristol on Saturday night of ye 10th between Sailors and our Militiamen which began in ye house of ye widow of late Morgan Morgan of our Goytre and continued through the whole street. Two Sailors were killed on ye spot and several of both Sailors and Militiamen wounded, and some of both sides cast into Newgate for ye Riots". And later — "Edward Jones of Porthkerry after receiving 1,000 lashes for letting out the French is to be shot, as a Warrant came from London to shoot him to death.[2]"

"Our Militia have made ye City of Bristol, as they did Exeter, a Brothel, of all the Militia in the Kingdom, the most viscious."

On the 31st October, Thomas gives more information on the affair in St. Nicholas Street, Bristol.

"Report confirmed of the killing in Bristol by Militia over a quarrel for five pennyworth of steak which the Militiamen wanted to have for four-pence. Butcher struck a Militiaman down with a spreading stick. Ye Militia beated ye Drum and gathered a number together, as did ye Butchers, and ye fighting was desperate, many wounded and one killed by Tom Jones of St. Fagan's, who swore another killed him. Tom Jones is in Prison in Irons and his pay taken. He is to be tried next Session for murder."

On the 2nd November, the *Gentleman's Magazine* adds more to the sorry tale — namely the sentencing of two Privates of the Regiment to 1,000 lashes each for taking money from French Prisoners of War confined at Knowle. In December the short and unhappy embodiment ended when the regiment, much to the relief of the inhabitants of Bristol, marched out of the garrison for Cardiff. On arrival there, Weapons and Accountrements were returned to Store, the men paid off and dismissed to their homes.

The conduct of the regiment during the embodiment reflects badly on the ability of both Officers and Non Commissioned Officers of the Corps. Happily, the situation was to change, and apart from some incidents during the Crimean War embodiment, the regiment was to build up for itself quite a fine reputation.

**Footnotes**

1. William Thomas (1727-1785) — an itinerant Schoolmaster who was a native of St. Fagan's near Cardiff.
2. Whether Edward Jones met his death before a Firing Party of the regiment is not known, but it is more than likely that his sentence was reduced to a heavy flogging.

# CHAPTER 4

# 1778-1783. The Second Embodiment

In 1763 came a Treaty which confirmed the Peace and the Militia for the next fifteen years was little seen except when drawn out for training. In 1778 France declared War in support of the American Colonists, and in Brittany an Army assembled in preparation for an invasion of our shores. The crisis resulted in an embodiment of Militia for Garrison Duty at home, in consequence of which the Glamorgan Militia assembled in preparation on the 26th March. Shortly thereafter the Regiment marched off to Warley in Essex where during the summer months it carried out periods of Regimental and Brigade training. Towards the end of the year the Corps returned to South Wales and took up its winter quarters in Cardiff.

Early in 1780 the regiment joined the Bristol Garrison where in May it was relieved by the Monmouthshire Militia. Ordered North to Lancashire, it was during its tour of duty in that County commended for its work in Aid of Civil Power during Riots which took place in Preston and Lancaster. The Diary of John David[1] who was serving with the Regiment at that time tells us that by July 1782 the Corps had returned to South Wales and was quartered in Swansea. From that town on the 29th of the same month it commenced its long march to Falmouth. At Bristol, the regiment stayed nine days and was issued with new clothing. It then marched on via Bridgewater, Exeter, Tavistock and Truro to the new station.

The Pay of Militiamen at this date ranged from 17 shillings (85p) per diem for a Lt. Colonel, through Sergeant at 1 shilling (5p) to the 6d (2½p) received by Privates. In like manner to Regular Regiments, a certain percentage of Other Ranks Wives and Children were allowed to accompany the Corps on service. Other dependents were left behind where the repsonsibility for their maintenance became a charge upon the respective Parishes.

In 1793 Peace was restored by the Treaty of Paris at which stage the Glamorgan Regiment returned to South Wales and was disembodied in Cardiff. The Order for Disembodiment was conveyed to the Lord Lieutenant in the following Circular Letter:

"My Lord,

The King having been pleased to sign Orders for the disembodying of the Corps of Militia for the County of Glamorgan under your command with all convenient speed, I am commanded by His Majesty, in his name, to express to you the great satisfaction he has received from the reasonable and meritorious service of the Militia of that County, and as a mark of His Royal approbation, I am commanded to acquaint you that His Majesty is pleased to permit each Non Commissioned

Officer, Drummer and Private Man to keep his Cloaths and Knapsack which are at present in wear; and also to allow them respectively fourteen days Pay from the day of their being disembodied exclusive, which you are hereby authorised to pay them taking from each man respectively a receipt for some."

Later the same Letter directs: "Before disembodying, you are to cause His Majesty's Orders, and also this Letter to be read at the head of each Company in your Corps, that they may be convinced of His Majesty's most gracious attention to them. Permit me, Sir, at the same time to express through you the satisfaction I feel in having the honour to communicate His Majesty's gracious approbation of the services of the Militia Forces and the marks of His Royal Bounty to the Non Commissioned Officers and Private Men.

I have the honour, etc., etc.,

G. Yonge."

The Regiment then reverted to the disembodied state until 1793, a period marked by sporadic periods of training and occasional enforcement of the Ballot in order to keep the required numbers up to strength.

## Footnote

1. Extracts of this Diary which relate to the activities of the Regiment are held in The Welch Regiment Museum Archives.

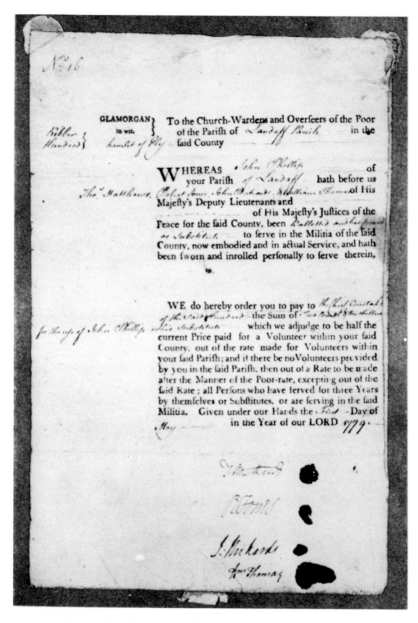

An order on the Church Wardens ond Overseers of the Parish of
Llandaff for the payment of a substitute.
*Courtesy of The Welch Regiment Museum*

The Silver Medal Depicted (Actual Size) was presented to H. Evans for
Service in 1778

Obverse: At the centre the Royal Cipher GR below a Crown and within
a wreath. Around the wreath is inscribed the regimental title
'GLAMORGANSHIRE MILITIA' and the date 1778.

Reverse: At the centre a Trophy of Colours and Pikes above a Cannon.
Above the design, the inscription 'PRESENTED BY COLONEL LORD
CARDIFF' and below it, 'TO H. EVANS FOR SERVICES'

The Medal is displayed in The Welch Regiment Museum at Cardiff Castle
*on loan from The Welsh Folk Museum Collection at St. Fagan's.*

MILITIA GRENADIER      MILITIA LIGHT INFANTRY

Militiamen c.1780
*Courtesy of W.Y. Carman, FSA, and Lord Danvers Osborn*

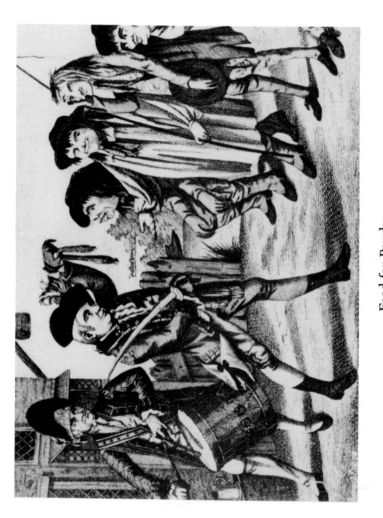

Food for Powder
A Contemporary Cartoon after Deighton portrays some of the indifferent
material available to Regular Army Recruiters of the early 18th Century
*Courtesy of The Welch Regiment Museum*

Enrolling the Supplementary Militia
A Caricature by Gillra lampooning the Supplementary Militia
*Courtesy of The Welch Regiment Museum*

Martello Towers, Hythe Ranges, c.1876

# CHAPTER 5

# 1793-1802. The Third Embodiment

Eleven years were to pass before the services of the Glamorgan Regiment were again required — a period which according to the eminent military historian, Sir John Fortescue, was a time of neglect, in which Government complacently allowed the Militia to slip back in terms of training and efficiency. Arousing itself to face the oncoming storm, the Government in December 1792 gave thought once again to Militia, and in a Circular Letter dated the 1st of that month ordered that immediate steps be taken to place the Weapons allocated to Militia Regiments in secure places and directed the Lords Lieutenant to ensure that at least one third of the Permanent Staff N.C.O.'s reside together in compliance with the terms of the Militia Act.

The outbreak of the French Revolutionary War on the 1st February, 1793, saw the Militia drawn out nationally. In Glamorgan, the Warrant for the embodiment of its regiment for Garrison Duty was issued to the Lord Lieutenant on February 2nd.

Under the command of Colonel, The Viscount Mountstuart the regiment marched away to the West Country to take up duties in the busy Naval Port of Plymouth. On March 3rd, 1793, the Lord Lieutenant of the various English and Welsh Counties met at the St. Alban's Tavern, London, for the purpose of drawing Lots to determine the precedence of the various Regiments of Militia. The result which appears in the Annual Register[1] saw the Glamorgan Regiment numbered 5th in the Order of Precedence nationally.

On the 21st April, 1794, Lt. Colonel Richard Awbrey of Ash Hall, near Cowbridge, assumed active command of the Regiment which continued its service in Plymouth and district.

By 1796 the demands of the War created a need for additional manpower, and the Government in an effort to resolve the problem set about raising a 'Supplementary Militia'[2] to strengthen the numbers already in service. Sometimes referred to as 'The New Militia' the scheme envisaged raising an additional 59,500 men from the English Counties and about 4,500 in Wales. As will be seen, the scheme was also intended to benefit Regular Army recruiting, and whilst the Ballot to raise Supplementary men was in progress, no additional exemptions were granted to would be members of the Volunteer Force until the additional quotas for Militia were completed.

The new quota for the Glamorgan Regiment was set at 622, and the training period for men selected for Supplementary Service set at twenty days. The raising of the additional numbers presented the Deputy Lieutenants with no easy task, as in addition to the demands of the Navy and Army, a mass of men already serving in Volunteer Corps were in return for that service exempt from the Militia Ballot. Strangely, Government made no move to ease the problem by insisting on personal service, but instead continued to allow the iniquitous Substitute system to flourish.

By May 1796, the Glamorgan Regiment was stationed at Wells with a detachment at Frome in Somerset. Before the end of the month, the Corps reassembled and marched on to Kent where it joined the Dover Garrison on June 16th. In October the regiment marched to Canterbury and there took up quarters for the winter. *The Hereford Journal*, 19th October, 1796, reports, "The Glamorganshire Militia have broke Camp at Dover and marched out for Canterbury."

The year 1797 saw the regiment serve variously at Canterbury, Shorncliffe and Dover, and in April a party was sent back to Glamorgan to supervise the training of the Supplementary Militia. In a General Order dated 24th of that month Lt. Colonel Awbrey was directed as follows:

"His Majesty having deemed it expedient that the whole of the Supplementary Militia of Glamorganshire should be embodied as soon as possible (that part only excepted, as may voluntarily engage to serve in His Majesty's Forces) I have the honour to signify to you, the Commander in Chief's Order, that you cause a Detachment from the Glamorganshire Regiment of Militia, consisting of a Field Officer, two Captains, four Subalterns, with as many Non Commissioned Officers and Drummers as can be spared from the duty of the regiment, to proceed without loss of time, agreeable to the route transmitted herewith, to Cardiff, the place appointed for the assembly of the Supplementary Militia of Glamorgan, there to receive and take charge of the Supplementary Militiamen. For the information of the Officers employed on this duty, I have the honour to acquaint you that the quota of Supplementary Militiamen allowed to enlist into His Majesty's Regular Forces is far from being completed. The Supplementary Militiamen assembled in Cardiff are for four days after their assembly to have the option of enlisting into the 44th Regiment of Foot[3]; and His Royal Highness, the Commander in Chief, will be actuated by a zeal for the good of His Majesty's Service to use their influence with the men, and will persuade them to enter as Volunteers by explaining to them the following terms under which they enlist.

That they will receive Seven Guineas Bounty[4], and are to serve during the War, and six months after the conclusion of a general Peace, and no longer, and that they shall not be liable to serve out of Europe.[5]

At the expiration of four days, or as soon as possible, the Officer Commanding the Detachment will receive a route by which he will march the Supplementary Militiamen whom he will have received (such only being excepted as may have engaged in the 44th Regiment of Foot) to your Headquarters."

January 1798 found the Glamorgan Regiment stationed in the Dover Garrison, but the Supplementary men, for reasons unexplained, were still in Cardiff.

The numbers of Glamorgan Supplementary Militiamen allowed the then doubtful privilege of enlisting as Regular Soldiers is given as 103. Presumably the Officers had some difficulty persuading them, but the numbers actually inlifted into the 44th are not known. The Regiment next moved to Ashford, and there absorbed the Supplementary Men who had arrived from Cardiff. Their arrival boosted the strength of the Corps to nine Companies.

A shortage of Regular Troops to deal with the Rebellion in Ireland resulted in Legislation[6] which permitted the Crown to use up to 12,000 Militiamen from England and Wales on Irish service. It is interesting to note that amongst the 13 Regiments selected from amongst those who had volunteered for such service, six were Welsh, and included amongst them was the Glamorgan Regiment.

In May 1799, the Regiment marched from Kent to Portsmouth, where on the 15th June, they were embarked on the Transports 'Hebe' and 'Dictator' for passage to Cork. On arrival, the Corps marched to Fermoy[7], and there remained some months, during which period the conduct of both Officers and Men so impressed the townsfolk, that on the 21st December, eve of the Regiment's departure from the town, the following letter was handed to Colonel Awbrey.

"Sir,

We, Subscribers, for ourselves and other inhabitants of Fermoy, feel as we ought, the loss of the Glamorganshire Regiment about to leave us. A Regiment whose Officers are Gentlemen and Christians, whose presence gave being to good order, and checked every irregularity of the lower classes. Indeed, the behaviour of the Privates, for honesty, sobriety and fair dealing, claims our heartfelt acknowledgements.

Accept from us the tribute of high esteem and gratitude, accompanied by warmest wishes for health and prosperity to your good self, the Officers and Privates of the Glamorgan Regiment.

Signed by

James McWhirter and Five other Townsmen of Fermoy".

Three Companies led the march from Fermoy to Dublin proceeding via Clogheen, Clonmel, Kilkenny, Carlow and Naas. The remainder of the Regiment followed within days.

The Fermoy Testimonial does much to show that the Militia were not always the indisciplined and drunken rascals that some accounts would have us believe them to be. Much however depended on the firmness and attitude of the Commanding Officer and Officers, and also in great part, the mettle of the Non Commissioned Officers which they selected.

In 1799, permission was given for a proportion of serving Militiamen from time to time to volunteer to transfer their service into the Line[9].

"His Royal Highness, The Commander in Chief, directs it to be declared to the Militia Forces that an Act of Parliament has passed with a view to enable His Majesty to provide for a vigorous prosecution of the War, in amongst which other provisions, it is enacted that it shall be lawful for one fourth of the Private Men of the Embodied Militia to enter as Volunteers into such of His Majesty's Regiments of Infantry as His Majesty shall by Order under His Royal Sign Manual think proper to appoint."

By that means, in the years that followed, the Militia supplied the Regiments of the Line with some of their best material — men who were fit, capable of marching long distances, and who were well trained and experienced in all apsects of the military duty other than actual combat. As will be seen, the Glamorganshire Regiment provided more than its expected share of such men to the Regular Army for the duration of hostilities.

The beginning of the year 1800 found the Regiment stationed in Dublin where they remained until May, a portion being on Guard at the Parliament Buildings when the Act of Union was passed. Embarking, the Corps took passage to Liverpool, and from there marched out for Cardiff, which route took them via Chester, the border Counties and Hereford. There on the 23rd July, the *Hereford Journal* recorded their arrival.

"Arrived at Hereford en route for Cardiff, the Glamorganshire Militia commanded by Colonel Awbrey, 400 strong, and with an excellent Band. The Regiment on volunteering for Irish Service, was in number, over a thousand, but has been much reduced due to men volunteering their services into the Line."

From Cardiff the Regiment moved on to Swansea and Haverfordwest in which Pembrokeshire town Headquarters were established. The Regiment throughout the year 1801 served in that County and had Detachments stationed thoughout the district.

The signing of the Peace of Amiens, March 27th, 1802, brought back an eagerly awaited Peace, in consequence of which the Regiment returned to Cardiff and was disembodied.


## Footnotes

1. Annual Register Vol.IXXXV. p.13
2. An addition to the County Militia above quota.
   (Manual of Military Law. WO. 1914 p.165)
3. 44th or East Essex Regiment
4. £7.35
5. The condition which stipulated that men would not be called upon to serve out of Europe was an important inducement, as in those days service in Tropical or Semi-tropical climates was tantamount to a Death Warrant. It was not uncommon for regiments called upon to serve in those parts to lose 50% and upwards of their strength to fever or other tropical diseases.
6. Act 38. Geo. 11. c.66
7. Other Welsh Militia Regiments selected were the Merionethshire, Montgomeryshire, Pembrokeshire, Denbighshire and Carmarthenshire Corps
8. Fermoy. Co. Cork

# CHAPTER 6

## 1802-1803.
## The Milita Act of 1802, Substitutes, Exemptions from Service, Deserters, The Militia Ballot.

The year 1802 saw the Laws relating to Militia consolidated under a new Act which became known as the Militia Act of 1802.[1]

The provisions of the Ballot were retained, and the Property Qualifications for Militia Officers reinforced.

Men between the ages of 18 and 45 were made eligible for service, and could, if not selected by Ballot, volunteer for a term of five years service with the Militia. Such Volunteers received a Bounty of £6, but were extremely hard to find, as men soon found that more money could be made by offering themselves as a Substitute. Sadly the Act did not kill off the Substitute system, but continued to support the iniquitous scheme, thus allowing those who could afford it to pay the sum of £10 to the Deputy Lieutenants and quite legally buy themselves five years exemption. The actual cost, as will be seen, could often amount to a much larger sum.

The Militia Quota for each County was fixed by the Privy Council every ten years, but the Crown still had authority to increase the number required in the event of Invasion, threatened Invasion or Rebellion. Counties who failed to produce the required Quota were fined an annual sum for each man deficient, the Fine being made a charge on the Parish responsible. The Act also directed that the Militia, when disembodied, would be called out every year for training, and that the Men, whilst undergoing same, would be subject to the Mutiny Act.

Later, the Act became subject to a series of amendments designed to assist the authorities bring Militia Regiments up to strength after the renewal of hostilities in 1803. Property Qualifications for Officers were also relaxed, and the Fine per man deficient from a County Quota was increased to £40 per annum, which for some Parishes was a crippling and intolerable burden. The price of five years exemption was increased to £15 on paper, but the real answer to the problem — Universal Service with no Substitutes allowed, was once again ignored.

Records of the period show that the price of obtaining a Substitute was often far in excess of the statutory sum. Prices ranged over the years from £20 in Denbighshire to a record £45 in Monmouthshire, and Insurance schemes were introduced to assist 'the dodgers' to meet the cost. The high prices demanded probably account for the large number of Principals serving in the Welsh Corps of Militia of the period.

Apart from those who had purchased exemption from service, there were others who by Law could not be touched. They included, Peers of the Realm, Officers of the Navy, Army and Marines on Full Pay, or Half Pay, Non Commissioned Officers and Men of the King's Forces, Officers serving, or who had completed four years Militia Service, Resident Members of Universities, Clergy, Constables and Other Law Officers, Articled Clerks and Apprentices, Seafaring Men, and Men employed in Naval Arsenals and Dockyards, The Company of Watermen of the Thames, Men having more than one child in wedlock and with an income of less than £100 per annum, Volunteers serving in Corps under the Volunteer Act of 1802, Men not physically fit, and men under the height of 5'4" provided they were not in receipt of an annual income, or were owners of property valued in excess of £100. If Income or Property was valued in excess of that figure, they were liable to serve as Principals, provide a Substitute, or pay the appropriate Fine.

## Deserters
Originally, Principals serving as Militiamen found guilty of Desertion were liable to a fine of £20 or a term of six months imprisonment on conviction before a Justice of the Peace.

A Substitute could be sentenced by Court Martial to a further term of Militia Service, or to Service with a Regiment of the Line for Life. In 1787 the whole matter was tightened up, a Royal Decree being read out at the head of each Regiment — "All Deserters from the Militia will be sent to the East Indies or the Coast of Africa for Life." This, as has been previously explained amounted to nothing less than a delayed sentence of death.

## The Ballot
Each County was for this purpose divided into sub-divisions under the control of the Deputy County Lieutenants. Upon the approach of the Ballot, the Constables of the Hundreds or other Administrative Sub-Divisions would draw up a list of all men between the ages of 18 and 45 resident in their districts together with any claims for exemption. These Lists would then be displayed upon the Doors of the Parish Church together with a notation of the numbers required from that district towards completing the County Quota.

Some weeks later, those concerned would be instructed to present themselves for Ballot, where at the time and place appointed the Deputy Lieutenant and Assistants having placed the names of those eligible to serve into a hat or box, would after mixing them up, draw out one name after another until the required numbers were completed. Balloted Men, provided they elected to render personal service, would be sworn in as Privates in the County

Militia. On discharge of their obligation, they would be exempted from further service for five years. Vacancies arising from death or disability in service, or from normal Discharge, were immediately filled by Ballot from the district concerned.

There exists in the Muniment Room of the Neath Antiquarian Society a most interesting social record titled Militia Drawing Book, and which is in fact a forty eight page listing of the men of the Neath Hundred, Glamorgan, eligible for service in the County Regiment of Militia in 1760, with notations indicating those who were selected for service by Ballot. The record opens as follows: "A List of proper persons to take their Chances in raising 52 Militia Men, being the number, fix'd to be rais'd within the said Hundred, to serve in, and for the said County, which were Drawn and Balloted, at the Guild of the Town of Neath, within the said Hundred, before Herbert Mackworth Senior, and Phillip Williams Esquires, Deptuy Lieutenants acting in and for the said Hundred, and Mathew Pryce Esqr one of his Majty's Justices of the Peace in and for the sd County, the 10th of Janry, 1760."

The List contains 1261 men, the last half of which, in addition to place of residence, also makes note of the candidate's occupation, mainly a mixture of skilled or semi-skilled workmen and labourers. Only three of those listed bear the style 'Gent', and two the appellation 'Mr' which bear out the fact that socially, the system was extremely biased in favour of the more affluent section of the community.

The 52 names selected have the letter 'D' alongside their names, of which only 10 elected to pay the appropriate fine and name an acceptable Substitute. This interesting document is discussed in more detail in an article by Elis Jenkins titled 'Neath's Citizen Army in 1760', Transactions of the Neath Antiquarian Society, 1979.

### Footnotes

1. Militia Act of 1802 — 56 Geo II,c.59

# CHAPTER 7

# 1803-14. The Fourth Embodiment

In May 1803, the shortlived Peace foundered as Britain declared War upon Napoleonic France. The renewal of hostilities once again saw the Militia drawn out to face what was to be its longest continuous period of service. With the military might of France directed against her, the situation was in many ways similar to 1940, when Britain stood alone facing the armed might of Nazi Germany. In 1803 however, the French were the threat, and it was British resistance alone which stood between them and their desire for the wholesale domination of Europe.

French efforts were concentrated on preparing a Fleet of Transports, and massing an Army of Invasion at the Channel Ports. On the British shore, the Militia, with a stiffening of Regular Troops awaited the onslaught, whilst behind them, and amongst them was the third line, the Citizen Army — part time Volunteer Soldiers, the Home Guard of that period. Their preparations were inspired by intentions similar to those made clear to Germany and his own countrymen by Winston S. Churchill some 137 years later — "We shall defend our Island, whatever the cost may be; we shall fight on the beaches, we shall fight on the landing grounds, we shall fight in the fields and in the streets, we shall fight in the hills; we shall never surrender."

In Glamorgan, the County Militia had been embodied in April, and by June was stationed at Winchester, later moving on to the military encampment at Stokes Bay, Gosport. On the 14th August, it was amongst Militia Regiments inspected by His Royal Highness, The Duke of York[1], then in November, moved into Winter Quarters at Haslar. At Gosport the Corps had been strengthened by an intake of Supplementary Militia, and shared its duties in that Garrison with the Monmouth, and Brecon Regiment, Merioneth Regiment and Herefordshire Regiment of Militia. The Garrison Guard consisted of 3 Officers and 131 Non Commissioned Officers and Privates which numbers were expected to furnish Sentries over the Guns at Fort Blockhouse, guard the boats lying in the Haslar Lake, as well as a multitude of other minor, but equally important duties.

Each Regiment provided a Detachment to make up the numbers required daily, but when in February 1804 the four Militia Regiments at Haslar were reinforced by the arrival of the 2/48th Foot (Northamptonshire Regiment) the provision of the full Guard became an individual regimental responsiblity.

Life in the Portsmouth Garrison included also many Inspections and Reviews due to visits by Senior Officers and occasionally Royalty. The Glamorgan Regiment when drawn up in Marching Order for such an event was paraded as follows:

The Advance Guard
The Regimental Colour Party
The Regimental Pioneers
Cart with Pioneer Tools and Equipment
The Battalion Guns
The Regiment in Column of Companies
Bat Horses with Ammunition
Bat Horses with Surgeon's Medicines
Bat Horses[3] with Battalion Company Stores
The Rear Guard

Heading the Regiment when actually on the March would be the Regimental Band and Drums — the size and quality of the Band depending entirely on the affluence of the Regimental Officers who were expected to maintain by private subscription its members and instruments.

The Regiment took its leave of Haslar in March 1804 and after short periods of duty at Southbourne, Eastbourne, and other places along its route arrived at Pevensey Barracks on June 22nd. At Pevensey, the regiment was almost continuously on the alert and involved in anti invasion duties. The year saw the Corps, together with other Welsh Regiments of Militia granted permission to use the prefix 'Royal', and as such was allowed the distinction of wearing Royal Blue Facings.

That Invasion was still considered to be a very real threat is confirmed by *The Cambrian*, which in its August 31st edition exhorts its military readers in the following terms:

"Cambrians, be on the alert! Your native courage, acknowledged proficiency and military discipline, and the recollections of the glorious deeds performed by your illustrious ancestors in former times, will stimulate you to imitate their noble example."

On the 19th July, Captain M. Cadoux took over the duties of Adjutant, and by the 24th August the Regiment had moved to Langley and was accommodated under canvas. In the Autumn it moved back to Pevensey and took up its winter quarters in the Barracks. It continued to serve in that town and district until November 1805 in which month it was posted to, and in due course occupied winter quarters in Hailsham Barracks.

Meanwhile, the victory over the combined enemy Fleets at Trafalgar removed for the duration the fear of invasion and on the French Channel coast the camps which some months previously had been overflowing with The Army of England were empty — the French Troops having been directed to military adventures further East. Neither Militia nor the Volunteer Force had been called to the test, but there can be little doubt that had such a situation arisen, they would have given the invader plenty to think about.

In May 1806, the Royal Glamorgan then stationed at Horsham was ordered to Bristol and marching in two Divisions arrived in the Garrison early that same month. At Bristol, in addition to normal garrison duties the regiment provided detachments to assist in manning the Guns in the Shirehampton and Avonmouth Forts and also Guards and Escorts for the Prisoners of War then housed in the Stapleton Gaol.

In 1807, a number of men not exceeding 25% of the regimental strength were allowed to assist with the harvest provided that the work was within one day's march of the Regimental Headquarters. September also found the regiments in garrison, viz, Royal Glamorgan, Royal Pembroke and 3rd Lancashire Militia encouraging their members to volunteer for service with the Line. Men of the Royal Glamorgan thus inclined, of which there were considerable numbers, were allowed the choice of the 43rd (Monmouthshire Light Infantry), 76th (later 2/Duke of Wellington's), 90th (Perthshire Regt) and 96th (later 2/Manchester).

The New Year 1808 found the Royal Glamorgan brigaded with the Royal North Gloucester and Wiltshire Regiments of Militia in the Bristol Garrison, but on the 10th January, the Glamorgan Corps marched out for Taunton where for a few weeks it was employed in that town and district. On the 28th, 29th and 30th March, the Royal Glamorgan moving in three Divisions commanded respectively by Major Morgan, Captain Robinson and Captain Bruce moved on to Exeter. The Press reporting the departure stated "Each individual of that orderly Regiment left behind him that character for discipline which constitutes the real meaning of what is usually termed the good Soldier." The year also saw the beginning of the Campaign in the Iberian Peninsula, and subsequent heavy demands on the Militia for volunteers to go out as reinforcements for the Regiments of the Line. The Militia generally, and the Glamorgan Regiment in particular responded magnificently, and many hundreds of men from the Militia of Wales contributed to Wellington's successes in the great battles which took place in Spain and Portugal.

In June 1808, the Corps was Brigaded with the South Devon Militia and Exeter Infantry Vounteers on Broad Clyst Common near Exeter, and there was inspected by Major General Thewles who expressed himself highly pleased with the steadiness, discipline and ability of the regiment. On the 4th of the same month, in company with the Exeter Volunteers and 3rd Dragoon Guards the Corps paraded in Exeter to fire a Feu de Joie in honour of His Majesty's Birthday.

In 1809, the Regimental Headquarters was located at Tiverton, and Detachments were stationed at Exeter, Crediton, Pensington and other places. The Regiment was then ordered to Cornwall, the main body arriving at Pendennis Castle, Falmouth, on the 7th May. On the 19th of the month, a letter from Headquarters Western District at Exeter states — "The Men of the Royal Glamorgan Militia stationed at the Signal Posts of Devon and Somerset will be relieved immediately by men of the North Hants Militia, and proceed to join their regiment at Pendennis."

That the Regiment provided its share of Volunteers for the line is confirmed by the following Circular and Letter:

47

"Horse Guards Circular 5th May, 1809,

It is desirable that the Regiments of Militia should immediately send parties into their respective counties for the purpose of commencing to recruit as soon as the Act which is now before Parliament shall have past." The Recruits being required as replacements for those who had left the Regiment by volunteering into the Line and also the following Letter — Assistant Quartermaster General to the Officer Commanding, Glamorgan Militia, dated 7th May, 1809.

"Sir,

I have to request you will be pleased to send into the Depot of Camp Equipage at Plymouth all articles of Camp Equipage and Light Equipment now in possession of the Royal Glamorgan Regiment of Militia above the establishment agreed due to the number of Volunteers lately taken from the Corps under your command."

In Glamorgan and neighbouring Counties the Regimental Recruiting Parties were not finding it an easy task to fill up the vacancies left in the Corps in spite of the cash inducement offered

## DISTRIBUTION OF LEVY MONEY FOR RECRUITS TO COMPLETE THE MILITIA OF GREAT BRITAIN VIDE 49 GEO 111, c.53 — JUNE 1809

| | Men not in the Local Militia | | | Men from the Local Militia | | |
|---|---|---|---|---|---|---|
| On being attested — in money | £5 | 5s | 0d | £4 | 4s | 0d |
| On joining the Regiment | £5 | 5s | 0d | £4 | 4s | 0d |
| Total Bounty Money to Recruits | £10 | 10s | 0d | £8 | 8s | 0d |
| Reward to Officers and Party to cover all expenses and to be distributed in such a manner as the Colonel or other Commandant directs | £2 | 2s | 0d | £2 | 2s | 0d |
| Total Levy Money | £12 | 12s | 0d | £10 | 10s | 0d |

In spite of replacement problems, Officers of the Militia were ordered to encourage by every means in their power their men to transfer into the Line. Quotas were set which Commanding Officers found hard to meet, the Commanding Officer of the Glamorgan Corps himself being reminded in a letter dated 21st July, 1809, that he had not met his Quota, and that a further 59 Volunteers were required. At the same time, seven other Militia Commandants were similarly admonished.

A Horse Guards Letter dated 17th October, granted an Amnesty for Military Offenders in the District, and is possibly also indirectly targeted at Recruiting.

"The Commander in Chief deeming it proper to mark by every possible means the approaching happy event of His Majesty entering upon the 50th year of his Reign, and it appearing to His Excellency, Sir David Dundas, that an event of this nature cannot be distinguished in a more appropriate manner than by an act of general amnesty and forgiveness.

I have received His Commands to signify to you that all Delinquents confined for offences of a military nature belonging to Regiments serving in the District under your Orders, are upon this joyful occasion to be released from confinement on the 25th of this month, the Anniversary of His Majesty's Accession to the Throne, and to be allowed to return to their duty."

It is not known how many Royal Glamorgan Militiamen benefited from this Act of Grace, for the general conduct of the Regiment during the embodiment appears up to that point to have been exemplary. At no time was there anything to compare with that which had occurred during the first, and what was to occur later, during the Crimean embodiment.

Key Officers serving with the Regiment at this time were,

| | |
|---|---|
| Colonel Henry Knight | 30 April, 1808 |
| Lt. Colonel R. Morgan of Llandough Castle | 18 August, 1808 |
| Major J. Robinson | 16 August, 1808 |
| Captain and Adjutant R.G. Thomas | 17 March, 1808 |

At Pendennis on October 25th, 1809, the Officers of the regiment regaled the men with porter to celebrate the Jubilee Year of the reign of King George III[6], and undoubtely the Detachment of the regiment which was stationed at Penrhyn were likewise treated. As was customary in the Regiments of the Line, a small percentage of wives and children were allowed to accompany each Militia Regiment on its travels, the Royal Glamorgan being no exception. These women were in the main, native Welsh, but there were others also who had married into the Corps during its service in various stations. In return for washing, cooking and nursing the sick, the families were included on the ration strength, and the children received a basic education, usually at the hands of a Non Commissioned Officer detailed for the duty of Regimental Schoolmaster. In a good regiment, the wives of the Officers, in particular, the Colonel's Lady, played a part in their general welfare, as for example in Royal Glamorgan on Christmas Day, 1809.

"On Christmas Day, the Wives and Children of the Non Commissioned Officers of the Royal Glamorgan Militia were regaled with an excellent Dinner of Roast Beef, Plum Pudding and Porter at the Barracks, Pendennis Castle, provided by Mrs Morgan, the Lieutenant Colonel's Lady."[7] By the end of June 1810 the Regiment had relieved the Lancashire Militia in the Bristol Garrison, and has also sent a Detachment to duty at Milford Haven. During this period the regiment was also responsible for maintaining Beacons on the North Somerset coast, providing Town Guards, a Detachment for duty with Prisoners of War at Stapleton, and manning the Avon Forts. In November, the Milford Detachment on being relieved by the Pembroke Militia rejoined the Headquarters at Bristol.

In May 1811 volunteering for the Line took place from amongst the Militia Regiments stationed at Bristol, *The Cambrian* reporting that 60 men of the Royal Glamorgan had so volunteered and had left the Corps to join the regiments of their choice.

An Order dated 9th July authorises Regiments of Militia to recruit 'By Beat of Drum' — a recruiting method long used by the Regulars. In that manner it was hoped that the various Corps could build up to their established strength, replacing those lost to the Line through volunteering. Additionally, a Letter to the Commanding Officer from Whitehall dated 15th July states: "Sir,

I have the honour of transmitting to you an Order of His Royal Highness, the Prince Regent in Council, authorising you in conformity with the provisions of the twenty third section of 51 Geo II, c.20, to raise by Beat of Drum, or otherwise, in the County of Glamorgan and adjoining Counties, such number of Volunteers for the Regiment under your command as will complete it to 403 Privates, being the original quota fixed for the County under 42 Geo II, c.90, Sec 19." And later, "I am further to acquaint you that His Royal Highness is pleased to permit you, in the event of your deeming it advisable, to enlist at a smaller rate of Bounty, a proportion of Boys of the age of fourteen years and upwards, not exceeding one fourth of the number you require to raise."

Recruiting by Beat of Drum demanded a high degree of persuasiveness, salesmanship and resilience, and as such was not every Non Commissioned Officers bent. Sergeant Jackson, a Guards Recruiting Sergeant and ex Militiaman disliked the task — "I said I disliked the Recruiting Service; however, another tour of that kind was marked out for me and another younger Sergeant, rather of a whimsical nature. It was to take a Drum and Fife and attend all Wakes, Races and Revels within twenty miles of London. There we had to strut about in our best Coats, and swaggering, Sword in hand, drumming our way through the masses, comingled with gazing clodpolls, gingerbread mechanics, and thimbleprick sharpeners. These pranks ended with the summer. We had not been very successful — our standard ran very high, and the 'free, able and willing', very low."[8]

In contrast one wonders how many Recruiters were as skilled in that business as was the noble Sergeant Kite of an earlier period — a man who had a shrewd understanding of the types most likely to accept the 'Shilling'.

"If any Gentleman, Soldiers or Others have a mind to serve Her Majesty and pull down a French King; if any Prentice have severe Masters, any children have undutiful Parents; if any Servants have too little Wages, or any Man too much Wife, let them repair to the noble Sergeant Kite at the Sign of the Raven in this good town of Shrewsbury, and they shall receive present relief and entertainment.

Gentlemen, I don't beat my Drum here to ensnare, or inveigle any man, for you must know Gentlemen, that I am a man of honour! Besides, I don't beat for common Soldiers: No, I list only Grenadiers — Grenadiers, Gentlemen!⁹

Doubtful also, the possibility of laying on such a spectacle as this which took place in Ireland in 1775, although some of the Militia Colonels were wealthy enough to be able to surpass it.

## "ORDER OF PROCESSION

Major Roche, bearing a large Purse of Gold
Captain Cowley
A Great number of Likely Recruits
An elegant Band of Musik consisting of
French Horns, Hautboys, Clarionets and Bassoons
playing 'GOD SAVE THE KING'
A Large Brewer's Dray with five Barrels of Beer
the Horse richly caparisoned and ornamented with Ribbons
Two Draymen with Cockades, to serve the Beer,
The Recruiting Sergeant
Another Division of Recruits and a prodigious
concourse of Spectators."¹⁰

On July 12th, *The Cambrian* reporting on the Regiment stated — "The major part of that excellent Regiment The Glamorgan Militia which has been so long stationed at Bristol, with equal credit to themselves and satisfactory to the inhabitants, volunteered on Wednesday for Ireland".

A Letter from the War Office dated October 11th states "That the Establishment of the Glamorgan Regiment of Militia under your command should be fixed from the 25th September last at the number specified in the margin hereof." In the margin was appended

1 Colonel as Lt. Colonel
1 Lt. Colonel as Major
1 Major as Captain
6 Captains
7 Lieutenants
5 Ensigns
1 Adjutant
1 Quartermaster
1 Surgeon
1 Sergeant Major
1 Quartermaster Sergeant
20 Sergeants
20 Corporals

1 Drum Major
13 Drummers
403 Privates

a total of 483 in 6 Companies

"The following Ranks, viz: Paymaster, Surgeon's Mate, Paymaster's Clerk, and Armourer not being borne on the Establishment, are not included in the above state, but Pay and Allowances will be granted to them as heretofore."

As the War dragged on, its demands for manpower made it progressively more difficult for Militia Regiments to maintain their established strengths. The demands of the Line, discharges, sickness and other causes regularly sapped the strength, the Royal Glamorgan being no exception. In Glamorgan and neighbouring Counties its Recruiting Parties faced with strong competition from the Navy, Line and other Militias reaped a poor harvest. In such circumstances a blind eye was often the answer to age, and several boys were recruited.

The practice gave rise to the following letter, which on the face of it appears to contradict the instructions given in the letter of July 15th, 1811.

> "Sir,
> There being reason to suppose that it has been the practice in several Militia Corps to enlist, or enrol Boys for the purpose of being trained as Drummers, and muster and pay them as Private Men, although from their age and height they were not fit for the service. I think it is my duty to point out to you the illegality of the practice and to acquaint you that no person hereafter received into the Militia will be allowed to be borne upon the strength of any Regiment as a Private Man unless he is of the age specified in the 26th Section of 51. Geo II, c.20."

Doubtless that in the face of such warning any youngsters who had enlisted in the Royal Glamorgan and were of that category were shortly thereafter discharged.

In March 1812 the Royal Glamorgan was converted to the Light Infantry role.

> "Horse Guards,
> 26th March, 1812,
> Sir,
> I have the honour to acquaint you by direction of the Commander in Chief that His Royal Highness, The Prince Regent has been pleased to approve of the Royal Glamorganshire Regiment of Militia being clothed, equipped and exercised as a Corps of Light Infantry.

It is not considered necessary that Arms should be changed, those in possession being considered perfectly applicable to that service, or that any alternation should be made to the Clothing and Appointments until the 25th December next; but on your transmitting to me a Return showing the number of Drums now in possession of the Regiment, the necessary application will be made to the Board of Ordnance for their being received into the Ordnance Store and for Bugles being issued instead of them.

    I have the honour, etc., etc.,

    Henry Calvert

    A.G."

 

On the 29th June, the Regiment on being ordered to the East Coast marched out of Bristol for Bath from which town it moved on the 13th July via Marlborough, Hungerford, Newbury, Maidenhead, Uxbridge and Ipswich to Woodbridge Barracks to arrive on July 26th.

*The Cambrian* reporting the move in its June 26th edition stated "The Glamorgan Militia are to march from Bristol in July en route to the Eastern District," and also "The Royal Glamorgan Militia commenced their march on Tuesday for North Yarmouth. The departure of this excellent Regiment from Bristol excited the regret of the inhabitants to whose esteem the Officers and Men had conciliated by their uniform and consistant deportment during the long period they have been quartered in that City." The stay in North Yarmouth was comparatively short as by 21st September the regiment was marching South via Colchester, Maldon, Billericay, Gravesend, Sittingbourne and Canterbury to Ramsgate. On arrival Headquarters were established and one Company sent on to Margate and a Detachment to Westgate. At Ramsgate a member of the Corps attempted to supplement his income, the case being reported in *The Cambrian*, November 6th.

"A Private in the Glamorganshire Militia and his Wife were on Monday apprehended at Ramsgate, being detected in the act of fabricating base Shillings and Sixpences, and were committed to Sandwich Gaol."

During October the Royal Glamorgan provided another crop of Volunteers for Regular service, the men being taken up by the Foot Guards, Line Infantry and Royal Waggon Train.

A Regimental Order published in Ramsgate on the 17th November, 1812, gives details of the Subscriptions required from Officers in respect of the Officers Mess and Band

| Field Officers | To the Mess Fund | 50 Guineas (£52.50) |
| | To the Band Fund | 50 Guineas |

| Captains | To the Mess Fund | 25 Guineas (£26.25) |
|---|---|---|
| | To the Band Fund | 25 Guineas |
| 1st Lieutenants | To the Mess Fund | 15 Guineas (£15.75) |
| | To the Band Fund | Nil |
| 2nd Lieutenants | To the Mess Fund | 10 Guineas (£10.50) |
| | To the Band Fund | Nil |

and in connection with conversion to Light Infantry the following Letter

"Sir,
    In consequence of a communication from the Commander in Chief the Board have ordered the following articles to be issued and forwarded to Ramsgate for the service of the Glamorgan Militia in exchange for the Pikes and Drums in possession of the Regiment, viz: 18 Fusils complete, 14 Bugles. I have it in command to request you will cause your Pikes and Drums to be delivered into the Ordnance Store at Dover, consigned to the Store Keeper at the Station as soon as the Fusils and Bugles shall have arrived at the Headquarters of the Regiment."

On December 31st, the Royal Glamorgan marched out of Ramsgate and Margate to assemble in Canterbury which had been nominated as its Headquarters.

1813 saw the Corps still in that town with a Detachment at Ashford. The Detail Book of the Regiment for that period is safely preserved in The Welch Regiment Museum, and gives considerable information about the day to day routines and duties of the regiments in Garrison. Included over a period were, The 4th Dragoon Guards, 5th Dragoon Guards, 3rd Dragoon Guards, 1st Dragoons, Rutland Militia, Royal Veteran Battalion, 2nd Battalion 9th Foot[11], 1st W. Yorkshire Militia, Galloway Militia, Fifeshire Militia, North Down Militia, South Down Militia and the Waterford Regiment. The Book shows that in addition to providing a Town Guard, Guards and Escorts for Prisoners of War, the Regiments in Garrison were regularly exercised with blank cartridge in the Field and with 'Ball' Cartridge on nearby Ranges. The Live Firing allowance per man rarely exceeded ten rounds.

A high proportion of the Private Men of the Royal Glamorgan Militia were unfamiliar with the English language, but as will be seen from the following Commanding Officers Order due attention was given to the matter. "All Orders should be read to the Men in the presence of an Officer of each Company at the next private Parade of the Company after the issue of such Orders, and it will be desirable that they should be explained to the Men by the Non Commissioned Officers in the Welsh Language."

The demand for Volunteers to serve with the Line continued, the Commanding Officer receiving a Letter from Whitehall dated 27th January, 1813, authorising him to allow 57 Private Men to enlist as Regulars should they wish to do so. In consequence of this, and past reductions, Recruiting Parties were sent back to South Wales to 'beat in' the required numbers. The Corps was not totally without its miscreants and deserters, one of whom received in April that year a just and 'suspended' sentence.

*The Cambrian* April 30th, 1813,

"On Saturday last the following Prisoners capitally convicted at Gloucester Assizes were executed in front of the County Gaol, namely Samuel Lee, a Gypsy, for Horse Stealing at Hartbury, and James Bailey, Edward Edwards, Ellis Rees and Thomas Edwards for robbing Mr Saxton on the highway near North Leach. Edward Edwards was a Deserter from the Glamorgan Militia, for which he received 150 Lashes upon delivering himself up to his Regiment after committing the robbery for which he suffered."

An Order dated 31st July authorises up to seven men per Company to assist the farmers of the Canterbury District bring in the harvest and on the 12th August, the Corps, together with other Troops in the Garrison paraded to fire a Feu de Joie in honour of the Prince Regent's Birthday.

Meanwhile, the Recruiting Parties previously mentioned were busy in Newport, Cardiff, Swansea, Neath and Merthyr Tydfil.

On the 29th October *The Cambrian* reported on the Inspection of the Regiment — "The Glamorgan Militia now quartered at Canterbury were inspected on Thursday 21st ult by the Hon. Major General Grey, who was pleased to express his high approbation of the manner in which they performed the Light Infantry evolutions, as well as the internal economy of the Regiment which had been twelve months under his Command."

On the 10th November, 1813, the Royal Glamorgan relieved in Garrison by the Kildare Corps marched off to Hythe in which Garrison it joined the 2/43rd Foot,[12] 2/52nd Foot[13] and the Royal Staff Corps. In addition to other garrison duties the regiment provided detachments to man Martello Towers in the district and also working parties for the Royal Staff Corps which body was much involved with military engineering. Later a Detachment of 1 Officer and 53 Other Ranks was posted to Folkestone.

Although writing some ten years later, William Cobbett *(Rural Rides)* describes how the coast near Hythe must have appeared to the eye in 1813, "When my eye in swinging round lighted upon a great round building standing upon the beach, I had scarcely time to think about what it could be, when twenty or thirty others standing along the coast caught my eye; and if anyone had been behind me, he might have heard me exclaim, in a voice which made my horse bound — "The Martello Towers by....!"

"Oh Lord!", to think I should be destined to behold these monuments of the wisdom of Pitt and Dundas and Perceval, "Good God!" Here they are, piles of brick in circular form, about three hundred feet (guess) circumference at base, about forty feet high and about one hundred and fifty feet circumference at the top. There is a door about half way up in each, and each has two windows. Cannons were to be fired from the top of these things in order to defend the country against French Jacobins." And also, "Hythe is half Barracks, the hills covered with Barracks."

"Here is a Canal (I crossed it at Appledore) made for the length of thirty miles (from Hythe in Kent to Rye in Sussex) to keep out the French." The military canal was in fact one of the defensive obstacles in the Kent/Sussex anti-invasion defence scheme and was constructed under the direction of the Royal Staff Corps. Parts of the Canal and several of the Martello Towers can still be seen in those districts in the present day.

Other units stationed in the district at this time were, The Aberdeenshire Militia and Derbyshire Militia, at Dover the Galway Regiment, at Deal the Londonderry Militia, and in the North East of the county at Chatham, the Fifeshire, North Down, South Down and Kerry Regiments of Militia.

On December 10th, *The Cambrian* reported the regiment's willingness to proceed on active service — "Highly to the honour of Ancient Britons, the Glamorgan Militia at present at Hythe have volunteered in a body, both Officers and Men, for General Service."

The Corps at this time under the temporary command of Major Robinson was further depleted, as in response to the constant demand it provided a substantial number of Volunteers for service with the Royal Staff Corps, 53rd Foot,[11] 86th Foot,[15] Royal Waggon Train and Royal Sappers and Miners. Several of the Officers also volunteered, and were accepted for the regular service.

Sergeant Thomas Jackson, a Recruiter for the Coldstream Guards, and an ex Militiaman himself was actively recruiting on the South Coast at this time and makes some interesting comments regarding the quality of men drawn into the Line from the Militia — "If taken from such a regiment as I was trained in, The King's Own, Stafford; the Militia Soldier is, in every point of order and discipline, not only his equal, but perhaps his superior." The comparison here being between the Regular and Militiaman. "The Militia Soldier, too, is governed by the same material as he of the Line; the Mutiny Act, or Articles of War, are read to him every month, and for any breach of these articles he is equally liable to punishment, as the Act reads, almost at the end of every Clause — 'he shall suffer death or such other punishment as by general or regimental court martial shall be awarded'."[16]

Between February and April 1814, a Detachment of the regiment was stationed at Ashford. Recalled, it joined the main body on the 12th April, the whole marching out the following day via Dover and Sandwich to arrive at Ramsgate on the 15th. A Circular Letter dated 26th of the same month instructed Regimental Recruiting Parties to discontinue their activities and to rendezvous with the Regiment in Bristol during the following month. On May 9th the Royal Glamorgan marched out from Ramsgate en route to join the Bristol Garrison. Its route instructions were as follows:

| | |
|---|---|
| Monday, May 9th | Canterbury |
| Tuesday, May 10th | Lenham and Adjacent District |

| | |
|---|---|
| Wednesday, May 11th | Tunbridge |
| Thursday, May 12th | Godstone |
| Friday, May 13th | Dorking |
| Saturday, May 14th | Guilford |
| Sunday, May 15th | Guilford (Rest) |
| Monday, May 16th | Odiham |
| Tuesday, May 17th | Whitechurch |
| Wednesday, May 18th | Lavington |
| Friday, May 20th | Trowbridge |
| Saturday, May 21st | Bath, Walcot and Bathwick |
| Sunday, May 22nd | **Bath and District (Halt)** |
| Monday, May 23rd | Bristol |

The Route Order dated May 5th commands Magistrates and all others concerned along the route to be of assistance in providing Quarters, impressing Carriages, and other necessaries.

During its short stay at Bristol the Regiment was mainly employed providing escorts for the movement of Prisoners of War between Portsmouth and Stapleton Prison.

On the 11th June the Regiment marched out of Bristol and proceeding via Aust, Chepstow and Newport arrived at Cardiff on the 13th. On the 16th June the following Circular, No.230 was issued to Commanding Officers of Militia:

"Sir,

His Royal Highness, the Prince Regent, having been pleased in the name of, and on behalf of His Majesty, to sign Orders for the disembodying of the Militia of the County of 'GLAMORGANSHIRE' with all convenient speed; I am commanded by His Royal Highness, for the exemplary and meritorious services of the Corps of Militia under your command, to acquaint you that His Royal Highness is pleased to grant the following allowances on the occasion to the Officers and Men hereinafter mentioned:

To each Subaltern, and to the Surgeon's Mate, if any, an allowance will be made equal to Two Months Pay from the day of disembodying exclusive which being granted to them in this shape, will not interfere with the receipt of Half Pay, nor any other allowance to which they may be entitled, or may hereafter obtain from Government. Officers holding two appointments are however to receive the allowance for one of them only.

The Adjutant, Paymaster, Surgeon and Quartermaster are not to have the allowance of Two Months Pay: it being intended that they shall be retained on duty, and to receive certain Rates of Pay commencing the day subsequent to that of the Disembodying, which Rates shall be communicated to you as soon as they shall have been determined upon."

This lengthy Circular continues with a List of the Payments and Privileges to be made to the Non Commissioned Officers, Privates, etc., e.g.:

Such Sergeants due for discharge and entitled to an out-Pension, and such Corporal and Drummers having a claim for Pension under the General Militia Laws were to receive an advance of Marching Allowance of 1s 10d per day, sufficient to carry them to London (reckoning ten miles for a day's march without halting days) where they could appear for examination before the Chelsea Board.

Non Commissioned Officers and Drummers discharged, and not recommended for a Chelsea Pension, and every Private disembodied was allowed to retain his regimental clothing for that year, and his Knapsack. Non Commissioned Officers and Drummers retained on the Disembodied Establishment were to receive Fourteen Days Bounty and to be paid new Rates of Pay, at that date not yet determined.

Arms, Accoutrements and Greatcoats were to be handed in, and in due course sent to store with the Tents, Camp Equipment and other necessaries.

On the 25th June, 1814, the Regiment was disembodied at Cardiff on completion of a period of over eleven years of continuous service. The following General Order was published to mark the end of that period of Militia History which came to be known as 'The Long Embodiment'.

"Horse Guards,
24th June, 1814,

The re-establishment of Peace having enabled His Royal Highness, The Prince Regent, in the name and on behalf of His Majesty to direct the disembodying of the Militia Forces. The Commander in Chief, previous to their return to their respective Countries and Counties desires thus publicly to offer to them his best acknowledgement for the zeal and perseverance with which they have during a long and eventful War shared with the Regular Army in every military duty which has fallen within their province.

From the gallant and patriotic spirit displayed by the Militia were derived at the most critical periods of the War, the means of reinforcing the disposable Force of the Country, a measure which most essentially contributed to its military renown, by placing the British Army foremost in those Confederate Bands which resisted the unbounded ambition and overwhelming power of the late Ruler of France, and by their bravery and discipline under the direction of Divine Providence, rescued that country from tyranny and oppression, and restored to Europe the blessing of Peace. The Commander in Chief feels personally indebted to the Militia Forces for the ready and cheerful obedience with which they have at all times received his Commands, and he requests that with

58

these heartfelt expressions of approbation, they will collectively and individually accept his warmest wishes for their welfare and happiness.
Sgd.
Frederick,
Commander-in-Chief.

Further Messages of thanks were received from the House of Lords to be read presumably to the regiment at the next Annual Training, or perhaps posted about the various Parishes for the Corps had disembodied weeks before its distribution. In the form of a Circular Letter it had this to say — "Sir, In pursuance of an Order of the House of Lords, I have the honour and satisfaction of transmitting to you a copy of two resolutions, which passed the House on the 5th inst(July) and I have to desire that you will take the earliest opportunity of communicating the same to Officers, Non Commissioned Officers and Men of the Corps under your command.
I have the honour to be, Sir,
Your most obedient humble servant,
(Signed) Sidmouth."

To the Officer commanding the Glamorganshire Militia."
"Die Martis, 5th July, 1814,
"Resolved nemine dissentiente, by the Lords Spiritual and Temporal in Parliament assembled, that the thanks of this House be given to the Officers of the several Corps of Militia, which have been embodied in Great Britain and Ireland during the course of the War, for the seasonable and meritorious services which they have rendered to their King and Country."

"Resolved nemine dissentiente, by the Lords Spiritual and Temoral in Parliament assembled, that this House do highly approve and acknowledge the services of the Non Commissioned Officers and Men of the several Corps of Militia which have been embodied in Great Britain and Ireland during the course of the War, and that the same be communicated to them by the Commanding Officers of the several Corps, who are desired to thank them for their meritorious conduct."

## Footnotes:

1. Frederick, Duke of York, Field Marshall, Commander in Chief of the British Army.
2. Second Battalion, 48th (Northamptonshire) Regt. of Foot
3. Pack Horses used to carry Officers and Regimental Baggage.
   The Soldiers detailed to look after them were known as 'Batmen' a term used in more modern times to describe an Officers Servant
4. T. Gilbey. *Britain at Arms*; p.10. Eyre & Spottiswood 1953
5. *Cambrian* 1804
6. *South Wales Daily News* 1.8.1899
7. *Cambrian* 1/1810

8. *Narrative of the Eventful Life of Thomas Jackson, late Sergeant of the Coldstream Guards* (Birmingham 1847)
9. *The Rambling Soldier* — edited by R. Palmer. Penguin Books 1977
10. T. Gilbey. *Britain at Arms* (p.9). Eyre & Spottiswood 1953
11. 2nd Battalion, 9th (The East Norfolk) Regt of Foot
12. 2nd Battalion (Monmouthshire Light Infantry Regt) 43rd Foot
13. 2nd Battalion, 52nd (Oxfordshire Light Infantry) Regiment
14. 53rd (Shropshire) Regt of Foot
15. 86th (Royal County Down) Regt of Foot
16. *Narrative of the Eventful Life of Thomas Jackson, late Sergeant of the Coldstream Guards* (Birmingham 1847)

# CHAPTER 8

# 1815-1816. The Fifth Embodiment

On March 1st, 1815, following his escape from Elba, Napoleon Bonaparte with eleven hundred men landed at Antibes in the South of France, an event which set Europe into turmoil. Of the Quadrouple Alliance, only Great Britain and Prussia were in any way ready to take the field against that force which rapidly expanded into an Army of two hundred thousand, most of them veterans of the Emperor's previous campaigns. The British Army was particularly handicapped due to the fact that most of its experienced Peninsular Veterans were serving in the Americas which left at home only a small core of experience backed up by a mass of fairly 'green' material. With such units committed to service in Europe, the Militia was once again called upon; certain regiments of the disembodied Force, the Royal Glamorgan included, being drawn out for Garrison duty in the United Kingdom.

In a Letter dated 14th April, 1815, Colonel Henry Knight was instructed as follows:

"Sir,
It being deemed expedient under the present circumstances that preparatory steps should be taken towards completing the Militia by Beat of Drum, I have to desire that you will lose no time in sending out Parties of your Non Commissioned Officers and Drummers to such stations within the County, or the adjacent Counties as you shall judge most desirable for that purpose.

As soon as it shall have been determined on that the recruiting should actually commence, you will be duly appraised thereof, and at the same time furnished with the necessary instructions for your guidance.

I am, Sir, etc, etc
(Signed) Sidmouth."

Where recruiting failed to produce the required numbers arrangements were also made in the County to enforce the Militia Ballot.

On the 25th April, a Circular Letter was received concerning Recruitment and Bounty —

"Sir,
Referring you to my Letter of the 14th inst., I have now the honour to transmit to you an Order of His Royal Highness, The Prince Regent in Council authorising and requiring you to proceed forthwith in raising Men by Beat of Drum for the Corps under your command.

The Amount of Levy Money for each Recruit will be as follows: viz,

| | | | |
|---|---|---|---|
| On being Attested | £1 | 1s | 0d |
| On Final Approval | £2 | 2s | 0d |
| On Joining the Corps when embodied | £1 | 1s | 0d |
| To the Officer and Party on Final Approval and to be distributed in such a manner as the Commanding Officer shall direct | £1 | 1s | 0d |
| Total Levy Money | £5 | 5s | 0d |

The Recruits are immediately upon enlisting to be examined and attested in the usual manner and they are to be sent up to Headquarters weekly or oftener if necessary, for the purpose of being finally approved by the Adjutant and Sergeant of your Corps.

After final approval, they are to be paid the second part of the Bounty and allowed to their homes, and you will not fail to cause it to be explained to them that should circumstances render it un-necessary or inexpedient to re-embody the Corps under your command, the Guinea which is hereby made payable upon its being embodied, will be paid to them at the first period of their assembly for Annual Training and Exercise, and you will also appraise them, that in the event of their being embodied, each man will be entitled to an additional Guinea for the purchase of necessaries under the provisions of the 125th Section of the General Militia Act.

Each Recruit will be entitled to Pay and Marching money for the days of march to and from Headquarters.

The Prince Regent has been pleased to direct that no Boys shall be enlisted until further orders.

In every respect the Recruiting is to be carried on under the same Rules and Regulations that were in force when it was discontinued in the month of April last.

You will take care to select the most active and intelligent Non-Commissioned Officers for the performance of this service, and you will not fail to transmit to me, on the 1st June next, and on every succeeding month a Return showing the number of Recruits which have been raised in the preceding month, and also the strength and stations of the various parties.

I have only to add that the Non-Commissioned Officers and Drummers who may be employed upon this service will receive the same Pay and Allowances as when embodied.

I am, Sir,

Yours etc, etc,

Sidmouth."

On the 25th April also, Colonel Henry Knight issued by Letter, the following instructions to Captain Ray, Adjutant at the Cardiff Headquarters.

"Sir,

As it appears to be the intention of the Government that the Militia be raised by Beat of Drum under the superintendence of the Staff of Regiments who will be employed on this service, you will from time to time issue such Orders, and give such Directions as you think most conducive to the end intended, and distribute the Recruiting Parties as you think best for the good of the service, etc." and on the 28th of the month reminds the Adjutant of his wishes in respect of that part of the Levy Money allocated to the Recruiters.

"Sir,

A certain sum from the Guinea due to the Officer and Parties, on final approval, will be expended in Hand Bills or Advertisment stating the amount of Bounty, and the conditions on which the Recruit is enlisted, as also a Cockade and a Bowl of Punch to be given to each Recruit.

I am, Sir

etc, etc,

Henry Knight (Colonel)."


Rates of Pay for Permanent Staff as authorised by Circular 232/June 1814 are listed in the Order Book, and are of interest, if only for comparison with present day rates.

| | |
|---|---|
| Adjutant | 8s per diem |
| Paymaster | 6s per diem (in a Corps consisting of 3 Companies and upwards) |
| Surgeon | 6s per diem |
| Quartermaster | 5s per diem (in a Corps exceeding 360 Private Men) |
| Sergeant Major | 1s 10d per diem (in a Corps consisting of two or more Companies) |
| Sergeants | 1s 6d |
| Corporal | 1s 2d |
| Drum Major | 1s 6d (in a Corps consisting of 3 or more Companies) |
| Drummers | 1s per diem |

On the 16th June *The Cambrian* gave notice of some impending movements — "The Glamorgan, Denbigh, Flint and sixteen English Regiments of Militia are destined to relieve those now serving in Ireland but the Order to embody the Royal Glamorgan was not issued until the 29th of the month when W.O. Circular Letter, No.283 gave the following instructions:

"Sir,

His Royal Highness has been pleased in the name and on behalf of His Majesty to Order the Regiment of Militia under your command to be drawn out and embodied.

I have the honour to acquaint you that the Establishment of the said Regiment as approved by His Royal Highness, and as signified to me by Lord Sidmouth, is to consist of the numbers detailed in the margin, in which are included that additional Sergeants, Corporals and Drummers allowed to the Militia when embodied for actual service."

The Establishment noted in the margin was as follows, no change having taken place from that laid down for the Corps in 1811.

1 Colonel as Lt. Colonel
1 Lt. Colonel as Major
1 Major as Captain
6 Captains
7 Lieutenants
5 Ensigns
1 Adjutant
1 Quartermaster
1 Surgeon
1 Sergeant Major
1 Quartermaster Sergeant
20 Sergeants
20 Corporals
1 Drum Major (or Bugle Major)
13 Drummers
and 403 Private Men

Upon receipt of the instructions immediate steps were taken to draw out the regiment, the embodiment taking place under the command of Colonel Henry Knight at Cardiff. There the 18 Officers, Non-Commissioned Officers and Private Men were divided into six Companies, and in accordance with the instructions given in Circular Letter No.283 already referred to.

On the 22nd July, the Regiment having assembled on the 7th at Cardiff, the following notice appeared in *The Cambrian* "Return of Militiamen who have not joined in pursuance of an Order from the Lord Lieutenant of the County of Glamorgan for embodying the said Militia on the 7th July, 1815.

| Name | Age | County | Occupation | Attested at | Date |
|------|-----|--------|-----------|-------------|------|
| William JOHN | 23 | Glamorgan | Labourer | Swansea | 23rd May, 1810 |
| Jacob JONES | 18 | Mon (Langstone) | Labourer | — | 1st May, 1815 |

| Name | Age | Origin | Occupation | Place | Date |
|---|---|---|---|---|---|
| David LEWIS | 27 | Pembroke | Labourer | — | 3rd May, 1815 |
| Patrick WELSH | 18 | Monaghan (Danmoine) | Tailor | Cardiff | 4th May,1815 |
| Walter DAVID | 34 | Carmarthen (St. Clears) | Labourer | — | 11th May, 1815 |
| John SWAIN | 24 | Dublin (St. Catherines) | Labourer | Cardiff | 20th May, 1815 |
| David JONES | — | Pembroke (Rossether) | Labourer | Swansea | 23rd May, 1815 |
| John GRIFFITHS | — | Glamorgan (Bishopston) | Labourer | Swansea | 29th May, 1815 |
| Llewelyn JOHN | 29 | Glamorgan (Bettws) | Butcher | — | 4th April, 1814 |
| Daniel WILLIAMS | 16 | Kent (Ashford) | Shoemaker | Bridgend | 9th Dec., 1813 |
| Abraham LEWIS | 23 | Monmouth (Wenallt) | — | Newport | 5th May, 1815 |
| William RICHARD | 23 | Carmarthen (Llandybie) | Labourer | Cardiff | 6th May, 1815 |
| William MATHEW | 24 | Glamorgan (Llantrisant) | Collier | Dyffryn | 22nd May, 1815 |
| John LLEWELYN | 26 | Pembroke (Redboxton) | Labourer | Aberdare | 23rd May, 1815 |
| Thomas REES | 30 | Carmarthen (Llandyfeiliog) | — | Swansea | 31st June, 1815 |
| Rees PARRY | 18 | Brecon (Brecon) | Labourer | Cardiff | 19th Nov., 1811 |
| Griffith WILLIAM | 25 | Glamorgan (Lougher) | Labourer | Swansea | 24th Feb., 1815 |
| Lot MAGGS | 20 | Gloucester (Frenchay) | Smith | Newport | 21st May, 1815 |
| Isaac PROSSER | — | Monmouth (Goytre) | Labourer | Cardiff | 9th Jan., 1814 |
| William HOWELL | 23 | Carmarthen (Laugharne) | Labourer | Merthyr | 11th May, 1815 |
| David MORGAN | 18 | Monmouth (Goytre) | Labourer | Cardiff | 9th Jan., 1814 |
| Jacob THOMAS | 18 | Carmarthen (Llanfihangel) | Labourer | Aberdare | 22nd May, 1815 |
| Thomas RICHARD | 20 | Glamorgan (Swansea) | Labourer | Newport | 20th May, 1815 |
| Rosser REES | — | Monmouth (Llanddewi) | Labourer | Newport | 9th June, 1815 |
| John CHILD | 23 | Hereford (Labrey) | Labourer | Newport | 5th May, 1815 |
| William DAVIES | 18 | Glamorgan (Llangyfelach) | Labourer | Swansea | 16th May, 1815 |
| Williams DAVIES | 19 | Glamorgan | Labourer | Neath | 26th Jan., 1814 |
| John GRIFFITHS | 19 | Carmarthen (Llandarrog) | Labourer | Cardiff | 31st May, 1815 |
| David RICHARD | 23 | Glamorgan (Tythegston) | Tailor | Cardiff | 28th Sept., 1813 |

| Samuel THOMAS | 18 | Monmouth (Bedwellty) | Shoemaker | Cardiff | 7th Jan., 1814 |
|---|---|---|---|---|---|
| Thomas WILLIAMS | 20 | Glamorgan (Llangynfyd) | Labourer | Swansea | 6th June, 1815 |
| Cadogan EVANS | 20 | Glamorgan (Llantrisant) | — | Cardiff | 4th May, 1815 |
| James DOWLAN | — | Cumberland (St. Mary) | Hatter | Aberdare | 25th May, 1815 |
| Henry HARRIS | 21 | Pembroke (St. Wynals) | Labourer | Cowbridge | 1st June, 1815 |
| Tom THOMAS | 15 | Monmouth (Liswene) | Labourer | Cardiff | 6th Sept., 1813 |
| Tom JONES | 20 | Glamorgan (Neath) | Weaver | Neath | 6th Dec., 1814 |
| Lewis JONES | 25 | Carmarthen (Llandyfeiliog) | Labourer | Cardiff | 1st Feb., 1814 |
| Thomas JONES | 15 | Carmarthen (Llandeilo) | Labourer | Neath | 27th Mar., 1815 |
| William BEVAN | 26 | Monmouth (Bishton) | Labourer | Newport | 19th May, 1814 |
| Patrick BREAN | — | Carlow (Birkarry) | Tailor | Newport | 19th May, 1814 |
| William DAVID | 19 | Carmarthen (Conwyl) | Labourer | Swansea | 6th May, 1814 |
| John EATON | 34 | Glamorgan (Bridgend) | Cordwainer | Cardiff | 25th Mar., 1815 |
| Thomas LEWIS | 29 | Glamorgan (Cowbridge) | Cordwainer | Cardiff | 17th May, 1815 |
| Evan MORGAN | 15 | Glamorgan | Cordwainer | Swansea | 30th Mar., 1813 |
| John REES | 17 | Glamorgan (Neath) | Copperman | Neath | 24th Jan., 1814 |
| Thomas THOMAS | 23 | Cardiganshire (Llandysul) | Saddler | — | 25th May, 1814 |

By Order of the Lord Lieutentant of Glamorgan
Wm Ray,
Captain and Adjutant,
Royal Glamorgan Regular Militia


**Extract from the Militia Law**
And be it further enacted that if any Militiaman ordered by the Lord
Lieutenant to be drawn out and embodied shall not appear in pursuance of
such Order, every such Militiaman shall be liable to be apprehended and
punished as a Deserter, and if any person shall harbour, employ or conceal
any such Militiaman when so ordered to be embodied, every such person
shall for every such offence forfeit and pay a sum of £100."
On 12th August the Royal Glamorgan Militia set out for Swansea, but on
arriving at Cowbridge were re-routed to Bristol and duties in that Garrison
where on the 8th September Orders were received that the Corps in company

with the Worcester Militia should embark as soon as Transports were available for Waterford in Ireland.

Disembarking at Waterford on the 20th September, the Corps rested a few days, before marching out on the 26th for Youghal, Co. Cork, where they arrived on the 8th. There it remained until early in the following year, as a military presence in that district was essential for the preservation of Law and Order.

On January 26th, 1816, the Regiment moved on to Clonmel, a town some 50 miles inland. There it was stationed until ordered back to England. On the 22nd April, the 1st Division marched out for Middleton near Cork being followed the next day by the 2nd Division. On the 29th, the whole embarked at Cove of Cork to arrive at Bristol on May 6th. Shortly thereafter, on being ordered back to its own County, the Regiment left Bristol, and marching via Chepstow and Newport arrived there on the 9th. At Cardiff, the accounts were settled, Arms and Accoutrements returned to Store and farewells made. On the 17th May, 1816, the Royal Glamorgan Militia was disembodied, its Officers and 403 Other Ranks being dismissed to their homes.

The long years of War had given the Militia the opportunity to prove its usefulness. Throughout, often in most difficult and trying circumstances, high standards were maintained, and the duty well done. This was particularly true of the Glamorgan Corps, for it had built up for itself an excellent reputation during the long years of conflict. Apart from the performance of its duties, it had produced a steady stream of Volunteers for service with the Line, a contribution which when combined with the total effort, did much towards ensuring the successful conclusion of the War. Sadly, such service was all too quickly forgotten, as on the return to Peace, the Government having had its 'Pound of Flesh' lost interest. The Militia was allowed to fall into a state of decline, and soon became little more than a military force on paper.

The disembodiment of 1816 saw the commencement of a long period of military inactivity with the regiments of Militia existing only as a permanent staff of NCOs and Drummers supervised by an Adjutant at the respective county headquarters, and sufficient only to provide a small armed party if called upon to assist the Civil Power.

In mid-October, the disturbances now remembered as the South Wales Strike of 1816 took place during which the Permanent Staff of the Royal Glamorgan undertook some useful service at Merthyr. David Jones in his excellent book *Before Rebecca* states that the root cause of the trouble lay in disputes over wages and the price of bread. Commencing on the 16th October, the striking iron workers succeeded in closing down almost every blast furnace from Blaenavon to Merthyr, and some having armed themselves were likely to prove more than a match for the Magistracy and a small force of Special Constables. A call for military assitance resulted, which saw the embodiment of the Swansea and Cardiff Troops of Yeomanry Cavalry and the rapid move by coach to Merthyr of Captain Ray, Adjutant of the Royal

Glamorgan, together with 24 armed Sergeants and Buglers of the Militia Permanent Staff. Arriving there on the 18th October, they found the town fairly quiet and had no difficulty in reporting to the Magistrates assembled in the Castle Inn. There Captain Ray organised a defence against attack, and was later reinforced by the arrival of 120 Officers and men of the 55th Regiment[2] and the Swansea Troop of Yeomanry Cavalry.

Later that day, the strikers assembled somewhat noisily outside the Inn — a number later estimated to be in the region of eight thousand. Encouraged by the presence of a determined and strongly positioned body of soldiers the Ironmasters (some of whom were also Magistrates) refused to negotiate with the workers whilst they remained in a riotous state. That decision having been made clear, the Riot Act was read, but without immediate effect. The Magistrates next ordered the Yeomanry Cavalry to disperse the crowd, and this they accomplished using only the flat of their Sabres as a means of persuasion. Some thirty arrests were made, and to give credit where due, the mounted Volunteers were able to complete a difficult and unwelcome task without bloodshed.

Captain Ray and his Militia Staff stayed on in Merthyr until the 28th of the month when the continued presence of Regular Troops in the town allowed them to return to Cardiff.

It is interesting to note that although Militia in the past had been used with great success in similar civil situations, there was a marked reluctance to call upon them to perform such duties within the boundaries of their own County. During the Merthyr Riots of 1800, the Ironmaster, Samuel Homfray, had informed General Rooke, then commanding the Severn Military District, that in his opinion the Glamorgan Militia "Would be of little service as there are a great many Merthyr people amongst them."

That opinion was to be proved wrong, particularly in 1831, when Glamorgan Militiamen additional to Permanent Staff were used to effect in a situation much more dangerous than the Merthyr Riots of both 1800 and 1816.

*Footnotes*
1  Jones, D., *Before Rebecca — Popular Protests in Wales, 1793-1835*
2. 55th or Westmoreland Regiment (after 1881, The Border Regiment)
3. *Cambrian Register*

68

# CHAPTER 9

# 1817-1854. The Years of Neglect. Revival in 1853

"A successful War seems to demoralise a national military spirit, and military inactivity is usually the sequence," so stated B.E. Sargeaunt in his *History of the Monmouthshire Militia*[1], and such was certainly the case in matters of home defence for many years after Waterloo. The Militia was allowed to slip away into obscurity, with the laws ordering its annual training rescinded, and the ballot which kept the force up to strength suspended, such matters being submitted annually to Parliament for decision. In consequence the Royal Glamorgan was not drawn out for training until 1820. The Permanent Staff however, remained reasonably active and were called out on the 16th March, 1818, to guard the cargo of a wreck which had come ashore near Aberthaw. In September of the same year, ten of the Staff were sworn in as Burgesses of Cardiff, an honour bestowed upon them in recognition of assistance given to Magistrates in preventing riot in the town on the 4th May.[2]

A Return dated 24th January, 1819, showed the Staff to consist of Captain and Adjutant William Ray, Quartermaster Henry Steel, Lt. and Paymaster John Langley, Surgeon William Hopkins, 1 Sergeant Major, 1 Bugle Major, 23 Sergeants, 14 Corporals and 7 Buglers.

In February 1820, they paraded with the Cardiff Troop of Yeomanry Cavalry to celebrate the Accession of King George IV together with town Officers and other dignitaries.

On the 13th May, notices appeared in the press announcing that the regiment would be drawn out for training commencing 29th May, and ordering the balloted men to assemble in Cardiff at 8 a.m. on the day stated. During training the men were billeted in the Public Houses and Lodging Houses of the town and paraded each day, in the forenoon and afternoon for Drill and other military exercise which took place on the Castle Green or the Cardiff Arms Field. The Press described them as young men who promised to shape up into good soldiers, and the Lord Lieutenant at the close of training on the 25th June expressed his satisfaction on their soldierlike appearance and good conduct. The men he said "were highly creditable to the County and to the Regiment".[3]

Outside these training periods, the townspeople of Cardiff were constantly reminded of the regiment by the appearance each Sunday in full dress at Church Parade of the Militia Permanent Staff. They created local interest, but outside of that, balloted service in the Corps was not particularly popular. Militia Societies flourished and advertised regularly in the weekly newspapers. For the sum of one guinea (£1.05) they promised Subscribers exemption from service in the event of their being selected by ballot. This was done by providing sufficient cash to pay the appropriate fine, or with which to purchase for themselves a substitute. The Regimental Band at this time was also in great demand to provide music at various Cardiff and County functions, but was maintaining with some difficulty the fine reputation that it had held during the war years. The Regiment assembled again in 1821 and trained in Cardiff for 21 days commencing May 3rd.

The Regiment was not drawn out again until 1825 as Government did not consider such activity necessary. In April 1825, the much respected Henry Knight who had commanded the Corps for seventeen years resigned, and was succeeded as Commanding Officer by John, Second Marquis of Bute, then also Lord Lieutenant of the County.

The Regiment assembled for training in Cardiff on the 26th May, and so pleased was the Marquis with their progress, that on the last day of training, every Private Man was given by him a Shilling with which to drink his health. On the following day he entertained both Non Commissioned Officers and the Band at Dinner in the Cardiff Arms to signify his particular pleasure on their efforts.[4]

The Royal Glamorgan next mustered in 1831, but during that long interval many changes had taken place. 1827 saw the death of William Ray who had been the Regimental Adjutant since 1814. He was succeeded by Captain Jonathan Howells who took up his appointment on the 20th September of that year.

The Government in its pursuit of economy sought reductions in the Militia Permanent Staff. In consequence the year 1829 saw that of the Royal Glamorgan reduced to 1 Adjutant, 1 Sergeant Major, 1 Acting Quartermaster Sergeant, 9 Sergeants and 4 Buglers. No provision was made by Government for a Band, its upkeep being a matter for the purse of the Officers. The Marquis of Bute stepped in to assist, and provided from his private pursse the wages for six musicians as also £100 per annum towards Band upkeep and expenses. In return, the small group provided music at his private functions and performed publicly on the Castle Green once every week. In 1899, Mr Hookstaff of Paradise Place, Cardiff, a member of that small band of music makers was still alive, and able to provide the local newspapers of the day with some interesting reminiscences.[5] The Permanent Staff meanwhile were accommodated in the St. Mary Street Armoury, near the site of the Bethany Chapel, which site is now occupied by the well known Howell's Department Store. An upsurge of civil unrest in 1830 and 1831 saw the Militia Ballot enforced for the last time by an Order in Council. In consequence, preparations were made by the Lieutenancy, and each County Sub-Division was in March 1831 informed of the numbers they were required to provide from the men eligible for Militia Service. The allocation list was as follows: Kibber — 10, Cardiff — 23. Caerphilly Upper — 76, Caerphilly Lower — 24, Dinas Powis — 16, Cowbridge — 20, Ogmore — 10, Miskin — 31, Neath

— 53, Newcastle — 39, Swansea — 61, Llangyfelach — 40. In all a total of 403 men.[6]

The prospect of Milita service was not at all well received by those liable for service, and a study of a sample of the 1819 Militia Lists which will be found in the appropriate appendix will show that there was much social bias. In Merthyr, for example, no less than 1,500 of the men listed appealed against being included in the ballot. Only those who had rupture, defective eyesight or had lost fingers were successful.[7] The main fear of workmen was the prospect of having to act in Aid of Civil Power during their period of service. In the light of events which took place in that town later that year, their fears were fully justified.

The Regiment assembled in Cardiff for 28 days training commencing 12th May, the Staff having to start from scratch due to the fact that very few of those present had any prior experience of military training. On June 1st, disturbances which had sparked off in Aberdare spread to Merthyr, and received such support from the workers of that district, that within hours they succeeded in bringing normal life and industrial work to a standstill. The Constables which Magistrates had at their disposal to keep the peace found themselves completely unable to cope with the situation, and in consequence urgent calls were made to the Lord Lieutenant for military assistance.

First to respond to the call was the Military Commander at Brecon, who immediately dispatched a Detachment of the 93rd (Sutherland) Highlanders[8] to Merthyr. By 10 a.m. on the following morning they arrived at the Cyfarthfa Iron Works. Meanwhile, that same day, Friday, June 3rd, the Permanent Staff of the Royal Glamorgan Light Infantry together with a Detachment of the Militiamen under training were sent off to Merthyr by coach under the command of the Adjutant and accompanied by Lt. Colonel Morgan of Llandough Castle.

In Merthyr, the Highlanders had been involved in a struggle with the Mob outside the Castle Inn, where a workers delegation had received no satisfaction from their negotiations with Ironmasters and Magistrates assembled therein. The mob outside on being made aware of that failure were spurred on by certain ringleaders to disarm the Soldiers with disastrous results. The Soldiers opened fire upon the crowd outside and many, mostly curious bystanders were killed or seriously wounded. Only one or two Soldiers were disarmed in the melee, but several were injured, two of them seriously, but as was usually the case in such confrontations it was the protesting crowd which suffered most, and without the satisfaction of having their grievancies remedied. Later in the day, the Highlanders were reinforced by the arrival of the Glamorgan Militia Detachment and the Eastern (or Cardiff) Troop of Yeomanry Cavalry. Thus strengthened, the military withdrew from the Castle Inn and moved off to set up Headquarters at Pen-y-Darren House. Fortunately for all concerned, there were no further clashes with the disgruntled workmen that day.

The military were not to have it all their own way, as amongst the Merthyr workforce were many ex-soldiers whose experience and organising ability was greatly underestimated. This was demonstrated clearly on Saturday, June 4th, when Captain Moggridge with 40 men of the Cardiff Troop of Yeomanry Cavalry, who had been sent out to meet and escort the Baggage and Ammunition Waggons of the 93rd Highlanders, then on their way to Brecon, were ambushed in the ravine at Cefn Coed y Cymmer, and were only able to extricate themselves from a dangerous situation with difficulty. Major Rickards with 100 Yeomen of the Central Glamorgan Troops moving up from Merthyr in support of Moggridge also met stiff opposition in the form of Musketry fire and stones. Unable to deploy his men for a charge, due to the narrowness of the front and the steep sides of the ravine, he was forced to withdraw, but Moggridge by that time had successfully extricated his detachment, and went on to meet the Waggons and escorted them in to Pen-y-Darren by another route. By far the most serious reverse of the day was the successful ambush by rioters of a half-Troop of the Swansea Troop of Yeomanry Cavalry on the Hirwaen/Merthyr Road, which event both heartened the workers, and was to have serious repercussions in connection with the future of Yeomanry Cavalry in the County.

Emboldened by this success, a strong force of rioters advanced later that day on Pen-y-Darren House, but withdrew on finding the military well prepared to disperse them.

Sunday, 5th June, passed off quietly, but on the Monday morning, the mob once again assembled and moved out to confront the military. Forewarned of their approach, Lt. Colonel Morgan, accompanied by Magistrates, and a force consisting of 110 Officers and Men of the 93rd, 50 Officers and Men of the Royal Glamorgan Militia, and 300 Mounted Men of the Glamorgan Yeomanry Corps, set out to meet the threat. The place of confrontation was at Dowlais Great Pond, where appeals by the Ironmasters followed by a reading of the Riot Act failed to persuade the angry workers to disperse. Having exhausted every peaceable method, the Magistrates handed over matters to the military. The Highlanders and Militia were ordered to load, and the Yeomanry to draw Sabres. Each word of command was given slowly and clearly, in order that the mob would be in no doubt as to the final intention. At the point when a bloody solution seemed unavoidable, the frontage of the mob gave way, and the Yeomen moving in then quickly dispersed the mass using as encouragement only the flat of their Sabres.

The conduct of the Militia throughout had been steadfast and exemplary and did much to silence the critics. Contrary to prediction, there had at no time been any sign of unreliability. They had performed well, one of the most difficult and trying tasks that can ever be asked of a Soldier.

After 1831, the Militia was once again allowed to slide back into semi-obscurity, and in 1836 had to suffer the indignity of having its very teeth drawn. On the 7th February of that year, instructions were received ordering all weapons on issue to the force to be returned to the Tower, sufficient only being retained by each regiment to arm, what by that date was a very much reduced Permanent Staff.

Contrary to some beliefs, the Glamorgan Regiment was never directly involved against the Chartist movement, but during the last two months of 1839, the Permanent Staff were involved in training Special Constables to meet any threat. The well known confrontation in Newport with Chartists was handled by Regular Troops, with Royal Glamorgan Permanent Staff standing by in Cardiff well clear of the situation.

Following the death on July 30th, 1844, of the Adjutant, Captain Howells, the post remained vacant until 1846, when Captain J.H. Armstrong took up the appointment.

The 18th March, 1848, saw the death of the Marquis of Bute. In his will he bequeathed to the Regiment the Band Instruments, which body he had so long maintained. Sadly, he was not to see the revival of the long dormant regiment which resulted from the Militia Act of 1852. By early 1853, the reawakened interest found voluntary recruitment for the Corps well advanced, and in Cardiff, preparations were being made to receive them for training.

On the 20th May, 1853, the Royal Glamorgan, having emerged from the doldrums assembled in Cardiff for 28 days training. There, in addition to the Permanent Staff were one Sergeant, one Corporal and 14 Private Men of the 85th Regiment,[9] as also a similar detachment from the 73rd[10] whose task it was to assist the Staff quickly whip the recruits into some recognisable military shape.

On arrival, some Militiamen were housed in Longcross Barracks,[11] but the majority of the men found themselves, as in past years, billeted in Inns and Lodging Houses about the town. The Drill ground was the large space situated between Cardiff Castle and the Westgate, then known as the Cardiff Arms Field, part of which is today occupied by the national Rugby Stadium. In the absence, due to indisposition of Lt. Colonel Tynte, the regiment was commanded by the Second in Command, Lt. Colonel Knox, who set up his Headquarters and Orderly Room at 3 Crockherbtown.

Although at that time unavoidable, the practice of billeting Militiamen in public houses was most undesirable. Away from the supervision of the Officers and NCOs during off duty hours, with pay or bounty money in their pockets. The men with nothing better to occupy their time, more often than not, took to heavy drinking. In consequence, the conduct of a minority became a source of nuisance about the town and adversly affected the good name of the regiment.

Their presence in town nevertheless, created great interest, and the CMG[12] reporting on progress 26th May, stated: "They are daily engaged in various exercises in which they have already attained creditable proficiency. It is a subject of general remark, that the appearance of the men in the short time that has elapsed has greatly improved, and there can be no doubt, that under the able supervision of the Officers in command, the Corps on the expiration of 28 days drill, will be found to be most efficient."

"In the Field, their appearance is very imposing. In the streets, their bearing is soldierlike and respectable. We are happy to have it in our power as public journalists to bear our testimony that their conduct has been hitherto, exemplary, and we congratulate the Adjutant, Captain Armstrong, whose care at enlistment, has contributed to the success which has crowned his efforts, as upwards of 900 Recruits, who in a short time, will be transformed into useful soldiers have answered to their names."

The social life of the town was livened by the presence of the Corps "We have to record a dejeuner dansante, given at the Cardiff Arms by Lt. Colonel Knox and the Officers of the Royal Glamorgan Light Infantry on Saturday 4th inst to the distinguished gentry of the County."[13]

On June 11th, an interesting letter was published in the same Newspaper,

"Sir

It has just occurred to me that the publication of a few brief reminiscences of the services of the old Glamorgan Militia might not altogether be uninteresting at a time when a new regiment of young Glamorgan blood is in the process of formation and are now training upon the same ground that their forefathers trod before them. It has gladdened the heart of many a veteran to find that the reputation and renown of the County for possessing the smartest and most efficient Militia Regiment in the service during the long and bloody war that prevailed half a century ago, bids fair to be maintained by the Corps at present assembled.

"The old Regiment had the good fortune always to be well commanded, and amply supplied with Officers of the highest County blood, and to all appearances, the young one has the same bright prospect before it at the present time, and doubtless both Men and Officers are well pleased with each other.

"The old Glamorgan Light Infantry had a high character for strict discipline and steady behaviour in Quarters and gallant conduct in the Field, and it was always held in great estimation when Brigaded with other Troops.

It was commanded, when first embodied by the Grandfather of the present Marquis of Bute, then Lord Mountstuart; and in later years by his noble Father. The regiment was embodied with very little intermission from the year 1790 to the Peace of 1814, and was re-embodied in 1815 on the escape of Bonaparte from Elba, and remained so until the War was terminated by the Victory at Waterloo and the Capitulation of Paris. During that long service, the regiment did Garrison Duty in various parts of England. It was encamped on Warley Common in Essex, at Dover, in Sussex and other places, and sailed from Portsmouth in the year 1799 for Ireland without leaving a man behind in Hospital. It was in Garrison in Dublin with a portion of the Guard on duty at the Houses of Parliament when the Act for the Union of Great Britain and Ireland was passed in the year 1800.

The Regiment is stated to have supplied the Line by voluntary enlistment with nearly 5,000 Men, and throughout the severe and hardfought Battles of the Peninsula and also at Waterloo, the Royal Glamorgan always furnished its quota to fill the ranks of many a gallant Regiment, the 4th[14], the 11th[15], the 53rd[16] and many others amongst the number. The Regiment was very popular everywhere, and its splendid Band under poor Owen, latterly of the Scots Greys, was an especial favourite. I will conclude this hasty sketch with an extract from a Letter I have just received from an old friend in London. The extract is as follows:

'Your Militia, I expect are crack men, unless they are much altered from when I knew them in 1805 in Sussex.

The Men were at that time good Soldiers and the Officers were Gentlemen, and I do not think Glamorganshire men will have deteriorated since that time.'

Cordially concurring with those sentiments,

I remain Sir,

Your very obedient Servant

The late Surgeon of the Regiment."

*The Guardian* continues its report on the regiment on June 18th — "The men of Glamorgan who behaved with such propriety during their stay amongst us imparted so much pleasurable animation to the inhabitants that we are confident the departure is witnessed with regret. We have reason to be proud of them. In former times, says a correspondent in this day's *Guardian*, when exercising in Brigade, with other Regiments, under the command of a General Officer, the Glamorgan Militia was made the regulating Battalion more than once, and from the proficiency which the successors of the old Glamorgan have attained in the Art of War, we have no doubt that were another opportunity of a similar nature to occur, the young Soldiers of the present day would be equally advanced in their gallant profession."

And later in the same issue.

"On Monday afternoon, after the Men had gone though their exercises, they were each presented with a handsomely bound Bible — Welshmen with a Welsh Bible, and those that understood English with one in that language. Nearly a thousand copies of the Scriptures have been provided by public subscription by the exertions of that most excellent lady, intimately connected with one of the principal families of the County, namely Mrs Armstrong, Wife of the gallant Adjutant of the Regiment.

The Bibles were presented by that Lady, assisted by the Rev. W. Leight Morgan, Rev. T.Ll. Griffiths, Rev. G.D. Wrenford, Rev. D. Noyle, Mr Andrews, Scripture Reader, Mrs Leigh Morgan and other Ladies.

It was an interesting sight. Previous to the distribution, the Rev. Leigh Morgan addressed the regiment to the following effect — 'Soldiers of the Royal Glamorgan Militia. By the kind permission of the Commanding Officer I am allowed to address a few words to you on this interesting and important occasion. You have now come to the last week of your training, but before you are dispersed and have gone to your separate homes, I have the privilege to inform you that everyone of you who is willing to receive it will be presented with a Bible, gifts of your Friends and neighbours throughout the County in which you dwell in token of their good wishes to you and the interest they feel in your welfare. I gladly thus publicly bear my testimony to your general good conduct during the time you have been in the town of Cardiff. You have been exposed to many and great temptations, unavoidable to some extent in a large seaport town like this. You have been billeted, necessarily so, in various Taverns and Beer Houses and you have had your evenings unoccupied. When all these and other circumstances are taken into consideration, it is not surprising if some of you have been overtaken in a fault: but the public testimony of this town as far as I know, is that you have behaved well and that your general character has been praisworthy, and I have no doubt that your bravery and military discipline are not inferior to your good conduct.'

The Inspection and Review of the Corps which took place on the 14th June was reported in great detail — "The Review took place on Tuesday by Colonel Barnard who commands Troops in South Wales. The weather was extremely favourable and the Park was attended by an immense concourse of spectators who evinced the warmest interest in the proceedings. The various Equipages of the neighbourhood families studded the ground. Large numbers of richly attired Ladies flitted to and fro, followed by groups of admiring swains, adding to the charm of the scene.

Soon after 11 o'clock the white plume of Colonel Bernard caught our eye. He was mounted on a very handsome Charger as was also Lt. Colonel Knox and Captain Armstrong the Adjutant. Colonel Barnard placed himself by the superb Saluting Flag which had been the evening before presented to the Corps by the Ladies of the regiment, and was received by the General Salute. He then, accompanied by Colonel Knox rode down the front and up the rear of the Line, the men standing as steadily as veterans, and as neat in their clothing as many ball room figures. As the regiment passed under inspection, but one feeling pervaded the thousands who were assembled as spectators — unqualified admiration for their magnificent and soldierlike appearance.

During the inspection, a Band of Drums and Fifes which had hurriedly got together, enlivened the Field, and immediately after Colonel Barnard had resumed his position at the Saluting Flag, the regiment broke into Open Column right in front and marched past in slow time to the fine old martial air, 'The Garb of Old Gaul' composed by two Officers of the 42nd Regiment[17]. This movement was admirably performed. The regiment then marched past in quick time to the tune 'Ap Shenkin';[18] and succeeded equally well. It then closed to Quarter Distance and marched past in that formation."

The account then goes on to describe the various complicated movements of Battalion Drill culminating in Forming Square. Into this formation rode the Inspecting Officer, and in his address to the regiment, complimented the men on their steadiness under Arms and stating that he would report most favourably on their state of efficiency to the Home Secretary. After dispersal of the parade, Colonel Barnard inspected the Regimental and Company Books in the Orderly Room where once again, he found everything as it should be, and to his entire satisfaction.

The Newsheet goes on to say: "An interesting incident occured in the course of the afternoon. As Colonel Knox and Colonel Barnard were passing through Angel Street, Colonel Barnard saw Mr Jenkins, who has care of the grounds of Cardiff Castle, with his Waterloo Medal suspended on his breast, and immediately went up to him saying, he could not pass an old Soldier without exchanging a few words with him. He made various enquiries relative to Mr Jenkins' services, and parted with many expressions of gratification on finding a brave man who had served his Country faithfully, having the means of spending the autumn of his life in comfortable repose. Mr Jenkins was for some years the Sergeant Major of the Royal Glamorgan, which post he relinquished when the regiment was recently embodied. He was succeeded by Sergeant Major Mitchell, whose conduct during the training has gained for him the respect of the Lieutenant Colonel, the Adjutant and Officers generally. Mr Mitchell is an experienced Soldier, and has a remarkable aptitude for imparting instructions to Recruits. He is most assiduous, persevering and firm, but never harsh in executing the very onerous duties attached to his office."

On the day following the inspection, the Commanding Officers, Lt. Colonel Kemeys Tynte, in a Regimental Order, warmly thanked all Ranks for the zealous and efficient manner with which they had performed their duties. The full establishment of the regiment on that date was: 3 Field Officers, 10 Captains, 20 Subalterns and Staff Officers, 1 Sergeant Major, 36 Sergeants, 36 Corporals, 7 Buglers and 1086 Private Men.

On the 16th June, having returned their weapons and kit, the men were dismissed from training taking with them the thanks as expressed by William Williams, the Mayor and Chairman of town Magistrates, for their good conduct during the training period.

In April 1854, Captain J.K. Erskine succeeded Captain Armstrong as Adjutant, and supervised the annual training which took place in Cardiff between 8th September and 3rd October. Sadly the conduct of the regiment on that occasion gave cause for complaint, which matter was at the time fully aired in *The Cambrian.*

"The Royal Glamorgan Militia have daily continued their exercises in the Field at Cardiff, and nightly also, when many of them have exercised the patience of the Townspeople and the Police about the streets. It must be admitted they are becoming a smart body of Soldiers, which does credit to their Instructors. The gentlemanly bearing of the Officers wins the respect of all classes."

Worse was to come! but for that experience the townspeople of Cardiff had to wait until the following year when the Crimean War crisis led to a full embodiment of the regiment.

The outbreak of the Crimean War and consequent demand for manpower led to some legislation relating to the Militia. An Act of December 1854 empowered the Crown to accept offers from Militia to voluntarily serve outside the United Kingdom and Bounty was offered to Militiamen who expressed themselves willing. The War also resulted in a mass of military appointments as young men came forward to serve as Militia Officers.

Some saw the force as a convenient back door approach to a Regular Army Commission and a taste of action. Others, however, found it a means of conveniently expressing patriotic fervour without being in the least exposed to the slighest risk or discomfort. As will be seen, the Royal Glamorgan did not serve abroad, but was confined instead to a long period of local Garrison duty.

## Footnotes

1. Sergeant B.E., *The Royal Monmouthshire Militia.* RUSI. 1910
2. *Cambrian.* 2 October, 1818
3. *Cambrian.* 30 June, 1820
4. *Cambrian.* 24 June, 1825
5. *Western Mail.* May, 1899
6. *Cambrian.* 19 March, 1831
7. *Cambrian.* 25 February, 1831
8. After 1882. Argyll and Sutherland Highlanders
9. King's Light Infantry. After 1882, 2nd Bn, King's Shropshire Lt. Infy.
10. Perthshire Regt. After 1881, 2nd Bn, The Black Watch
11. Once on the site of the present Cardiff Royal Infirmary, Newport Road
12. *Cardiff and Merthyr Guardian*
13. Cardiff Arms. An Inn on a site near to the present day Angel Hotel
14. After 1881, King's Own Royal Lancaster Regt.
15. After 1881, The Devonshire Regt.
16. After 1881, 1st Bn, King's Shropshire Light Infantry
17. After 1881, 1st Bn, The Black Watch
18. Composed by John Parry *(Bardd Alaw)* one time Bandmaster of the Denbighshire Militia. Appeared c.1803, and was later adopted (at a date not known, but after 1831) by the 41st Foot (later 1st Bn, The Welch Regiment) as its March Past in Quick Time. As a March, the tune may well have been in earlier use by the Royal Glamorgan.

Cardiff Castle — Inside Grouds
West Frontage c.1820
*Courtesy of The Welch Regiment Museum*

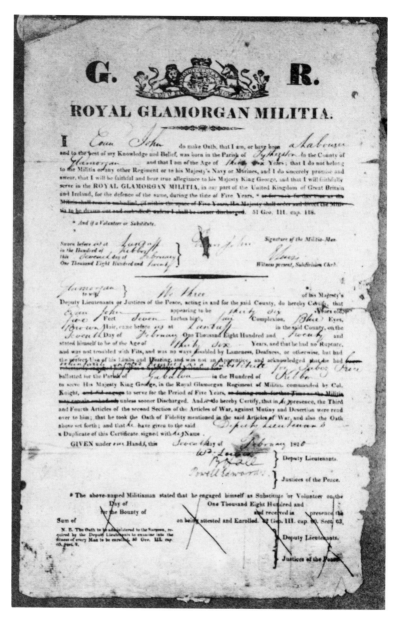

Attestation Certificate of Evan John for the Royal Glamorgan Militia,
1820
*Courtesy of The Welch Regiment Museum*

# *GLAMORGAN*

# MILITIA.

NOTICE is hereby Given, That the MILITIA of the COUNTY of GLAMORGAN is appointed to be trained and exercised (as the several Acts of Parliament in that behalf made direct) for TWENTY-ONE DAYS together, to commence on THURSDAY, the 3rd Day of MAY next, at the TOWN of CARDIFF; and all Men enrolled in and belonging to the said Militia are hereby required to assemble in the said Town of Cardiff, at Eight o'Clock in the Morning of the same Day.

By Order of HENRY KNIGHT, Esq. Vice-Lieutenant,

### *EDWARD PRIEST RICHARDS*,

### Clerk to the Lieutenancy.

N. B. Every Person belonging to the said Militia, who shall not appear and join the said Regiment of Militia, at the time and place appointed will be subject to the penalty of Twenty Pounds, or Six Months Imprisonment.

*Cardiff, 16th April, 1821.*

R. LLOYD, PRINTER, HIGH-STREET, CARDIFF.

Militia Training Notice, 1821

SITE OF THE
**ROYAL GLAMORGAN MILITIA BARRACKS (THE ARMOURY)**

Circa 1856

1844 1855          1863 1866

RESPONDING TO THE MILITIA ACT OF 1757, THE LORD LIEUTENANT, THE EARL OF PLYMOUTH, RAISED THE ROYAL GLAMORGAN MILITIA IN 1760.. IT BECAME THE ROYAL GLAMORGAN LIGHT INFANTRY MILITIA IN 1812 AND THE 3rd (MILITIA) BATTALION,THE WELSH REGIMENT, FROM 1881 TO 1908..THE WELCH SPELLING DATES FROM 1920.. FIRST EMBODIED IN 1761, IT SAW NUMEROUS PERIODS OF SERVICE IN BRITAIN, IN THE CHARTIST RIOTS, IRELAND AND IN SOUTH AFRICA (1899-1902)..
THE ORIGINAL HEADQUARTERS WERE THE MILITIA BARRACKS ON THIS SITE..
THE HOUSE, KNOWN AS THE ARMOURY, ACCOMMODATED THE CAPTAIN/ADJUTANT AND HELD THE ARMS & ACCOUTREMENTS OF THE FORCE..
THE SITE BECAME PART OF THE ST. MARY STREET COMMERCIAL FRONTAGE FOLLOWING THE ERECTION OF LONGCROSS BARRACKS AT NEWPORT ROAD IN 1843.

GLAMORGAN MILITIA
DONATED BY CARDIFF CITY COUNCIL

16

Plaque sited on the corner of St. Mary St. and
Wharton St., Cardiff, to mark the site of the old Militia Store and
Armoury.
*Courtesy of The Welch Regiment Museum*

# GLAMORGANSHIRE MILITIA.

NOTICE IS HEREBY GIVEN, that pursuant to
the Order and Authority of CHRISTOPHER
RICE MANSEL TALBOT, Esq., M.P., Her Majesty's
Lieutenant of the County of Glamorgan, and of Sir
GEORGE TYLER, K.H., M.P., and JOHN BRUCE
PRYCE, Esq., two of the Deputy Lieutenants of the
same County, a GENERAL MEETING of the
LIEUTENANCY of the said County of GLA-
MORGAN, will be holden at the TOWN HALL, in
the Town of BRIDGEND, in the said County, on
MONDAY, the 20th day of SEPTEMBER INSTANT, at
One o'Clock in the Afternoon of the same day, for the
purpose of RAISING and ENROLLING 676 MEN
to serve in the MILITIA of the said County, being the
number required to be raised in the Year 1852, under
and by virtue of an Act of Parliament passed in the last
Session of Parliament for Consolidating and Amending
the Laws relating to the Militia in England, and for
general purposes.

Dated the 1st day of September, 1852.

E. P. RICHARDS,

Clerk to the General Meetings of Lieutenancy,

Cardiff.

Militia Notice, 1852
General Meeting of the Lieutenancy

*Cardiff, 3rd May, 1853.*

# ROYAL GLAMORGAN MILITIA.

NOTICE is hereby given, that the MILITIA of the County of Glamorgan is appointed to be trained and exercised (pursuant to the several Acts of Parliament made in that behalf), for **Twenty-eight** Days together, to commence on FRIDAY, the Twentieth day of **May** instant, at the **Town** of Cardiff, in the said County ; and all **Men** belonging to the said Militia are hereby required to assemble in the said Town of Cardiff, at Eleven o'Clock, on the Morning of the same day ; and every **Man**, not labouring under any **Infirmity** incapacitating him, who shall not appear at the time and place aforesaid, will be deemed a Deserter, and incur the Penalties provided by Law in such a case.

By order of Her Majesty's Lieutenant.

## E. P. RICHARDS,

Clerk of the Lieutenancy.

W. BIRD AND SON, PRINTERS, CARDIFF.

Militia Training Notice, 1853

The Rummer Tavern, Castle Street, Cardiff, c.1856
Typical of the inns on which the Militia were billeted
*Courtesy of The Welch Regiment Museum*

Ex Sergeant Major William Findlay
Sergeant Major of the Regiment c.1855 and later Gatekeeper, Cardiff
Castle
*Courtesy of The Welch Regiment Museum*

# CHAPTER 10

# 1855-1856. The Sixth Embodiment

The Regiment assembled in Cardiff on January 4th, 1855, under the command of Lt. Colonel Kemeys Tynte for its sixth wartime embodiment. A small number of the men were accommodated in Longcross Barracks, but the majority were billeted upon Inns and Public Lodging Houses about the town — a necessity which was over sixteen months to result in conduct which gravely tarnished the regiment's reputation.

In early February, a heavy fall of snow brought all training to a standstill, but by mid month had cleared sufficiently for the training programme to continue. The thaw also saw the commencement of an intensive recruiting drive, a part of which was concentrated on Cardiff.

*The Cardiff and Merthyr Guardian* (or *CMG*) reporting the activity stated "The Band belonging to this Corps turned out from the rendezvous on Saturday last headed by two Sergeants holding before them naked Swords and with many coloured ribbons streaming from their caps. A considerable concourse of people attended them in their perigrinations about the town, where at different intervals, one of the Sergeants in a loud voice, informed the glory loving Britons, who seemed not a little gratified at these martial emblems, that the Royal Glamorgan Light Infantry Militia were then wanting Recruits, and that all active young men of 5'4" and upwards were invited to join them." Similar parties were soon at work on market days the length and breadth of Glamorgan. At this time also moves were made amongst the Gentry of the County to subscribe towards the purchase of some pieces of silver Mess Plate for the Officers Mess. The move was strongly supported by the *CMG* which stated "Subscriptions have been entered into by the County Gentry for presenting the Militia with their Mess Plate, and we think it nothing but courtesy that every County should act in the same manner." Examples of the Plate and Cutlery presented to the Regiment as a result of that appeal are still in use with the 3rd Battalion, Royal Regiment of Wales or are preserved in the Regimental Museum.

Being a Welsh Corps, the Regiment was in the habit of celebrating St. David's Day, and this is confirmed by the *CMG* in its March 3rd edition.

"Colonel Kemeys Tynte has resumed command of the regiment, which during his absence on Parliamentary duties has been commanded by Lt. Colonel Wheatley. Thursday last, 1st March, being the day dedicated to the tutelar Patron Saint of 'Gwlad ein Genedigaeth'[1] the majority of the Privates of the Royal Glamorgan Militia mounted the Leek, the National Emblem of Old Cambria. The Leeks were worn a la mode of a military plume, and no doubt many of the gallant fellows pledged their Saint and each other during the day in 'Cwrw Da'[2]. It is highly creditable to the regiment that no excesses occurred on this Anniversary so much honoured by Welshmen. We rejoice to state that the health of the regiment is excellent, there being but five cases of sick in Hospital. A handsome white Goat has been presented to the Regiment, and the gallant Lt. Colonel has presented a beautifully wrought silver Goat carrying panniers for snuff for the Mess Table. Recruiting goes on favourably."

The report is most interesting in that it indicates that the Royal Glamorgan were in the habit of wearing the Leek in their caps on St. David's Day many years before a similar custom was adopted by the 1st Battalion, The Welch Regiment. That Regiment then known as the 41st or The Welch Regiment of Infantry was at that date serving in the Crimea and had itself adopted a Goat of Russian origins as a Regimental Mascot. It is likely however that in view of the above report that the Royal Glamorgan Light Infantry (later to be 3rd Battalion, The Welch Regiment) were ahead of the regular regiment in adopting that custom.

The custom was by no means new, being considered old in the 23rd Foot, The Royal Welch Fusiliers as far back as 1777. The Denbighshire Militia also had a Goat which accompanied that Corps during the long Napoleonic Wars embodiment. As far as is known, the Royal Glamorgan carried no official Motto until 1881, when on becoming 3rd Battalion, The Welsh Regiment it took into use the existing Welsh Motto of that Corps.

On March 10th, the *CMG* recorded — "On Thursday last, two Companies of the Royal Glamorgan Light Infantry made their debut in the neat and becoming red Frock Coat[3] which is to be supplied to all Militia Regiments on the 1st April. Since the embodiment of the above regiment about 190 new Recruits have been obtained."

On March 17th it reported the first of a series of disgraceful off duty conduct and clashes with the police by members of the regiment which were to mar the Regiment's reputation, but which could have been greatly minimised had the military authorities of the day applied some forethought to the matter of billeting and payment of Bounty. Such disturbances were not confined to the Royal Glamorgan, but became commonplace amongst embodied Militia Regiments throughout the country.

"On Thursday before D. Lewis, Esq., J. Batchelor, Esq., and E.P. Richards, Esq., of Plasnewydd, Thomas John a Militiaman, was fined £5 or 2 months imprisonment for assaulting P.C. Wallbridge."

Before the end of the month an additional 27 Recruits had been enrolled and the Regiment issued with new knapsacks and clothing. Regimental strength on March 31st stood at:

1 Colonel,
1 Lt. Colonel,
1 Major,

7 Captains,
12 Subaltern Officers
26 Sergeants (inc. 1 Sergeant Major)
18 Corporal, 10 Buglers and 479 Privates (exclusive of absentees).
A Circular Instruction dated 27th March gave all Militiamen who had voluntarily enrolled prior to 12th May, 1854, the option of being re-attested to serve the unexpired period of their service or of being discharged. This was in consequence of their Conditions of Service being varied by the Act of 1854, previous to which the Crown could embody Militia "On actual Invasion, or imminent danger thereof". That wording the Act changed to read "Whenever a state of War exists between Her Majesty and any Foreign Power." As War had been the impetus for embodying Militia and not Invasion or threat of same; within strict terms of Law, numbers of men were illegaly embodied.

Not for many years prior to 1855 had the Publicans and Lodging House proprietors of Cardiff been called upon to accommodate troops for such a long period. In peacetime during the normal short period of Militia annual training the obligation was welcomed as a boost to normal trading. The prospect of having troops billeted on them for an indeterminate period was a different matter, and within less than three months they commenced to complain. The March 2nd edition of *Cambrian* tells us "The Publicans of Cardiff begin to feel the pressure of having to provide Quarters for the Militia. Many Tradesmen, whose business is limited, and have young families to maintain, feel that the continuation of the burden will be intolerable." It also suggested a part solution to the problem. "It occured to us that some steps should be taken to afford the Militia-men amusements of an instructing and elevating character. Here they are distributed amongst the Public Houses of the Town, spending their time, as do persons who frequent those places, and we know well the demoralising effect of such a way of passing through life. It is true that there has been no serious outrage to complain of, but who knows what idleness and drink may bring forth." A prophetic statement, as the danger signs were clear, and to accentuate even further its point, the paper reported the death of a Militiaman from overindulgence of drink.

"On Sunday night a Private named Daniel Watkins, a native of Caerphilly, died awfully suddenly in the Glove and Shears Public House from the effects of drinking. What an end! It appears he had returned to the above house in a state of intoxication, and was shortly afterwards summoned to another world."

During the last few days of March, and the first week or so in April, the Militia commenced to 'paint the town red'. *The Cambrian* reporting these events stated "The Militia, the Royal Glamorgan, has been much crippled in its strength by the withdrawal of hundreds, who having served the period for which they enlisted, have for the present retired to their respective homes. The conduct of the Men during the last week or nine days, has been most reprehensible. It appears that they received some accumulated Pay or Bounty, and were allowed a certain time to spend the money, which they did by getting drunk.

We will not enter into particulars, as our account would certainly tarnish any laurel which the Corps may have gained, but Superintendent Stockdale, could, we are sure, unfold a tale which would greatly surprise parties who have never witnessed the irregularities which dissolute Soldiery will commit, and it occurs to us very forcibly, that the Militia should not be called out unless a Barracks can be provided for them."

The loss of strength which had occurred was of course due to the change in conditions of service brought about by the Act of 1854, and which has been heretofore described. The *CMG* published somewhat conflicting reports, the first of which on March 31st suggested that the regiment was not overmuch affected.

"The Royal Glamorgan Militia paraded on Sunday morning and attended St. John's and St. Mary's Churches in their new Uniforms. They looked remarkably well. On Thursday those of the Men who had enlisted previous to March 12th, 1854, and were liable to be called out 56 days in every year were informed that they would be paid a further Bounty of £1 in addition to the yearly Bounty of £1 if they stayed with the Regiment for Permanent Duty. Much disaffection has occurred in several Militia Regiments in consequence of those who enlisted before the above date fancying that they were not bound to serve more than 56 days in one year. We are happy to state that nothing of the kind has occurred here. Indeed, such is the popularity of the Corps that nearly the whole of those entitled by Order of the War Office to go home volunteered at once for Permanent Duty."

The fact of the matter was that far from volunteering to stay on, the majority of those concerned seem to have opted for discharge, for the *CMG* of April 7th had to state "On the 1st of the month, 104 Men had availed themselves of the terms of their attestation and had left their Billets for their homes. Twenty of the Men however, have returned. It is expected that many more will rejoin the regiment in the course of a few days."

On April 21st permission was given for Militiamen to volunteer their services into the Line, and event which was to further weaken the Corps and also contribute to the reprehensible conduct of some of the Men due to the distribution of Bounty. The *CMG* reporting on that development stated "Special Instructions having been received to permit open volunteering from the Militia into the Line, the Men were informed of the same yesterday morning (the Friday) on Parade.

They were formed into a Square, and Major E.R. Wood being in command of the regiment seated on a beautiful cream Charger addressed them to the following effect — 'In the absence of their Commandant Lt. Colonel Kemeys Tynte who was unavoidably detained in London on urgent Parliamentary business, it became his duty to inform them, that an Officer had been sent down here to receive Volunteers for Regiments of Cavalry, Artillery, Sappers and Miners,[4] Foot Guards, Infantry and Royal Marines. By the instructions sent out to the Officers commanding the Militia, they are strictly enjoined to afford every facility for the volunteering of their Men, and incase they should refuse to discharge any Private who should be desirous of volunteering, they must transmit their reason in writing for such refusal to the General Officer Commanding the District, for reference to Headquarters. Colonel Tynte and all his Officers were desirous that the Men should volunteer for the Army, and that he, Major Wood, felt assured that the Men of the regiment who would volunteer would exhibit that spirit of determination which Welshmen always had, and if they ever came into the presence of the enemy would also fight like the Welshmen who had distinguished themselves so nobly. He trusted that they would continue to evince that soldierlike conduct which they uniformly had shown since their connection with the Regiment, and then they could not fail to satisfy the Commanding Officers of those regiments into which they might Volunteer.

The Major's address was listened to with breathless attention. The Men appeared exceedingly pleased with the opportunity of showing their gallantry. During the course of the day, nearly 100 volunteered into different Regiments of the Line."

On April 27th *The Cambrian* carried a report which described the break down of discipline brought about by the Bounty Money paid to those men who had volunteered for regular service.

"During the past week, large numbers of Men in the Uniform of the Royal Glamorgan Militia have daily been committing the most disgraceful excesses apparently unchecked by the Authorities. Drunkeness, profane Swearing, Obscenities, Street fighting, etc., have been perpetrated on a scale never in our recollection witnessed here before. It is said the delinquents are Men who have joined the Regular Forces of Her Majesty, and that the Funds with which they have degraded themselves, alarmed, disgusted and intimidated respectable persons, formed a portion of the Bounty to be paid to them for turning out to serve their Queen and Country.

Some time ago, the Regiment were paid arrears due to them, upon which occasion they were allowed a week in which to spend the money and from what we have written, readers may well imagine in what manner it was laid out. Now is all this necessary? Is it essential to the well doing of the Service that Militiamen should at stated intervals be tolerated in the commission of revolting brutalities? Would it not be better if they were encouraged to save their money, and to form habits of forethought, economy, steadiness and sobriety? So bad has been the conduct of the Men during the week that on Thursday (yesterday) the Magistrates publicly commented upon it.

On the part of the inhabitants, we protest against the system hitherto followed."

Meanwhile, recruiting for the Line continued with the Militiamen blowing their Bounty about the town. There was however some relief in sight, for the Regular Army having got hold of their men were not all that slow in removing them. Strangely, the *CMG*, unlike *The Cambrian* says very little about the misconduct described, and is more than kind in its reporting on the culprits as they finally left the town. On Saturday, May 5th, it commented as follows: "The Royal Glamorgan Light Infantry Militia — 169 fine Fellows, the flower of this Corps have volunteered for service with the Line. On Wednesday and Saturday the 11 who had enlisted in the Royal Marines left Cardiff for Plymouth and on Friday 36 left to join the 11th[5] at Brecon. On Sunday, 10 left for the Scots Fusilier Guards in London, and on the same day 21 left for the Royal Artillery at Woolwich. The remaining 91 left on Tuesday, 33 of whom had enlisted in the 85th (Sunderland) and 58 in the 8th[6] at Chatham.

The morning previous to their departure the streets presented the appearance of a Garrison Town and Soldiers were seen hurrying in every direction bidding adieu to their friends and comrades and preparing for their departure. A portion left Cardiff by the South Wales Railway, and the remainder embarked by Packet.

They mustered in the Square in front of the Town Hall and were accompanied by Major Wood and their Officers to the Pier Head and Railway Station preceded by the Band playing 'Cheer, Boys, Cheer', 'The Girl I left behind me' and other favourite military airs. They were also attended by a large concourse of spectators who appeared to take interest in these brave fellows who have shown great courage in leaving their peaceful homes in Old Cambria to fight their Country's Battles in a Foreign Land, nothing daunted by the privations and hardships which have been endured by our Army in the East." The comments of the more respectable elements of the Cardiff community on the departure of those patriotic reprobates are not recorded.

The Regimental Band which since the death of its benefactor, the Marquis of Bute, had been somewhat neglected, was at this time strengthened and by dint of much practice was beginning to recover something of its past reputation. The *CMG* commenting in its May 12th edition states "It affords us much pleasure to notice the improvement of the performance of the Militia Band. The Bandmaster, Mr C.W. Riddle, is untiring in his exertions to increase the efficiency of his pupils who are now 20 in number. On last Sunday morning the Band accompanied the Regiment to Church for the first time."

In London meanwhile, Sir G. Tyler, Member for the Borough took up the vexed problem of billeting v Barracks for the Militia and received from the Minister some surprisingly vague replies to his questions. Observing that in Cardiff a considerable number of Militiamen were billeted on the town in spite of the presence of Longcross Barracks, he was told that the Board were not aware that such a place existed (much laughter). In reply, the Hon. Member stated that in pursuance of a previous application to have Militiamen occupy the Barracks he had been told it was not possible due to the fact that the establishment was already occupied by a Depot. Investigation revealed that the Depot consisted of one Sergeant and one Private of the Pensioner Corps (more laughter) which led him to believe that although the Barracks was not large enough to accommodate the whole of the County Regiment, begged that its use could be extended to accommodate a larger portion of the Regiment than had hitherto been allowed."

On May 24th, the Regiment was Reviewed in the Castle Park by Colonel Barnard, and in spite of their bad conduct in the town, the event drew a large gathering of spectators. Due to discharges and volunteering for the Line, the numbers on Parade were smaller than usual, but for all that, they were still capable of making a good impression. *The Cambrian* reporting the event stated — "There still remain a considerable body of able men, whose soldierly appearance and expertness under arms won for them the unfeigned applause of all who beheld the rapidity and ease with which they performed their graceful evolutions." Commenting on the Band, the report said — "A pleasing and exhilarating feature in the day's proceedings was a Band attired in new and appropriate uniform. In the last War, when the Militia of the Kingdom was mustered in large force, and when it was not an uncommon circumstance to see several Regiments exercised in Brigade, not only was the Royal Glamorgan, under Colonel Knight of Tythegston Court justly accounted one of the most perfect regiments in the service, but its Band was celebrated wherever it went. Mr David Owen[7] the Bandmaster, was an accomplished Musician, and led by him, the famous old Welsh Airs, which first were heard amongst the din of Border warfare, and which served to nerve the arm of the Ancient Cambrian to do battle bravely against the invaders of his native soil, might be found influencing the most fashionable and courtly assemblages of the Saxon. The Glamorgan is still a smart Regiment, and its Band will probably attain high proficiency in the delightful science of Music. But why not give us our native Music, which is so superior to the purilities that float their hour upon the flight of popular fancy, and then sink into deserved oblivion? We trust to see a Revival."

The next to bring the name of the regiment into disrepute was, very sadly, to be one of its Officers, and *The Cambrian* lost no time in reporting the matter. Its June 1st issue stated — "Yesterday at Cardiff Police Court, before David Lewis, Esq., Mayor, and John Batchelor, Esq., ex Mayor, Lieutenant Adams of the Royal Glamorgan Militia was charged with assaulting P.C. Basham at a late hour on the night of the 8th inst whilst the latter was in the execution of his duty."

At the request of the Lieutenant's Solicitor, the Case was adjourned for a few days, but on the 22nd, the story continued.

"Lieutenant Adams of the Royal Glamorgan Militia was convicted in the Penalty of £5 on Monday last by the Borough Magistrates for assaulting P.C. Basham."

It appeared, that the worthy, but inappropriately named Constable, was escorting a Prostitute to the Police Station at about 3 a.m. one morning, when he was accosted by the inebriated Officer. Adams, in an ill timed display of gallantry interfered with the Constable and his charge, and ended up striking him. The Magistrates expressing their disapproval of his conduct, imposed upon him the maximum fine they were empowered to award, five pounds being a considerable sum of money in those days.

The Militia Band meanwhile had become quite proficient, and being considered to have arrived at an acceptable standard, was given the Commanding Officers' permission to give evening Concerts to the Public on fine evenings at the Militia training ground.

In July, Colonel Kemeys Tynte was pleased to recognise the valuable services rendered to the Corps by its Sergeant Major, and arranged for the Adjutant to present him with a Gold Watch and Chain, the Watch bearing the inscription — "Presented to Sergeant Major Findlay by Colonel Kemeys Tyne, MP, Commanding, Royal Glamorgan Light Infantry, as a testimony of his approbation. Cardiff, July 3rd, 1855."

In August, Captain W.H. Bennett succeeded Captain Erskine as Adjutant and in the same month the regiment received a new precedence number to mark its place amongst the Militia Regiments of the United Kingdom. The *CMG* described the procedure — "The large increase of the Militia which under Her Majesty's Regulations and Orders for the Army take rank after the Line according to a numerical roster as fixed by Lot, and the organisation of a portion of that Force as Artillery, have rendered it necessary to determine the precedence of the new regiments recently enrolled. A Board of Militia Officers was ordered to assemble in the Camp at Aldershot for the purpose of declaring the Precedence alphabetically of the Militia Artillery, which in virtue of its organisation, will take the right of the Infantry. It is to be clearly understood that this List has reference mearly to circumstances of Parade."

In the List which follows, the following Welsh Regiments of Militia are mentioned — Glamorgan Militia Artillery 15, Royal Pembroke Artillery Militia 24, Royal Carmarthen 24, Royal Monmouth 31, Royal Flint 32, Royal Glamorgan 44, Royal Brecknock 132, Royal Denbigh 46, Royal Radnor 50, Royal Carnarvon 56, Royal Montgomery 57, Royal Merioneth 60, Royal Anglesey 61, Royal Cardigan 64.

The report went on to say — "The Militia Regiments will in future wear these numbers on their Caps." True for some, but not for all, and certainly not in the case of the Royal Glamorgan.

In September, due to a shortage of farm labourers and a bumper harvest a certain proportion of each Militia Regiment were given leave of absence to assist with that work, the numbers temporarily released from the Royal Glamorgan being 165.

The Regiment continued to give generously of its ranks to the Regular Army, being under constant and intense pressure to that end from the Recruiting Teams. The *CMG* commented on those proceedings on September the 8th and gives us some idea of the Line Regiments competing.

"During the past week, the military ardour of the Privates of the Royal Glamgoran Militia have been successfully roused by the active Recruiting Sergeants who have held out every inducement for them duly to enrol themselves among Her Majesty's Regular Forces, and have profusely offered them every inducement which is naturally to stimulate the Recruit — Bounty, Promotion, Glory, Pillage, Frolic and Fun, and cleverly hinting of the possibility in this merit rewarding age, of the sanguine Recruit possessing a Marshall's Baton at some distant period. The eloquence, materially assisted by a copious supply of Sir John Barleycorn was productive of success, and from the 31st ult until Wednesday, no less than 42 well drilled and efficient Volunteers have enrolled themselves in the 7th,[8] 8th,[9] 12th[10] 23rd[11] 85th[12] and other regiments of Rifle Brigade and Fusilier Guards.

A little merriment has being going on during the past week amonsgt the Men on the occasion of their commencing a military career and on leaving their Comrades in Arms."

The merriment appears to have cost at least one Militiaman a sore head, the CMG, 29th July, 1855 telling us that "A Private of the Royal Glamorgan Militia received a severe wound in the head on Sunday night. It appears that he had been drinking in some of the notorious houses in Charlotte Street and conducting himself in an aggrevating and insulting manner. Eventually he picked up a quarrel with a female in the Caledonian Beer House, who at once broke a Ginger Beer Bottle on his head, inflicting thereupon a wound. In the circumstances she has not been apprehended as the injury sustained was not of a dangerous character."

On October 12th, *The Cambrian* which at that time appeared to be keener on reporting the less savoury side of the Royal Glamorgan activities gave details of another clash between Officers of the Corps and the Police.

"At Cardiff Police Court yesterday, Lieutenant Adams and Lieutenant O'Grady of the Royal Glamorgan Militia appeared before David Lewis, Esq., Mayor of Cardiff and John Batchelor, Esq., ex Mayor, to answer a charge of having assaulted a Police Constable while in the execution of his duty. Fining Lt. Adams £5 and Lt. O'Grady 40/-, including Costs, the Bench stated, 'We have no desire to bring the Regiment into hostile collision with the civil force, but we must preserve the peace of the town, and we will do so!' "

On October 13th, the Magistrates in writing to Colonel Kemeys Tynte to further express their concern stated as follows:

"Sir,

I am directed by the Magistrates of the Borough to inform you that complaints have lately been made to them as to the conduct of some of the Officers of the Royal Glamorgan Militia, and two cases of assaulting the Police in the execution of their duty having also been brought before them, they beg to express a hope that you will endeavour to prevent a repetition of such practices for the future.

The Magistrates direct me to address to you in the first instance, and to state that should any further complaints be brought before them, they

will feel it their duty to report those complaints to the Secretary at War, a course they would exceedingly regret being forced to adopt.
I have the honour to be, Sir
etc., etc.
John Morris (Clerk to the Justices)."

Colonel Tynte's reply, far from expressing regret, and a promise of stiff consequential military punishment to such offenders was high handed and arrogant in the extreme and did him absolutely no credit.

"London,
October 18th, 1855,

Sir,
I have the honour to inform you that I am directed by Lt. Colonel Kemeys Tynte, M.P., to acknowledge receipt of your Letter dated Cardiff, October 15th, 1855, and to state that for the information of the Magistrates he considers the first part of your communication requesting the Officer Commanding to prevent a repetition of an irregularity on the part of two Officers of the Regiment an unmerited imputation upon himself and the Officer temporarily Commanding the Regiment, as well as an uncalled for reflection upon the discipline of the Corps.
With reference to the latter part of your letter, he begs me to add that he is quite prepared to meet any charge which the Magistrates may think fit to make against the regiment under his command.
I have the honour to be, Sir,
etc, etc,
J.K. Erskine,
Captain and Adjutant, RGLI."

In spite of the high handed replies (Lt. Colonel Wood had penned a similarly worded missive to the Magistrates), the two Colonels were furious and far from unconcerned. It is interesting to note that during the remainder of the embodiment, the conduct of both Officers and Other Ranks of the Royal Glamorgan gave no cause for complaint or reproach. During the last week of October 1855, the Regiment was inspected by Colonel Tynte and was drawn up for the event along St. Mary Street, Cardiff. Normally, events of that type were held on the Cardiff Arms Field, but the state of tide together with a river in flood made that venue unsuitable on the day selected.
Desertion, although not heavy, was not uncommon, and once a man was away, it was no easy task to apprehend him once he reached the conglomeration of mines and industrial workings which abounded in the mineral valleys. *The Cambrian*, 23rd November reports the apprehending of such an offender. "William David Francis was charged at Neath with having

deserted from the Royal Glamorgan Militia and committed to the House of Correction to await orders from the Authorities." In that month also a fire came close to destroying the Officers Mess and property, but complete loss was avoided by the prompt action of men on duty.

On November 30th, the Press reported that Government facing difficulty in maintaining the Militia at strength had decided to re-introduce the Ballot. Men from the age bracket 18 to 40 would be liable for service, and if selected would serve for five years. Here once again the authorities had not the courage to insist upon universal service, and declared their intention of allowing Substitutes on the payment of £5 by any man not wishing to meet the obligation. Fortunately the War came to an end before the machinery for re-introducing the Ballot could be properly organised. In consequence, the plan was shelved and soon forgotten.

The Royal Glamorgan at this stage volunteered to serve abroad in Garrison which offer was reported in the Press on December 14th.

"The Royal Glamorgan Militia having volunteered for foreign service will leave early in the spring for the West Indies to relieve a Regiment of the Line ordered to the Crimea." Fortunately for its members that requirement was cancelled, otherwise fever,[13] still the scourge of those parts would have thinned out all ranks considerably.

On December 15th the *CMG*, always ready to defend the County Regiment stated "Considering the temptation to which the Privates of the Royal Glamorgan Militia are exposed by being billeted in some of the lowest Public Houses and necessarily brought into contact with some of the worst characters, it is only a matter of surprise that they are so well conducted. We trust that Government will shortly adopt measures to remedy the system of billeting which exposes the Soldier to unnecessary temptation and is productive of a general physical and spiritual deterioration."

On New Year's Day the Non Commissioned Officers and Private Men were regaled at a good dinner provided at the expense of their Colonel, and during the week the Regular Army gained another 50 recurits.

On February 9th the Regiment turned out to inter with full military honours Captain Mylo Myers, an Officer of the Regiment who had suffocated whilst asleep in his lodgings in Swansea.

On April 19th the Corps underwent a most satisfactory inspection carried out by Colonel Shirley. It was to be the last inspection of the embodiment as during the month orders were received to disembody the Militia.

On the 16th May, 1856, the order to disembody the Royal Glamorgan was received from the Horse Guards, the *CMG* giving details of the regiment's preparations for the stand down on the 24th.

"The Royal Glamorgan Light Infantry Militia — The Order for the disembodiment of this regiment of Militia on Tuesday next 27th inst having arrived last Friday, the Men have been busily engaged during the week returning Regimental Stores, etc. Colonel Kemeys Tyne, M.P., is expected to arrive tonight, but whether there will be any public inspection of the regiment before it is disbanded we do not know at present. We take the opportunity of saying however, that the general conduct of the Men during the time they have been embodied in this town has been with some few exceptional cases, which could not but be expected should occur, has been of a most orderly and respectable character, and the Officers and Men of the regiment will carry with them the best wishes of the inhabitants for their future well being." On that generous note the story of the sixth embodiment ends, the Men being dismissed to their homes on the date stated.

*Footnotes*

1. Land of our Birth
2. Good Beer
3. Refers to the rather short lived double breasted Tunic introduced in 1855.
4. Forerunners of The Corps of Royal Engineers
5. 11th (North Devon) Regt. of Foot after 1881, The Devonshire Regt.
6. 8th (The King's) Regt. after 1881, The King's (Liverpool Regt.)
7. Mr David Owen, one time Bandmaster, The Scots Greys
8. 7th Foot after 1881, The Royal Fusiliers (City of London Regt.)
9. 8th Foot — King's (Liverpool Regt.)
10. 12th Foot (East Suffolk) after 1881, The Suffolk Regt.
11. 23rd Foot — Royal Welch Fusiliers
12. 85th (The King's Light Infantry) Regt. after 1882, 2nd Battalion, King's (Shropshire Light Infantry)
13. Yellow Fever

# CHAPTER 11

# 1857-1880.
# Activities and Reorganisation

Due to the recent wartime embodiment the Royal Glamorgan was not drawn out for training in 1857. In 1858 a Commission was appointed to enquire into "the Establishment and Organisation of the Militia with a view to rendering it more efficient for military purposes."

Amongst several recommendations, the Commission proposed that the annual training be extended to 28 days, that the Permanent Staff be increased, and that the Recruits should undergo a period of preliminary training. It was also recommended that a recognised Musketry Course be included as part of the annual training syllabus. Rather strangely, and in contradiction to what was long accepted practice, the Commission opined that the practice of encouraging Militiamen to volunteer for service with the Line, was "undesirable and inconvenient", predjudicial to the discipline of the Force and disruptive to its organisation.

The Royal Glamorgan assembled for 21 days training in Cardiff on the 28th September, 1858. Due to desertion, sickness and other causes only 250 men were mustered, but nevertheless were described by Colonel Patton, the Inspecting Officer, as being a fine body of well disciplined soldiers. *The Cambrian* described their conduct during training as excellent and records that considerable numbers had volunteered for service with the Line. Commenting on the low turn out the paper stated — "The constantly changing population of Cardiff and neighbourhood, and the fact of its being a seaport town whereby so many facilities of changing residence are afforded to the working classes are the chief causes of absenteeism." It also opined that had the period of training been longer, more men would have been present, as they were still reporting for training on the day of the regiment's dismissal. It hoped however, that the Royal Commission in its wisdom would find a means whereby the number of desertions, fraudulent enlistment and double enrolment which so plagued the Militia nationally would be drastically decreased. That a problem existed, there could be no doubt, as of the 800 men who had accepted a cash bounty on joining the regiment, only 200 had honoured their obligation by appearing as required on the first day of training.

In 1859, it was ordained that the recommendations of the Royal Commission namely, the introduction of preliminary training for Recruits and extending the period of annual training of Militia to 28 days be implemented, but neither change was effected by the Royal Glamorgan. In June notices were placed which announced that the regiment would assemble for training in July, and that men who had failed to report for training in 1858 would not be punished provided that they reported for duty in 1859. On the 14th July, the day of assembly, the situation was even worse than it had been in the previous year with only 147 men answering their names from a roll of 850. Only 7 of those who assembled were men taking advantage of the amnesty offered. On August 2nd, 200 Militiamen and their Officers were inspected on the Cardiff Arms Field by Colonel Raymond, Officer Commanding the Pembroke Dock Garrison. He complimented the regiment, in spite of the disappointing numbers, on its conduct and steadiness under arms. Towards the end of the year, the Volunteer Revival and consequent raising of Volunteer Corps of all arms within the County gave the Permanent Staff of the Regiment a great deal of additional duties, as the demand for their services as Instructors on a temporary basis to the newly raised Corps had to be fitted in on top of their normal regimental activities.

In 1860 the Royal Glamorgan trained in Cardiff from the 20th September to 16th October, and during the year the Militia Armoury and Store was moved from the Old Guild Hall to Blackweir to a site allocated for that purpose between Blackweir Terrace and Colum Place. A number of the Drill Sergeants continued with the work of training the County Rifle Volunteer Corps in Foot Drill and Musketry.

In August 1861, Captain M.B. Harrison succeeded Captain Bennett as Adjutant, and the regiment trained from 18th September to October 14th. During the annual training the men received live firing instruction, the first use of ball cartridge by the Corps in many a long year.

In 1862, the regiment trained from 8th to the 21st May and was commanded by Lt. Colonel E.R. Wood who succeeded Colonel Kemeys Tynte as Commanding Officer on the 29th of that month. In 1863, the Preliminary Training recommended for Recruits was introduced and commenced 10th April. The main body assembled on the 24th April. The whole then training together until 14th May. Longcross Barracks accommodated the Men whilst the Officers set up Mess in Winstone's Hotel. In October, Captain H.A. Palmer succeeded Captain Harrison as Adjutant, and he was able to note that the numbers who had attended annual training were greatly improved.

Between 1864 and 1866 both recruits and main body assembled annualy and were trained in Cardiff during the months of April and May. In 1867 the main body trained from 13th May to 8th June. A Militia Reserve Act of that year allowed Militamen, subject to the Commanding Officers approval to enlist in the Milita Reserve, provided the numbers involved did not exceed one quarter of the effective strength of any Corps. Men enlisting did so for a five year period, and received in addition to the usual Militia Bounty, £1 for every annual training period attended, which training would, with approval be carried out with a Regiment of the Line. In time of War or of threatened invasion, the Militia Reserve would serve with the Regular Army, but for no greater period than that of the emergency, and six months after its ending or of a Declaration of Peace.

In 1868, the main body trained from 28th May to 23rd June when due to lack of space at Longcross Barracks the men were billeted in the Public Houses and Lodging Houses of the town. An inspection of those quarters by the regimental Surgeon found many to be in an insanitary condition, as a result of which the men involved were moved to better class hotel accommodation. 13 Officers and 721 Other Ranks attended training and their conduct in the town was throughout most satisfactory.

In 1870 the main body of the regiment assembled on May 2nd, the Officers messing in the Royal Hotel, St. Mary Street and the men accommodated at Longcross Barracks. On the 24th May on the Cardiff Arms Field, new Colours were presented to the regiment by Miss Talbot of Margam, daughter of the Lord Lieutenant. The stand replaced that which had been in use since c.1855, the remnants of which are today preserved in The Welch Regiment Museum. 15 Officers and 764 Other Ranks were present during training, and apart from one incident involving one Militiaman and the Police, their conduct throughout was exemplary.

The year brought about a change in the wording of the 1854 Act which related to the circumstances under which Militia could be embodied. Hence that wording was to read "Imminent National Danger or of Great Emergency". In 1871 the Regulation of the Forces Act transferred the responsibility for the Militia, Yeomanry Cavalry and Volunteers from the jurisdiction of the Lords Lieutenant to the Crown, and hence the War Secretary. By that means the regulation of the Regular and Auxiliary Land Forces were brought under the umbrella of one government office. Preliminary Training for Militia recruits was also extended to 28 days. The main body of the regiment trained in Cardiff for 28 days commencing May 1st, the men once again being billeted on the town due to the presence in the Longcross accommodation of a detachment of the 23rd, The Royal Welsh Fusiliers. Two houses were rented by the regiment close to the Cardiff Arms Field, one for use as a Hospital, and the other as Regimental Orderly Room. 16 Officers and 773 Other Ranks paraded for annual inspection on May 26th. 54 Militiamen were listed as 'Absent from Training'. In 1872 the regiment trained from 22nd April to 18th May, which period was fairly uneventful. For the following year preliminary training for Recruits was extended to 56 days and commenced June 9th at Longcross Barracks. On August 1st, 1873, the Recruits moved out to Maindy Field and there set up a tented encampment large enough to house the whole Corps. They were joined there by the main body on August 4th, and although few of the Militiamen had any previous experience of life under canvas, the experiment proved to be a great success. Training was carried out in the vicinity of the camp, the men were healthier due to the outdoor life and due to the greater control which could be exercised over the men by the Officers and Non Commissioned Officers, the discipline of the regiment was greatly improved. 17 Officers and 680 Other Ranks benefitted from that experience, and thereafter the Royal Glamorgan and its successor Battalion housed all ranks together under canvas during annual training.

Officers Group. Cardiff Arms Field 1871
L. Heyworth, R.W. Llewellyn, H.C. Gould, H.S. Gordon, C.R. Reade

OFFICERS, ROYAL GLAMORGAN LT. INFANTRY AND OTHERS
MAINDY FIELD 1871

(1) Mr Noble 16th GRV; (2) W.H.R. Boyle 23rd R.W.F.; (3) Capt. Grayham 23rd R.W.F.; (4) J.J. Ross, Lt. 13th Lt. Infty; (5) Lt. A.t. Crawshay; (6) Capt. Gould; (7) Capt. Morris; (8) S.B. Blyth 23rd R.W.F.; (9) H.J. Knox 23rd R.W.F.; (10) Capt. L. Hayworth; (11) Capt. Fennell; (12) Capt. Gordon; (13) Lt. Reade; (14) Capt. G. Heyworth; (15) Lt. Col. Wood; (16) Lt. R.W. Llewelyn; (17) Major Deacon

*The Band of the Royal Glamorgan Militia and the Regiment drawn up in Cardiff Arms Field, 1871.*

A DETACHMENT OF THE ROYAL GLAMORGAN INFANTRY
PREPARE TO RECEIVE CAVALRY, CARDIFF ARMS FIELD, 1871.

ROYAL GLAMORGAN MILITIA CAMP — MAINDY FIELD, c.1875
WITH THE COMPANIES IN SQUARE IN THE BACKGROUND

*Courtesy of The Welch Regiment Museum*
Lt. Colonel Hubert Churchill Gould
Commanding Officer — 1875 to 1884

By General Regulation and Instructions, 2nd July, 1873, the United Kingdom was for military purposes divided into 70 Sub-Districts to each of which was allocated a Sub-District Brigade. In South Wales this resulted in the 41st (The Welch) Regiment of Infantry and 69th (South Lincolnshire) Regiment establishing a common Depot at Fort Hubberstone, Pembrokeshire and being lined with the Royal Glamorgan Militia and the Rifle Volunteer Corps of Pembrokeshire, Carmarthenshire, South Cardiganshire and Glamorgan in the 24th Sub District with Brigade Headquarters in Cardiff. This change was the first of several reorganisations which were by 1887 to link together under the Territorial Line Regiment title, the Infantry Militia of Glamorgan and the Rifle Volunteer Battalions of four South Wales Counties.

In 1874 the Royal Glamorgan held a successful camp at Maindy, the last to be held under the command of Lt. Colonel Woods. On February 24th, 1875, Lt. Colonel Hubert Churchill Gould became Commanding Officer, and on 24th October received as his Adjutant, Captain P. French, 69th Regiment, the first Officer of the linked Line Regiments to be appointed to that post. Prior to the arrival of the main body of the regiment for training on the 21st June, the recruits as in previous years had set up the camp on Maindy Field. A few days before the main training commenced the camp was struck and resited on the nearby Crwys Field. The reason for the change is uncertain, but was probably due to construction work then taking place on the new Barracks site on Maindy Field.

In 1876, the Stanley Committee recommended a strengthening of existing links between the Line Regiments of the various Sub-District Brigades and the Militia. It proposed that this could best be accomplished by treating them all as Battalions of the same regiment sharing a common depot. The recommendation although accepted, was not brought into full effect until 1881. In Cardiff the regiment trained on Maindy Field from 6th August to 2nd September with good results.

Early in 1877 the new 24th Brigade Depot (Maindy Barracks) was completed and the Militia Stores and Armoury hitherto housed near Blackweir moved into custom built accommodation near which were Quarters to house the Permanent Staff. In March, Captain French, having resigned his commission, was succeeded as Adjutant by Captain B.N. Anley, 41st (The Welch) Regiment. He was to guide the Royal Glamorgan through the many changes that were to take place during the next few years. 14 Officers and 701 Other Ranks attended training during the summer, 675 in 1878, and 777 in 1879.

In 1880 the Royal Glamorgan was from April 1st increased in strength from 8 to 12 Companies. The increase was part of a plan to form a second Glamorgan Militia Battalion, but for reasons not known that proposal was shortly thereafter shelved. Annual Training commenced on the 26th June and was attended by 843 Other Ranks. At the annual inspection 21st July, the regiment was complimented on its efficiency, conduct and appearance.

The year 1881 was to be an important milestone in the history of the regiment and brought an end to 121 years service as an independent Corps. Although sad, it was in no way the end of the road, as the Corps continued in unbroken service as the 3rd (Militia) Battalion, The Welsh Regiment.

The changes were in fact the culmination of a series of Army Reforms and reorganisation set in motion by War Secretary Cardwell some years before and which were being carried through the final stages by his successor Mr Childers. Meanwhile in Cardiff, the Recruits had assembled for preliminary training at Blackweir and were joined by the main body on the 26th June. Under canvas in Maindy Field they remained for a few days under the title Royal Glamorgan Light Infantry Militia. Shortly before midnight on June 30th, the Officers raised their glasses in final tribute to the old Corps, and after the stroke of the hour, in similar fashion wished success to the new. The changes implimented on July 1st, 1881, saw the 41st and 69th Regiments linked and redesignated respectively, 1st and 2nd Battalions, The Welsh Regiment. The new Regimental Depot was established at Maindy Barracks, Cardiff, as also the Headquarters of the new 41st Regimental District which replaced the old 24th Brigade Sub District. Included in the new district was also the 3rd (Militia) Battalion, The Welsh Regiment (late Royal Glamorgan) and also the affiliated Battalions of Rifle Volunteers from Glamorgan, Carmarthenshire and Pembrokeshire.

# CHAPTER 12

# 3rd (Militia) Battalion,
# The Welsh Regiment, 1881-1898

With the change accomplished the new 3rd Battalion, The Welsh Regiment continued with its annual training which included live firing practice on the Ely Range (a site close by the Cowbridge Road). On the 19th July the annual inspection of the Battalion was carried out by Colonel G. Carden, Officer Commanding, 41st Regimental District, which event was reported the next day in the *Western Mail*.

"The Annual Inspection of the Glamorganshire Militia took place on the Barracks Field, Cardiff on Tuesday afternoon in the presence of a large number of spectators. Present were, Colonel Gould in command, and the number of men who fell in was about 780, the total strength of the Battalion being upwards of 950. Officers present were Lt. Colonel Heyworth (Second in Command), Captain and Acting Major Hayworth, Captain and Adjutant Anley, Captains, Morris, Wilson, Callan, Tynte, Crespigny, O'Brien (3rd Middlesex), Brimley (7th Lancaster), Newell (Dorset Militia), Surgeon Major Taylor, Quartermaster Wilson and nine Lieutenants. The Regiment was divided into ten strong Companies and was drawn up in Line to receive Colonel Carden, who was accompanied by Captain Butler, 2nd Battalion, The Welsh Regiment, acting as Aide de Camp. The Inspecting Officer complimented the men very highly on their efficiency at drill and their excellent turn out in Marching Order. Several Companies were after the inspection marched into the Barracks where they gave up their Arms preparatory to their final dismissal." The account incorrectly names Quartermaster Wiltshire as Wilson, and the official record lists 193 Other Ranks as being absent without leave, a figure which does not take into account deaths, sickness or men who were abroad or had left the district to seek work elsewhere. In March 1882, Martini Henry Rifles were issued to the Battalion to replace the Snider, and changes in the method of training recruits were announced. Hitherto, recruits had trained for 56 days in Camp and then mustered for annual training with the main body. Henceforth they were to train in the Barracks at Maindy for 63 days immediately following enrolment for which they would receive £1 as Bounty and then be dismissed to their homes. If dismissed one month before the assembly of the Battalion for annual training they would be required to attend and be paid another twenty shillings. If dismissed in less than a month before annual training they would not be required to report again until the following year. At that date some 80 recruits for the Battalion were present in the Barracks.

The Battalion assembled on the 27th May. During training new clothing was issued; the old Scarlet and Royal Blue Facings of the old regiment being replaced by the Scarlet and White Facings of The Welsh Regiment. 19 Officers and 867 Other Ranks attended and were as had then become customary housed under canvas in Maindy Field. During training live firing was carried out on the Ely Range and Major F.L. Wade Dalton, The Welsh Regiment succeeded Major Anley as Adjutant. The Battalion was dismissed on the 23rd June, but on the 27th, Colonel Gould in a letter to the Officer Commanding the district offered the services of the Battalion to Egypt.

"Sir,

In view of the present state of affairs in Egypt and the likelyhood of their being War, I beg to offer the services of the Battalion under my command for foreign or any other service that may be required of them." The offer was greatly appreciated by the authorities and duly acknowledged but no call was made for the 3rd Battalion to serve in the Egyptian War. In 1883 the Battalion trained for 27 days commencing May 26th. During that period opportunity was given for the Militiamen to work in Brigade with troops housed in the Barracks. Apart from two incidents involving individual Militiamen who were imprisoned for disorderly conduct and assault, the conduct of the remainder in Camp was exemplary.

Of 152 Militiamen who failed to present themselves for training, some were later found to have fraudulently enlisted in other Militia Regiments in order to draw the Bounty. Proceedings were instituted against them in due course for fraudulent enlistment.

On the 14th March, 1884, Lt. Colonel Lawrence Heyworth succeeded Lt. Colonel Gould as Commanding Officer of the Battalion which assembled for training on May 5th. On the 27th May, the Battalion escorted a Colour Party of the 1st Battalion, The Welsh Regiment to Llandaff Cathedral where with due ceremony the Colours which had been carried by the old 41st Foot in the period 1815-1826 were laid up. Annual Inspection took place on May 28th when present on parade were 1 Lieutenant Colonel, 2 Majors, 10 Captains, 8 Subaltern Officers, 3 Staff Officers, 1 Sergeant Major, 39 Sergeants, 26 Corporals, 10 Buglers and 532 Private Men.

In June 1885, the knapsack equipment in use by the Battalion was replaced by the first pattern valise equipment. Annual Training commenced 27th July and was attended by 18 Officers and 896 Other Ranks. Absenteeism was still high and stood at 145. No live firing practice took place due to unavailability of suitable ranges.

The 1886 training commenced May 31st and much use was made of the Ely Range. 20 Officers and 936 Other Ranks attended. 130 Militiamen were absent without leave. On the 23rd October Lt. Colonel J.C.R. Reade succeeded Lt. Colonel Heyworth as Commanding Officer of the Battalion.

On the 15th June, 1887, Captain Arthur Russell Reade, 1st Battalion, The Welsh Regiment succeeded Major Wade Dalton as Adjutant. The Battalion assembled on June 27th. During training, and in order to obtain maximum value from the Ely Range a Camp was set up there capable of housing and feeding two Companies. In that manner the whole Battalion was able to increase its musketry efficiency.

April 1888 saw the establishment of the Battalion once again increased to 12 Companies in pursuance of a plan similar to that of 1881, namely the formation of a second Militia Battalion, which had it been formed, would presumably have been known as the 4th Battalion, The Welsh Regiment. As in 1881, the proposed second Militia Battalion was never formed.

Annual Training commenced July 2nd and was attended by 32 Officers and 937 Other Ranks. At the annual inspection, Colonel Rawlings, Officer commanding 41st Regimental District, commended the Battalion for its smartness and precision at the same time expressing the opinion that whilst at Drill they were not the equal of the Guards, he could safely say that they could take the shine off some of the Regular Line Battalions. Absenteeism remained high with 154 Militiamen absent from training. In 1889, Annual Training commenced 8th July and was attended by 34 Officers and 861 Other Ranks. On Wednesday 31st July in Cathays Park, the Battalion paraded to receive a new Stand of Colours from the Marchioness of Bute which Colours replaced those which had been carried since 1870 by the old Royal Glamorgan Light Infantry Militia.

In her address to the Battalion the Marchioness spoke as follows:

"Colonel Reade, Officers, Non Commissioned Officers and Men of the 3rd Battalion, The Welsh Regiment. I now hand over these Colours to your keeping. I thank you for having asked me to do so. I pray that it may never be your duty to carry them through the bloody tempest of War; but whether in War or Peace, I know that the hands to which I now commit them are as true as those which have borne the Colours of your bretheren from Bourbon to Sebastapol. I know that you will guard these Colours with faithfulness and cherish them with jealous affection. I know that as you look upon them they will serve to quicken within you the feeling of loyalty to your Sovereign, of love for your Country, and of devotion to your Regiment; and that when you resign them to those who come after you, you will hand on with them untarnished the reputation of your Native Land and the good name of the body to which you belong."

The new Colours were of a design similar to those carried by the Regular Battalions of The Welsh Regiment less certain distinctions. The Old Colours were afterwards presented to the Marchioness as a gift to hang in Cardiff Castle. The centrepiece of one (viz, the Regimental Colour) has survived and is now part of The Welch Regiment Museum Collection. The 1890 and 1891 training periods were held in July of each year. Numbers absent from training remained high, in spite of the fact that the Battalion was at this time one of the strongest in Great Britain and had no difficulty attracting recruits. Commenting in April 1890, the *Western Mail* stated — "The 3rd Battalion,

The Welsh Regiment is one of the smartest Militia Battalions in the service. This is mainly due to the efforts of the Commanding Officer, Colonel Reade, who since he assumed command of the Corps in 1886, has raised it to a high standard of efficiency.

Annual training in 1892 commenced 16th May and was attended by 21 Officers and 622 Other Ranks. On the 15th June Captain A.H.W. Tindal, 2nd Battalion, The Welsh Regiment succeeded Captain Reade as Adjutant, and to him must be given the credit for collating much of the information available in regimental records concerning the service of the Royal Glamorgan Light Infantry and its successor Battalion. 983 Other Ranks attended the 1893 training and approximately similar numbers in 1894. On the 29th September of that year, the Battalion in keeping with the custom of the Regular Battalions took onto its strength a pure white Billy Goat, a gift from Her Majesty Queen Victoria, and drawn from the Royal Herd which then still roamed Windsor Great Park. Sgt. Drummer Keeley was appointed its keeper, and a pen set up to house it in the Barracks' Skittle Alley. The goat was one of several to serve with the 3rd Battalion, the last of which was still alive in retirement in the early 1930s.

In June 1895, the Battalion received Lee Metford Rifles as replacements for the Martini Henry, but 100 of the old pattern were held back for the use of recruits. The change was no doubt welcomed by the men as the old Martini Henry was renowned for its kick and ability to badly bruise the shoulder.

On the 15th July, the Battalion numbering 20 Officers and 985 Other Ranks moved into a previously prepared Camp which had been set up by an Advance Party in a field close to the Esplanade Hotel, Porthcawl. During its stay in the town, the Battalion commanded by Lt. Colonel Alfred Thrale Perkins carried out Field Training on Lock's Common and Musketry practice on the Volunteer Range at Merthyr Mawr. The training period was both exciting and eventful as on the 4th August, the Severn Volunteer Infantry Brigade arrived and set up camp close by, and on the 6th, the 1st Battalion, The Welsh Regiment, then on the final stages of its Flag March through South Wales also arrived in town. This gave both the Militia and Volunteers an opportunity to work alongside their regular comrades in arms, and all participated in joint field exercises and a grand Review at Margam Abbey. Due to a smallpox epidemic, no annual training took place in 1896, but Training Bounties were paid to all men of the Battalion listed as 'effective' on June 1st. The Battalion Band in spite of the restrictions was able to meet its obligations and under the direction of Sergeant Drummer Kelly, and accompanied by the popular goat made an appearance at the summer Cardiff Exhibition and Military Tattoo. On the 27th June it provided music on the occasion of the opening by H.R.H. The Prince of Wales of the Free Library in the Hayes, Cardiff. The Battalion to a man was gratified when in December it was told that Captain Tindal, the popular Adjutant, was to be allowed to extend his service with the Battalion until October 1897.

An Order in Council dated May 3rd, 1897, allowed Militia Training to be extended beyond 28 days, but not to exceed 56 days in any one year. To compensate for the loss of the 1896 training period, Battalion training in 1897 was extended to 34 days, the venue being Cowshot Camp near Brookwood. The training commenced on 26th July with the arrival of Recruits. They were joined by the main body on Monday, August 9th, an event which caused a great deal of interest. *The London Daily Press* stated "They are from a class not usually found in the Militia," whilst other newspapers commented favourably on the fine appearnace and physique of the men. What undoubtedly stole the thunder was the Regimental Goat which led the march of the Battalion from Brookwood to Cowshot. *The South Wales Daily News* was equally effusive, stating, "Lt. Colonel Perkins has good reason to feel proud of such a fine Battalion, not only in the matter of numerical strength, but of physique and ability." It went on to say that the 3rd Welsh compared favourably with any Regiment of the Line to be found at Aldershot.

The Battalion at the time was fortunate in its Regimental Sergeant Major, Sgt. Major Murphy, a genial, but firm character who was proud of his Battalion. Quartermaster Sergeant Hanson Hill also made certain that their rations and accommodation were of the best available standard. The 11th August saw the Militia Brigade at Aldershot inspected by H.R.H. The Duke of Connaught, and on the 21st and 23rd of the month the Battalion were involved with regular troops in Divisional Field Days at Foxhill and Barrossa.

Whilst at Cowshot, the Other Ranks were issued with the new Home Service Pattern Blue Cloth Helmet which replaced the last Shako worn by the British Army, but only new to the Private Men of the Battalion, as it had long been in use elsewhere. Off duty, the men of the Battlion were particularly popular due to their singing ability. They gave voice at Church Parades, and their harmony was much admired in other places of worship throughout the district. The Battalion struck Camp on the 10th September, entrained for Cardiff at Brookwood and were dismissed from training the following day. Of the 182 recruits joining the Battalion in the last quarter of the year, approximately one half enlisted in the Regular Army, many opting for service with The Welch. On the 15th November, Captain G.D. Williams, Royal Berkshire Regiment succeeded Captain Tindal as Adjutant of the Battalion.

A Battalion Recruiting Drive commenced in January 1898, with Clr. Sgt. Fidler based at Pontypridd, Clr. Sgt. Rowley at Pentre, and Clr. Sgt. Smith at Merthyr. Their efforts resulted in a total of 271 men joining the Battalion by April 30th. Of that number however, some 130 were within a short period to purchase their discharge.

Venue for Camp in 1898 was Slwch, near Brecon, commencing 23rd May with the arrival of 270 recruits from the Cardiff Depot. They were joined by the main body on the 4th June, but the training was somewhat hampered due to the then small sized range and the fact that the Camp field was insufficiently large to be able to manoeuvre at drill the whole Battalion. That difficulty was compensated by some excellent Field Days on Mynydd Illtyd Common and long route marches. Open to the public at the weekends, the Camp was well patronised by visitors. A great attraction was the Church Parade, and also Band performances, which last, under the baton of Bandmaster Stockey had a wide and popular repertoire.

During training the Battalion was inspected by General Sir Forestier Walker, KCB, General Officer Commanding, Western District, and also by Colonel H.B. McCall, C.B., Officer Commanding, 41st Regimental District. Reporting the first inspection *The Brecon and Radnor Express* stated — "The General who witnessed the splendid swing of the Glamorganshire Men had a smile which could only suggest surprise and gratification. As the 12 Companies came by, one after the other, one could not help but admire the splendidly drilled Battalion."

Breaking Camp on the 2nd July, the Battalion consisting of 16 Officers, 50 Sergeants, 34 Corporals, 12 Drummers and 823 Private Men, headed by the Goat Mascot and Band marched to Brecon Station to entrain for Cardiff, where on the following day they were dismissed from training.

Meanwhile in South Africa, war clouds were gathering and soon a situation was to develop which would call upon the Battalion to proceed on active service abroad for the first time in its long history.

Major George Frederick Heyworth (late 5th Dragoon Guards)
served from 1869 to 1884
*Courtesy of The Welch Regiment Museum*

2nd Lt. REGINALD P. THOMAS — 3rd (MILITIA) BN — 1881-1884
*Courtesy of The Welch Regiment Museum*

*Lt. Colonel Lawrence Hayworth — Commanding Officer
— 1884 to 1886
Courtesy of The Welch Regiment Museum*

*OFFICERS 3rd WELCH. MAINDY. c.1885*
*TOGETHER WITH ATTACHED MILITIA OFFICERS*

*Courtesy of The Welch Regiment Museum*
*Lieutenant, later*
Lt. Colonel Arthur Russell Crewe Reade — Commanding Officer —
1886 to 1895
The Glengarry Cap Badge consists of a two part design consisting of a
gilded Victorian Crown and a Gilt/Silver Other Ranks patter Helmet
Plact Centre below.
The gilded letter 'M' which identifies him as a Militia Officer can be
seen below the Badges of Rank on the Shoulder Strap

OFFICERS. 3rd WELCH. JULY 1886
*Courtesy of The Welch Regiment Museum*

Lt. Clifford John Cory — Resigned 1895
*Courtesy of The Welch Regiment Museum*

Lt. I.H. Prior — 3rd Battalion
To Plymouth Division Submarine Miners Militia 1895
*Courtesy of The Welch Regiment Museum*

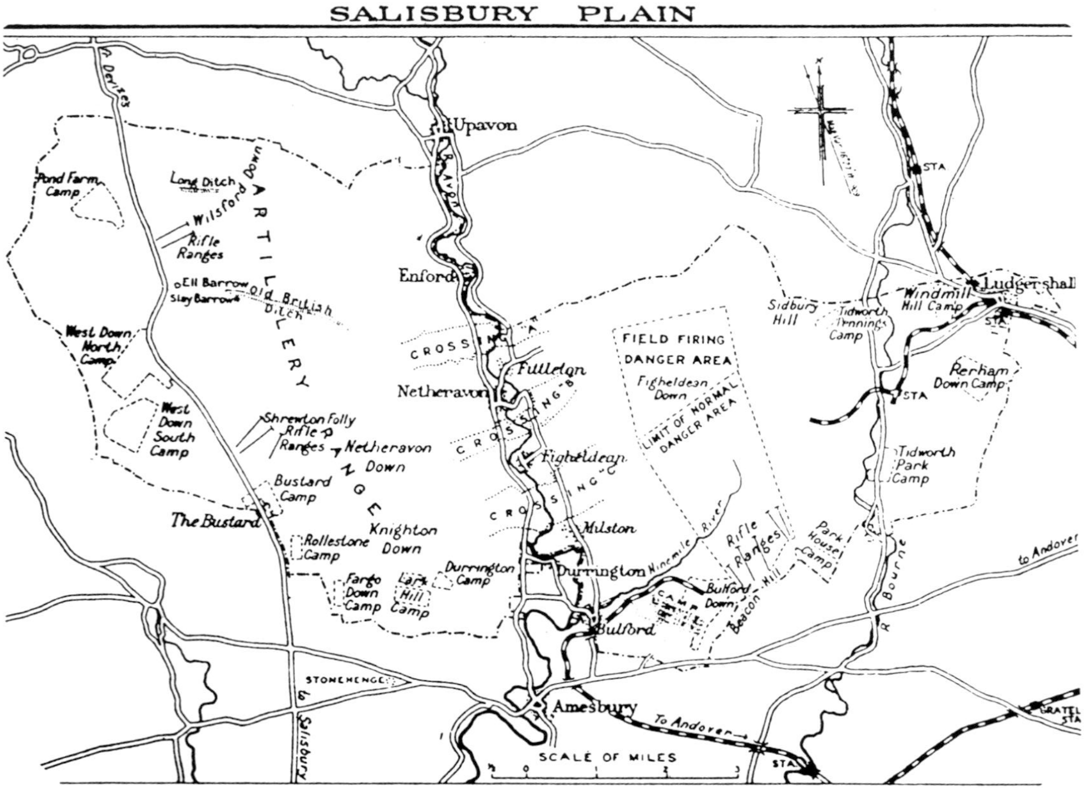

SALISBURY PLAIN

SALISBURY PLAIN TRAINING AREA

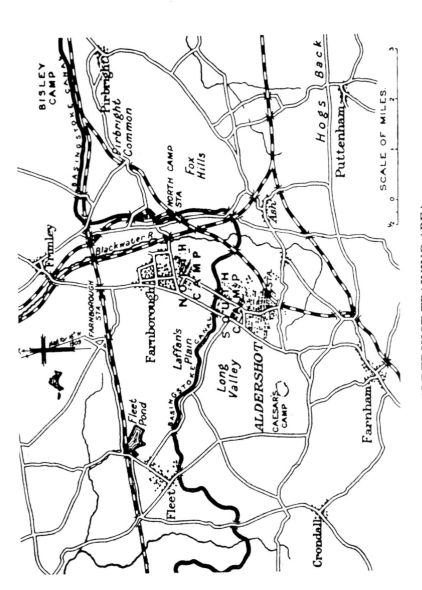

ALDERSHOT TRAINING AREA

3rd (Militia) Bn, The Welch Regt. c.1890
Officers, Wives and Guests. Maindy Field, Cardiff.
*Courtesy of The Welch Regiment Museum*

MAINDY BARRACKS, CARDIFF, DEPOT, THE WELSH REGIMENT, c.1878

A DETACHMENT OF THE 3rd (MILITIA) BATTALION, THE
WELSH REGIMENT MARCHING OUT OF FORT TREGANTLE,
Nr. TORPOINT, EAST CORNWALL IN THE 1890s

# CHAPTER 13

# 1889-1908. The Seventh Embodiment, South Africa, 1900- 1901.

The year 1899 was as far as Battalion activities were concerned, for the greater part, not much different to the previous year with the Permanent Staff much occupied in the Spring and early summer months with Recruiting, the instruction of Recruits and in preparations for annual training. On the 7th June an Advance Party consisting of Lieutenant (QM) Tinnock, two Sergeants and 21 Men proceeded to Porton to take over Camp Equipment at Porton Down. The Recruits assembled in Cardiff on the 12th June and entrained. On arrival at Porton they marched under the command of Major G.D. Williams to Bulford Camp. The preliminary training on this occasion extended over 14 days. Other Officers and Staff present were Captains, Taylor, Aldridge, Wilcox. Lieutenants, Nash, Hobbs and Williams, 27 Staff Sergeants and 21 Corporals. Recruits numbered 285 Private Men.

On the 26th June the Battalion assembled at Maindy Barracks and under the command of Lt Colonel A. Thrale Perkins proceeded that same day by Special Train to join the Recruits at Bulford.

During training the Battalion was Brigaded with the 2nd Dorsets, 2nd Royal Berkshire and 3rd Leinster Battalions commanded by Colonel R.A.P. Clements, DSO, ADC, the whole forming part of the 2nd Division commanded by General Sir W. Gateacre, KCB, DSO. Musketry Training was carried out on the Bulford Ranges, the course being completed on the 10th July. From the 12th to the 25th inclusive the Battalion was exercised in Brigade and Divisional Drills culminating in a night march on the 26th.

The 4th Brigade in which the Battalion was included was inspected by Colonel Clements on the 27th following which preparations were made to break camp. On the 28th Camp Stores and Equipment were handed over to an advance party of the 7th Rifle Brigade on completion of which the Battalion formed up and marched to Porton. Entraining later in the day it arrived in Cardiff early on the 29th July. After Arms and Equipment had been returned to Store at Maindy Barracks the Battalion was dismissed from training. Other Ranks in Camp numbered 883, and Battalion Officers were joined by six Militia Officers from other regiments who were attached as Observers.

During the Autumn months of 1899 the situation in South Africa deteriorated rapidly, in consequence of which instructions were issued to

embody the Militia for Home Garrison Duty. On the 3rd November, the following instructions were issued:-
"EMBODIMENT OF THE MILITIA

Her Majesty, The Queen, having graciously pleased by Royal Proclamation dated 26th October, 1899, to Order the Secretary of State for War to give the necessary directions for embodying all or any part of the Militia, the following instructions are promulated for the information of all concerned. 1. The undermentioned Militia Infantry Units will be embodied at their respective Headquarters on dates to be hereafter notified, but not earlier than the 20th November, 1899, and they will remain there, or proceed to other Stations under such Orders as may be hereafter issued:-
3rd BATTALION, THE WELSH REGIMENT."

On the 9th November, 1899, the Boer Republics handed in their ultimatum to the British Agent in Pretoria, couched in such terms as made War inevitable. The die was cast, and on the 12th November the first shots of the Boer War were fired.
In a Letter to the Commanding Officer, 3rd Battalion, The Welsh Regiment, dated 21st November, the War Office directed:

"Sir,
I am directed by the Secretary of State for War to inform you that the Barracks which your Battalion will occupy on embodiment will accomodate only 660 Non Commisioned Officers and Men in addition to the Regular details which will be attached to you. You must therefore make arrangements not to call up for embodiment more than 660 Men.
I am, etc, etc,
Evelyn Wood,
A.G."

In accordance with instructions only 55 Men from each Company were called upon to embody. They assembled at Maindy Barracks under the Command of Lt Colonel Thrale Perkins on Monday, 4th December, 1899, and from there proceeded to their War Stations.
The Battalion consisting of 12 Companies was distributed as follows:-
Headquarters, 'A', 'B' and 'D' Companies at Pembroke Dock,
'C', 'F' and 'K' Companies commanded by Lt Colonel Watts at Newport, Monmouthshire,
'E' and 'L' Companies commanded by Major Dashwood at Penally, Pembrokeshire,
'G', 'I' and 'M' Companies commanded by Captain Taylor ar Fort Popton, Milford Haven.
The following Officers and Members of the Permanent Staff were embodied with the Battalion as follows:

Lt Colonel and Hon Colonel A. Thrale-Perkins — Officer Commanding
Major and Hon Lt Colonel W. Watts
Major S.M. Thomas
Major E. Dashwood
Major W. Forrest
Captain A. Thrale Perkins
Captain R.W. Taylor
Captain J.W. Aldridge
Captain E.L. Wilcox
Captain R.L. Stevens
Captain E.A. Pope
Captain W. Elton
Captain H.W. Masterman
Lieut. H.H Esplin
Lieut. D. How
Lieut. D.W. Panton
Lieut. G.H.S. Williams
Lieut. J. Nash
Lieut. A.H. Hobbs
Lieut. Oakes (Royal Engineers) attached
Capt. and Adjutant H.E. Taylor (Royal Berkshire Regt)
Lieut. and Quartermaster T. Tinnock

*Permanent Staff*
Sergeant Major W.P. Murphy
Quarter Master Sergeant D. Gaughan
Sergeant H. Stockey
Colour Sergeant L.H. Davies
Colour Sergeant J. Fidler
Colour Sergeant W.H. Rees
Colour Sergeant C. Rowley
Colour Sergeant W. Evans
Colour Sergeant J.A. Bryant
Colour Sergeant W. Smith
Colour Sergeant G. Cadogan
Colour Sergeant J. Kerr
Colour Sergeant W. Rawlings
Colour Sergeant R. Foster
Colour Sergeant H. Williams
Sergeant W.H. Chattin
Sergeant W. Shears
Sergeant G.W. Paish
Sergeant J. Wigley
Sergeant D. Jones

Sergeant W. J Kelly
Sergeant D. Lovering
Sergeant E. Fowler
Sergeant W. Paine
Sergeant E. Tuck
Sergeant L.E. Williams
Sergeant E. Lewis

*Drummers — Permanent Staff*
Drummer H. Higgs
Drummer F. Chaplin
Drummer A. Sutton
Drummer R. Browne
Drummer W. Cowell
Drummer E. Hoey
Drummer W. Sergeant
Drummer G. Wheeler
Drummer A. Andrews
Drummer J. Cross
Drummer A. Lyons

Whilst the Battalion was at Pembroke Dock, men of the Milita Reserve were organised and made ready to proceed to join the Regular Battalion at the Front. The detachment, numbering 186, entrained for Southampton on the 16th December under the command of Captain Prothero and Lieutenant Smith of the 1st Welch.

Reveille for the Reservists sounded at 1.15 a.m. on the morning of their departure, then having breakfasted the Draft fell in, and were marched to the Station headed by the Battalion Band. At 4.10 a.m. the train steamed out from Pembroke Dock to the sound of farewell tunes from the Band and the cheers of Comrades and Spectators who had turned out to see them off despite the early hour. At Landore, near Swansea, each man received a pipe, half a pound of tobacco, cigarettes and cigars supplied by the South Wales Daily Post Fund. On arriving at Southampton, the Draft embarked onboard the S.S. Avoca which sailed for South Africa on Sunday 17th.

On January 8th, 1900, a second embodiment took place, the men assembling at Maindy Barracks, Cardiff. In this manner an additional 190 Other Ranks were called in for service, thus replacing the Militia Reservists already on their way to the Cape.

On the 17th January the Battalion volunteered for active service and commenced preparing itself for that event, by reorganising into eight Companies, a change accomplished without any reduction in strength. Within days, 31 Officers, 580 Other Ranks and a Civil Surgeon were ready to proceed. The Colours were destined to be returned to the Town of Cardiff and handed over to the Council for safe keeping. The Colour Party consisting of Captain

Forrest, Lieutenants Ryder and Ellis left Pembroke Dock on February 3rd. At Cardiff Station they were met by Colonel Perkins and a Guard of Honour of Recruits from the Depot together with the Band of the 3rd Volunteer Battalion, The Welsh Regiment. Present also were Detachments of the Glamorgan Artillery, Severn Division Submarine Miners (RE) Volunteers, and the Cardiff Company, 3rd Volunteer Battalion, The Welsh Regiment, the whole under the command of Colonel John Owen Quirk, Officer Commanding the District. From the station, the Colours were moved in procession through St Mary Street, High Street and Duke Street to Park Hall where during an impressive ceremony they were received by the Lord Mayor, Councillor S.A. Brain. They were in due course deposited in the Council Chamber to await the Battalion's return.

The Battalion left Pembroke Dock on February 12th travelling in two Special Trains. At Swansea the Troops received a warm welcome together with many gifts and again in Cardiff, where the train carrying the left half Battalion arrived at 6 a.m. The Battalion left to the sound of cheers and their Welsh National Anthem — 'Mae Hen Wlad Fy Nhadau'.

> "Who serves the Queen, and who will go
> to fight for her against the foe?
> Cries Tommy Atkins, I'm the man,
> I'll fight for Her as fight I can,
> When Queen and Country call, you need not fear,
> for I respond with hearty cheer,
> Where'er I go, Her Flag shall fly,
> In its defence I live and die."

On arrival at Southampton the Battalion embarked on the S.S. Majestic together with a large draft for the Guards Brigade commanded by Major Leigh, Coldstream Guards. Also taking passage were drafts of the 3rd Battalion, Royal Lancaster Regiment and the Highland Light Infantry — in all, a total of 1,864 men and five horses. The Press described the Welsh Battalion as "A fine body of Men, most of whom are Miners," their sturdy physique being a source for much comment as also their harmonious singing. Officer Commanding Troops onboard was Lt Colonel A. Thrale Perkins with Captain Taylor as Ship's Adjutant and Lieutenant Tinnock as Army Quartermaster.

The Majestic arrived at Capetown on March 1st, 1900, which from a Welsh point of view was most auspicious. The voyage South had been uneventful, apart from one death amongst the 3rd Royal Lancaster draft. Disembarking on March 3rd, the Battalion entrained for De Aar, Cape Province, where it arrived on the 5th. It then camped on a site near the railway station until March 15th when it joined a Flying Column under General Kitchener on a forced march to Prieska. No action took place, as the Boers which the Column had been sent to intercept evaded battle by withdrawing across the Orange River.

On the 3rd April, 1900, a Detachment of 240 from 3 Welsh commanded by Lt Colonel Perkins marched as escort to a Convoy from De Aar to Prieska. Other Officers present were Captains, H.E. Taylor, Forrest, Perkins, How and Captain W. Taylor. Lieutenants, Hobbs, Nash, Barker, Ellis, Carey, Woodfull and Campbell.

Moving out at dusk, the Convoy consisting of ten Bullock Waggons together with Mule and Donkey Waggons, rested the first night after crossing the Brak River. On the 5th it arrived at Britstown where an overnight stop was made in order to rest the bullocks. Moving on next day, the Convoy reached Prieska on the 12th having marched via Oomdraivlei and Kaarabee. The total distance covered was 120 miles during which the detachment lost three men through sickness — Drummer Higgs, Pte Smith and Pte Toben, all of whom were left behind at Britstown.

This nine day march, together with the previous experience in the Flying Column gave the Battalion a taste of life on the Veldt. The cold nights, hot days combined with an acute shortage of water soon showed all ranks that manning the lines of communication was certainly going to be no picnic.

At Prieska the Detachment bivouacked under blankets on high ground just north of the village, but after three days of heavy rain they were moved into empty houses which gave them slightly more comfort. The arrival of 3rd Welch provided a welcome relief for a Detachment of the 1st Suffolk Regiment who returned to De Aar with the empty convoy on April 15th.

On Easter Monday, the Vedettes were fired upon by the enemy. The following day, 20th April, Mounted Infantry supported by a Company of 3rd Welch carried out a reconaissance in force. In the sweep of the Kopjes on the other side of the Orange River, no Boer force was met, but one or two enemy were taken prisoner. The Prieska Garrison at this date was commanded by Colonel Adye, Royal Field Artillery with Captain Tindal, 1st Welch as his Staff Officer. Other units in the Garrison were two Sections of the 44th Battery, Royal Field Artillery equipped with 15 Pdr, B.L. Guns, Mounted Infantry of the Gloucestershire Regiment and Nesbitt's Horse.

For the remainder of the Battalion and its H.Q. at De Aar, life was somewhat quieter, and is described in a letter from Private Evan James Jones of 'C' Company to his parents at 2 Greenfield Row, Cwmdare:

"This is a very hot place to live in daytime, and so cold at night, that most of us have a cold. We are now stationed at De Aar. There has been some fighting here before we came out, but I have not encountered a Boer yet. I dont believe we shall have any fighting because I think Lord Roberts is going to clear the lot of them before we shall have a chance, for he relieved Ladysmith when we are on the way out. As soon as we arrived in Capetown, the good news reached us. The flags were sent up on every ship around, and that night Rockets of every kind and colour were sent up from every ship. We went up from Cape Town to De Aar, and here we are now. There are no English or

Welsh people here except the regiment, but there are plenty of blacks and foreign people. I am quite happy out here and I am enjoying myself first rate talking to the blacks. They have such a funny language, and it is difficult to know what they are saying. There is a great deal of these Blacks working under our Government. I do not believe we shall be here long, as there is talk of our being in London on the Queen's Birthday (24th May), for the greatest part of the War is over, and thank the Lord for it. There are a great many wounded here in the hospital, some with legs off, others with arms off, but they are full of jokes even in that way, yet little think of the time when they will be home. It is too hot for us to Drill by day, only once in the morning and again at night, so you see we dont work hard here."

Meanwhile at Cardiff, far from expecting the Battalion home, a Draft of 100 Militia Recruits, their training completed entrained for Devonport to embark for service with the Battalion in South Africa. The majority were still in their teens, but it was said of them, "A Smarter lot of Men have never left this Depot."

366 Pte R. George, a member of this draft wrote of the voyage:
"The Voyage has been a very pleasant one, and since we have been on board we have had a Concert in which the Welsh were very prominent. Their singing was much admired by the Captain and the Officers on board, and we were asked to form a Glee Party under Private Berti Beauchamp. We have 400 Horses on board which are in the care of 3rd Welsh. Since taking over that job we have been nicknamed the 3rd Welsh Dragoons. We are in excellent health and spirits and I am pleased to say, well respected and well treated onboard."

Battalion activities in South Africa meanwhile were extremely routine and in the main unexciting. Nevertheless the part played by the Militiamen freed the Regular Troops for the tasks which they were best trained to tackle whilst knowing full well that the lines of communication were secure.

The beginning of May found the Battalion dispersed as follows:
The Headquarters and major part of the Battalion were under canvas at Prieska which move had been made gradually between 15th April and 15th May. Captain Latham, 2nd Lt O'Brien plus 58 Other Ranks were stationed at Deelfontein, but a detachment commanded by Lt Colonel Watts remained at De Aar. The De Aar detachment also included Captain Esplin's Maxim Section, newly arrived from England on April 20th.

On the 4th May, 'D' Company commanded by Captain Latham returned to De Aar from Deelfontein and remained there as part of Lt Colonel Watt's Detachment. On the 11th May, 'E' and 'G' Companies commanded by Captain Taylor and Captain How marched out of Prieska for Kenhardt some 120 miles to the East where they were to be stationed until further orders. Some of the Officers and N.C.O.s included in this Detachment were, Lieutenants Panton, How, Woodfall and Berry, Colour Sergeants Evans and Smith, Sergeants D. Jones, D. Lovering, 298 E. Lewis and Cpl Andrews. This

Detachment was later joined by Lt Colonel Watts who took over as Officer Commanding the outpost. His previous duty as Officer Commanding the De Aart Detachment was taken over by Captain Aldridge.

On May 15th the men of 3rd Welch stationed at Prieska took part in a foray across the Orange River to round up sheep. 400 were eventually driven back across the river after which the daily rations were considerably improved.

On the 19th May, Lt Colonel Thrale Perkins was appointed Commandant, Prieska, vice Colonel Adye and Lt R.W. Carey was appointed Garrison Adjutant. RSM Bryant became Garrison Sergeant Major, QMS Gaughan, Garrison Quartermaster Sergeant and Sergeant Shears, Garrison Provost Sergeant. Colonel Adye's Column then moved out to attack the Boer Laager at Kies — Civil Surgeon Smith, 236 Pte Loach and 644 Private Harris of 3rd Welch being present during that action.

A description of life in the Priska Garrison is given in the Regimental Journal of August 1900, the letter which is unsigned having been written some time previously.

"We have been stationary for three weeks, and are comfortably billeted except for a lot of cursed flies which are crawling over my face. When we first arrived, either the Boers or own soldiers commandeered, looted or sold everything from the Stores and fresh supplies were prevented from coming in due to military authorities commandeering every available waggon here and at De Aar. However, things are beginning to right themselves, and such luxuries as Tobacco, Potatoes and Jam are now arriving in small quantities. Some of the troops are getting Tents from the Base, and the two Hotels have reopened their doors. At the 'PRIESKA' the Officers mess, and several others live. The food is not appetising and there is precious little of it, but one is glad to get it even at six shillings a day with rations thrown in. Whiskey at eleven shillings a bottle. Fresh meat is plentiful and the Mutton excellent, but the Troops badly require Bread and Tobacco. Kind friends at home have sent out large quantities of the latter for Tommy, but it does not penetrate into the back country."

The tone of the above suggests the pen of an Officer. The 27th May saw the arrival in South Africa of the draft heretofore mentioned when 99 men commanded by Sergeant Tuck of the Permanent Staff arrived from Devonport onboard the S.S Pindari. At Prieska, Captain Masterman succeeded Lt Carey as Garrison Adjutant, the latter having received a regular commision in the Loyal North Lancashire Regiment. In a letter written from De Aar at about this date, Pte Johns describes an incident in the life of the Troops stationed there — "We have three Companies here and five up at Prieska. Last Thursday when we were over on the Football Ground, one of our Officers came galloping over and ordered us back to Camp at once as Rebels were advancing towards Phillipstown. We all ran back. By that time our tents were down and we were ready to march to the station by half past three. There we were placed in Trucks and had to wait there for three hours perishing with the cold before we started. The Train took us as far as Hout Kraal, an hour's ride from here then we had 34 miles of marching to do.

It was after ten in the night when we started, so we marched all night until five in the morning, then we lay down on the veldt for an hour and a half. We could not sleep as it was too cold. After this rest we started again on the march until we came to some water. Here we were to have some breakfast. There was a muddy pool in the middle of the road from which we made some coffee. The water was so dirty that the Mules would not drink it, but we did. It went down up to the mark with one biscuit between two men. This is all we had on the march, and when we entered Phillipstown there was no sign of the enemy. We were all disappointed as we all thought to have an engagement. Our Maxim was ready too. We stopped there one day, and at three o clock the next morning started back to De Aar. We were treated splendid coming back, but we had to rough it going. Each man was in full Marching Order and also carried a Blanket."

On August 2nd, 1900, the De Aar Detachment commanded by Captain Aldridge entrained for Vryburg, Bechuanaland, where on arrival they took up quarters in West Camp. They were joined on the 24th by the Headquarters of the Battalion. On the 2nd September a draft of 88 men accompanied by Second Lieutenants Woosnam, Linton and Boyd arrived at Vryburg. This draft had arrived in Capetown onboard the S.S. Dilwara on the 29th August.

With the departure of General Sittle's Column on the 16th September, Lt Colonel Perkins, 3 Welsh, was appointed Commandant Vryburg with Captain H.E. Taylor as Station Staff Officer. The Garrison consisted of one Section Australian Artillery, 200 details of the Northampton and North Lancashire Regiments, 3rd Battalion, The Welsh Regiment, seven Mounted Infantry details and the Cape Police Division II.

Shortly after arriving at Vryburg, ten men of 3 Welsh volunteered for Mounted Infantry duty and were placed under the command of Captain Anthill, Royal Australian Artillery. Rebel Patrols frequently raided the Vryburg district in search of cattle and clashes between them and the outposts were not infrequent. When required, a mounted Patrol and a Gun would be sent to intercept the Raiders, but were rarely successful in bringing them in due to the speed at which they scattered.

In November, Colonel Milne arrived at Vryburg to organise and command a Convoy to proceed to Schwitzer Reneke in the Transvaal. The Infantry Escort was to be supplied by 3rd Welch and consisted of 200 Other Ranks commanded by Captain Aldridge. The Convoy left Vryburg on the 22nd November and had a brush with the Boers when its Cavalry escort was fired upon the next day. On the 24th, the Boers made a determined attack on the Convoy at Du Toit's Kopje, but were beaten off. Convoy casualties were confined to the Mounted Infantry. Schweitzer Reneke was reached on the 25th, the Convoy commencing its return journey on the 27th. During the journey, the Boers harrased the van and rear of the Convoy almost continuously and forced it to halt at O'Reilly's Pan. There, over 500 Boers made a determined attack over a three hour period which tried the defenders to the limit. The Convoy suffered many casualties amongst which were the following seriously wounded men of 3rd Welch.

576 Pte E. Davies of 'F' Company
552 Pte D. Evans of 'F' Company
601 Pte M. Thomas of 'G' Company

The Convoy arrived back at Vryburg on the 30th November.

In January 1901, Colonel Perkins was placed in command of a Convoy which was to proceed from Vryburg to Kuruman — a distance of some 98 miles and over bad roads. In a letter to his wife he stated:

"I am off tomorrow on an expedition across country which will take up eighteen to twenty days. By Lord Methuen's Orders I am going in command of a column of about 200 men of 3rd Welch, 150 Mounted Men, two 15 Pounders and a Pom Pom to relieve Kuruman.

We lost a convoy of 25 Wagons full of stores and forage between here and there about ten days ago. Lord Methuen has determined to have the place evacuated, and I am going to bring in the Garrison. There are a good many Boers still about in this part of the country, and I hope we shall get in touch with them."

As will be seen later, the Garrison at Kuruman was not evacuated, so there must have been a change of heart in that respect after the letter was written. The Convoy left Vryburg on January 2nd and covered the distance to Kuruman by the 9th. The Cavalry screen was fired upon by the Boers at one point during the outward journey, but the enemy soon dispersed when fired upon by the Convoy's Artillery. Having unloaded, the Convoy returned to Vryburg via Swatfontein to arrive back safely on the 26th.

On the 13th April, the Battalion was detailed to provide an escort for another Kuruman Convoy. The full escort consisted of 150 Mounted Troops, Captain Pope and 100 men of 3rd Welch, 150 Volunteer Riflemen and one 7 Pdr Gun Section. Also accompanying the Convoy was Lt Linton and 40 Other Ranks from the Battalion who were detailed to reinforce the Kuruman Garrison. Both outward and return journey were uneventful, the Convoy returning to Vryburg on the 29th of the month. On the 5th July, Colonel Perkins commanded a Convoy carrying Rifles to arm the natives of the Takoon district, the Mule Waggons having an Escort of 100 Men of Cullinan's Horse, 1 Section of 88th Battery, Royal Field Artillery, Lt Herd and 30 Other Ranks from the 3rd Welch. The Convoy had an uneventful journey both ways and returned to Vryburg on the 15th July after marching a round distance of 124 miles.

On the 10th August Colonel Perkins commanded a large Convoy consisting of 120 Ox Waggons from Vryburg to Kuruman. The escort consisted of 200 Mounted Rifles, 1 Section of 88th Battery, RFA, one Pom Pom Section and four Officers and 200 Other Ranks of 3rd Welch.

In the vicinity of Geluk, the Convoy was fired upon from a house flying a white flag. In due course a mounted Patrol took three prisoners, due to the prompt action of Pte Cavely of the 3rd Welsh Mounted Infantry who shot the Boer Horses and thus prevented their escape. Boer Patrols were sighted during the outward journey, but they did not attempt to attack the Convoy.

The empty Convoy and Escort returned via the Tungo Valley and reached Vryburg without incident on the 29th after a round trip of some 200 miles.

On the 29th September, 1901, the Headquarters of the Battalion moved from Vryburg to Kimberley. Shortly thereafter, two Officers and 160 Other Ranks found themselves manning the Blockhouses to the North and South of the town.

By this time the novelty of active service in South Africa had worn off, and many of the Soldiers were thinking in terms of home. That feeling is illustrated in a letter written by Sergeant Cadogan of the Battalion Permanent Staff which was reproduced in the Regimental Journal some time later.

"And now, of course, all our cries are 'we want to go home', but goodness knows when we shall go. However, we are all living in hope of being home for Christmas. Our men are all home sick and fed up with this country. We have seen none of the sights of South Africa, for we have not been out of Cape Colony, only just to fetch or take a Convoy to some place, or taking a stroll through Griqualand for 70 to 160 miles and back. I may tell you that we here, that is, 'A', 'B', 'E', 'G' and 'H' Companies with the following Non-Commissioned Officers of the Permanent Staff — Colour Sergeants Fidler, Evans, Smith, Cadogan. Sergeants Lewis, Williams and Jones have not seen any of the others for the past 16 months. They are hundreds of miles away from us. Our Companies here are only skeletons of what they used to be. Out of 74 NCOs and Men whom I brought out from home, I have 29; in fact the total of the five Companies is only 205 NCOs and Men. One cause of it is that we are so far from the nearest railway station — 120 miles, so that all the Recruits who have come out have gone on up to Headquarters, guarding the Railway Line.

Colour Sergeant Williams met with an accident and he is now at the Depot. Colour Sergeant Kerr is paying a Company at the Base Depot, Cape Town, and Colour Sergeant Foster is doing Orderly Room work out here. Colour Sergeant Smith and his Company have been away from here on Column duty down in the Colony since last April. They are now about 470 miles from here near the Namaqualand Border. We have got a Company of Mounted Infantry here under Sergeant Lewis (Darkey). They had a brush with the enemy on the 6th August. We had one man wounded, No 9533 Pte T. Jones of 'G' Company.

He was shot through the fleshy part of the thigh — glad to say he has now completely recovered and returned to duty again.

Very sorry to tell you that Colour Sergeant Davies is in Hospital suffering with enteric fever. He is reported dangerously ill, and does not recognise anyone."

The letter illustrates more than most documents the widespread activities of the Battalion — sadly, their hopes of being home for Christmas were not realised as they were to see the commencement of another year on active service before turning their faces in that direction.

On the 23rd December, three Officers and 120 Other Ranks marched out from Kimberley to Windsonton Road where they joined Major Paris's Column en route for Boshof. Other detachments of the Battalion Headquarters were employed in the Kimblerley district.

Mentioned in the Despatches of Lord Kitchener at this time were three Soldiers of the 3rd Welch. *The London Gazette* report later published stated as follows:-

"3rd Battalion Welsh Regiment — Corporal Sims, No 9224 Pte Donoghue, No 749 Pte Moore. Near Dornbult, on the Western line, on July 19th, 1901, hearing that the line was mined, Sims took the two men with him and proceeded to the spot on a trolley, and although fired at from the bush, removed the mine. Corpl Sims promoted Sergeant by the Commander in Chief."

At Prieska, earlier in the month, Major W. Forrest received an illuminated address from the inhabitants as a token of appreciation of his services to them whilst serving as Commandant of the Detachment stationed there. It expressed the regret of the loyal citizens of that district that he was about to leave, and an appreciation of his kind and gentlemanly behaviour to all classes.

It ended by stating that the citizens could not sufficiently thank him, his Officers and his Men for their ever ready help in all matters concerning the community.

Notes on the activities of the Battalion during its lst month of active service in South Africa show that in no way was the pressure of duty on the lines of communication relaxed, the type of work being exemplified in the examples which follow:-

*January 2nd, 1902.*
Lieutenant Furber and 70 Other Ranks escort an empty Convoy to Kimberley Captain Perkins and Lt Herd with 50 Other Ranks attached to the Armoured Train protecting the Railway north of Windsonton Road.

*January 15th, 1902.*
Captain Perkins, Lt Herd, Lt Furber with 120 Other Ranks proceed with Convoy from Vryburg to Kuruman.

*25th January, 1902.*
Lieutenant Todd with 91 Other Ranks complete a period of duty in the blockhouse north of Kimberley.

*4th Februarty, 1902.*
Four Officers and 175 Other Ranks return from duty with Major Paris's Kuruman Convoy.

On the 6th February the Battalion was inspected by the Officer Commanding Kly District at Dynamite Siding Camp. Two days later, the 8th, all Ranks entrained at Kimberley for Cape Town, where on arrival they embarked on the Transport 'Lake Erie' which sailed on the 11th for England. The Officers and 601 Other Ranks enjoyed a comfortable voyage home, arriving at Southampton on the 7th March. Entraining that same evening the Battalion arrived in Cardiff early the next day. From Roath Station they marched through streets crowded with spectators, whose welcome was at times, more than enthusiastic, via Crwys Road to Maindy Barracks which was reached by 6.30 a.m. After breakfast and some preparation the Battalion was by 9.45 a.m. formed up in quarter column, and headed by 'De Wet' the rather stubborn goat captured from the Boers at Boshof, the Battalion stepped off for Cardiff Arms Park. Once again, the Militia received a tremendous reception, particularly as they passed through Queen Street and Castle Street. There the drab Khaki of the South African veterans contrasted sharply with the Scarlet and Blue of the 3rd Volunteer Battalion, The Welsh Regiment, Submarine Miners and 2nd Glamorgan Artillery Volunteers whose members lined the route.

Played on by the Bands of the Artillery Volunteers and Submarine Miners the Militia drew up in Line before the main stand, the Volunteers and their Bands forming up behind them. There the Battalion waited in the presence of some 35,000 spectators, for the arrival of Lord Windsor, Lord Lieutenant of the County, who was to present all ranks with the South Africa Campaign Medal.

Following upon the arrival of the dignitaries which included in addition to the Lord Lieutenant, Mr Tudor Crawshay, Deputy Lieutenant, the Mayor of Cardiff, Mr F.J. Beavan, the Town Clerk, Mr J.L. Wheatley, and Sir William Thomas Lewis, Bart, the Colours of the Battalion, which had been placed in the care of the town Fathers were brought onto the field with due ceremony and handed back to the Battalion by the Mayor. The Colours were received by Lieutenant Boyd and Lieutenant Herd, and marched back into position in front of the Battalion.

The ceremony of presenting the Medals then commenced, the Officers, Non Commissioned Officers and Men coming up in turn to receive them from the hands of Lord Windsor. At mid-day, the presentation ceremony completed, the Militia and other Troops present marched past, the Militia proceeding to the Park Hall where they were to be entertained to a Dinner. *The Western Mail* of that day reports the departure as follows:-

"The march of the men from the park after the ceremony to the Park Hall was marked with less incident than the downward march had been. Throughout, the men passed between barriers, and there was nothing to impede their swinging quick march. Yet this short section had in it something more of a brightness, and a truer approximation to the tradition of a military pagent. First went a detachment of the Volunteer Artillery, followed by the Submarine Miners and the 3rd V.B. Welsh Regiment, passing by the Town Hall, High Street, Duke Street and Queen Street. In these auxiliary contingents there were three Bands of Music, and therein lay the secret of the smartness that marked that short march so distinctly. 'The March of the Men of Harlech', 'Llwyn Onn', and other Welsh airs were played in turn with 'Tommy Atkins' and 'Red, White and Blue'. In the middle of the column was a Guard with fixed Bayonets, escorting the just returned Colours, and whenever the two Standards were perceived, the crowd raised a shout. As the Men defiled into the Park Hall, they were cheered to the echo."

After the 'Lunch' and speeches together with numerous toasts, the proceedings terminated and the Battalion once again formed up for the march back to Maindy Barracks. The march, via Newport Road, Castle Road and Crwys Road developed into rather a straggle, for relatives and friends broke into the ranks and insisted upon accompanying the Men. A blind eye was turned to march discipline on this occasion, and the barracks were reached without incident.

Prior to their dismissal, Colonel Perkins addressed and thanked the Men. Afterwards Arms and Equipment were returned and the men issued with their civilian clothes. After receiving arrears of pay (the main part of which had already been sent to their homes) the Battalion dispersed, the Men returning to the receptions which awaited them in towns and villages throughout the County. At Cardiff, Swansea, Merthyr, Neath, Resolven and Pontypridd they were met by enthusiastic crowds, and festivities continued long into the night.

The splendid service of the Battalion in South Africa is well summed up in Lord Windsor's Arms Park speech:- "It is more than two years since the Battalion was embodied. The country was proud of it at that time; it is more proud of it now, after its services in South Africa and the way in which it has upheld the honour of the country." A *Western Mail* Correspondent went further: "They endured much. To march from point to point and camp out on the African veldt for two years, scorched by the burning sun in daytime, and frozen by night, was an ordeal that none but the strongest constitutions could have borne. But they endured it as all Soldiers, and as British Soldiers — patiently, heroically, without a murmur or complaint."

Authority for Annual Training for the year 1902 was received on the 31st May, the venue for that year being Aldershot. On Monday, 9th June, the Battalion assembled at Cardiff for 27 days annual training. The Battalion strength at this date is given as 15 Officers, 1 Warrant Officer and 851 Other Ranks, of which 13 Officers, 1 Warrant Officer and 548 Other Ranks were present. On the 16th June the Battalion attended a Review at Aldershot and was inspected by Her Majesty Queen Alexandra. On this occasion No.1 Company was commanded by Major Elton, No.2 Company by Captain B. Perkins, No.3 Company by Major Forrest, DSO, No.4 Company by Captain Latham, No 5 Coy by Captain R.W. Taylor and No 6 Coy by Captain W. Masterman. The Battalion Colours were carried by Lt H.F. Herd and Lt F.H. Linton.

After the Review, the following message was read to all Ranks.
"The Queen, in the unavoidable absence of the King, due to indisposition, has been pleased to express the pleasure which the appearance and soldierlike bearing of the Troops reviewed gave Her Majesty on June 16th."

The Battalion returned to Cardiff by Special Train to arrive early on the 6th July. Having returned Arms and Equipment to the Armoury and Stores, the men were dismissed to their homes at Noon.

On the 4th February, 1903, Lt. Colonel W. Watts, CB., succeeded Lt. Colonel A.T. Perkins, CB. as Commanding Officer of the Battalion, Colonel Perkins assuming the responsibilities of Hon. Colonel.

On the 12th March, Colonel Watts announced that he had applied to His Majesty The King for a white goat from the Windsor Great Park Herd to replace 'Taffy 1' of the 3rd Battalion which had died whilst on service with the Battalion in South Africa during the Boer War. He also announced that the King had been graciously pleased to approve the request. The goat arrived in Cardiff on the 17th April and was taken onto the Battalion strength as 'Taffy 11'.

The venue for the Annual Training of 1903 was Penally, an Advance Party commanded by Lieutenant Herd proceeding to the site on the 22nd May to pitch camp and prepare for the arrival of the Battalion.

Recruits for Preliminary Training proceeded to Penally by train on the 25th May, and were followed by the main body of the Battalion on the 9th June, they having assembled at Maindy Barracks the previous day. At Penally, the Battalion formed part of the 3rd Militia Infantry Brigade under the command of A/Brigadier General, Colonel A.G. Watson, 28th Regimental District. Other units in the Brigade were the 3rd and 4th Battalions, Gloucestershire Regiment and the 3rd and 4th Battalions, South Wales Borderers. 19 Officers and 954 Other Ranks were present at Penally but 63 Trained Men and 110 Recruits were listed as absent for various reasons.

During this training Colonel Watts, in order to encourage a high standard of shooting presented the Battalion with two Cups. One was to be competed for by Company Officers and the other by Companies of the Battalion. Winners for 1903 were Major W. Elton and 'A' Company.

On the 23rd June, the Battalion marched to Pembroke Dock and were transported by boat to Fort Popton. There they were instructed in Field Operations, including a scheme for the defence of Milford Haven.

The 26th June being His Majesty's Birthday, the Battalion paraded in Review Order and fired a Feu de Joie in honour of the occasion. After the Parade the Men were each given a pint of beer with which to drink the King's health.

Inspection took place on the following day, the Battalion acquitting itself well and meriting the praise of the Brigade Commander. On the 3rd July, the Battalion paraded early and marched to Pembroke Dock Station on completion of breaking camp later that day. Entraining for Cardiff that evening, they arrived back early the following morning, where after Breakfast and some rapid preparation they marched headed by the Colours to Llandaff Cathedral. There all Ranks attended the Service and Ceremony of the unveiling of Welsh Regiment Memorial Plaques, including one commemorating Members of the Battalion who had lost their lives during the recent South African Campaign. On completion of the ceremony the Battalion marched back to Maindy Barracks where after returning weapons and equipment they were marched to the Railway Station, handed the balance of their pay, and dismissed to their homes.

During this very successful annual training, the thirty strong Band of the Battalion under the direction of Bandmaster Prentice entertained the Public at Tenby each Sunday on Castle Hill. During the stay at Penally 511 Other Ranks were presented with the King's Medal for service in South Africa, they having received The Queen's Medal at Cardiff Arms Park on their return to Cardiff from the Cape.

On the 26th February, 1904, Captain and Quartermaster T. Tinnock retired from the Army, after serving eleven years with the Battalion. He was succeeded as Quartermaster by Lieutenant and Quartermaster I. MacDonald, late 2nd Battalion, The Welch Regiment.

The venue for the 1904 Camp was Porthcawl, an Advance Party of 32 Other Ranks under the command of Lieutenant N. Biggs proceeding to that town on the 6th August in order to pitch camp and make other preparations. Recruits for Preliminary Training assembled at Maindy Barracks on August 8th and then proceeded to Camp by rail, its site being on Fields close to the Church at Newton. The main body of the Battalion assembled at Cardiff on the 22nd and travelled down to Porthcawl the same day, the total present that night being 25 Officers, 7 Attached Officers, 30 Permanent Staff and 838 Other Ranks of the Battalion. 67 Trained Men and 76 Recruits were listed as being absent from training.

The Battalion was organised as follows for the occasion:-

Colonel W. Watts, CB, Commanding Officer
Major W. Forrest, DSO, Second in Command
Lt. Col. Parsons (Royal Fusiliers) 2nd Major
Major H.E. Taylor (1st R. Berkshire Regt) Adjutant
Captain B. Perkins Instructor of Musketry
Lt. J. Macdonald Quartermaster
'A' Company — Captain Herd, 2/Lt. Johns
'B' Company — Captain Perkins, Lt. Biggs, 2/Lt. Gaskell (3rd VB The Welsh Regt)
'C' Company — Captain Aldridge, Lt. Mandley, Lt. Ogden
'D' Company — Captain Latham, Lt. Ponter
'E' Company — Captain Jackson, 2/Lt. Sergeant
'F' Company — Captain Esplin, 2/Lt. Oppenheim
'G' Company — Lt Kesley, 2/Lt. Smith

'H' Company — Captain Masterman, Lt. Clarson
'I' Company — Major Huntington, Lt. Homer
'K' Company — Captain Hole (3rd Buffs), 2/Lt. Hayman
'L' Company — Lt. Furber, 2/Lt. Furber, 2/Lt. Montefiore
'M' Company — Major Dresser, 2/Lt. Rowthorn

During its stay at Porthcawl, the Battalion was able to make use of the newly constructed Porthcawl Range, which was opened on the 10th August. Lt General Sir William Butler, KCB, also visited the Battalion. As an old Officer of the 69th, he had a critical eye, but was well pleased with all that he saw.

The official Annual Inspection was carried out by Colonel A.W. Hill, Officer Commanding the 41st Regiment District. The activities of the day included a tactical exercise, but all went well, and Colonel Hill expresed himself well satisfied.

The soldierly bearing and irreproachable conduct of the men during their stay in Porthcawl produced a most complimentary letter from the Porthcawl Urban District Council, and in thanking the Battalion, expressed the hope that the district would be selected for its future annual training.

The Battalion returned to Cardiff on Saturday, 17th September, and were dismissed to their homes the same day.

In November, Major Taylor's term as Adjutant ended, and he was temporarily replaced by Lt Torkington of the 1st Welch pending the arrangement of a more long term appointment.

On the 11th February, 1905, Captain C. Lewis, Essex Regiment, succeeded Lt Torkington as Adjutant of the Battalion. Venue for the Annual Training was again Porthcawl, the Battalion assembling at Maindy Barracks, Cardiff, on the 10th July and moving on to camp on the same day. Inspected by Colonel A.W. Hill on August 2nd, it received, as in the previous year a good report. To encourage good shooting in Welsh Militia Battalions, Colonel W. Watts had presented a handsome Trophy styled The Red Dragon Cup. The Winners for the year were 3 Welsh. The Battalion was dismissed from training on August 4th. The damp conditions experienced during the 1905 Camp resulted in the death of the Battalion Goat, Taffy II, following which Colonel Watts applied to the King for a replacement. A suitable beast was selected by the Chief Ranger of Windsor Great Park and reported for duty with the Battalion on the 20th October, 1905, where he was officially christened 'Taffy III'.

Annual Training in 1906 commenced June 18th, the venue being Ross on Wye, Herefordshire. There the Battalion took over the ground and camp equipment from the 4th Shropshire Light Infantry, and were fortunate in having good weather throughout the stay. On the 12th and 13th of July, the Battalion were inspected by Brigadier General Ommany, CB, and as in previous years received a good report. Present in Camp were 27 Officers, 1 Sergeant Major, 49 Sergeants, 37 Corporals, 10 Drummers and 666 Private Men. The Battalion was dismissed from training on the 14th July.

The year 1907 saw the Regular Army short of officers and Reservists and unable to meet its establishment of 6,494 Officers and 160,200 Men. The Militia and Volunteers,although below strength were not considered sufficiently trained and organised to meet the demands of warfare of the day in spite of their enthusiasm. The seeds of the reorganisation which followed had been sown much earlier, but the growing process was rapidly pushed forward by the energetic Mr Haldane who had taken over responsibility for the War Office following the Liberal victory at the polls in November 1905. He set in motion plans for an entirely new force on modern ideas and the pattern of the Regular Army, which plan saw the Volunteers reorganised as a Territorial Force, and the Militia as a Special Reserve for his new Expeditionary Force. These changes best known as The Haldane Reforms became law under the Territorial and Reserve Forces Act of 1907 under which the Militia (that part of the force which survived) became for the first time a real reserve of Officers and Men for the Regular Army with the general role of providing complete units on mobilisation if required, but more importantly to maintain a regular flow of reinforcements to replace casualties and other wastage when the Regular Army was committed to War. The Special Reserve Battalions were to be administered in all respects through Regular Army channels. Training was to be based on the appropriate Regimental Depots, which in the case of 3 Welsh was Maindy Barracks, Cardiff. Officers and Other Ranks joining would receive 6 months initial training and thereafter assemble for 27 days annually.

The long history of the 3rd (Militia) Battalion, The Welsh Regiment, formerly the Militia of the County of Glamorgan ended at midnight, March 31st, 1908. The following day, April 1st, the Battalion continued in service as the 3rd (Special Reserve) Battalion, The Welsh Regiment, which although never again to see active service, provided for the Regular Battalions of the parent Regiment many hundreds of all ranks for active service during World War 1, thereby continuing the custom set by its predecessor regiment during the War against Napoleonic France early in the past century. Here the story ends, but the proud traditions of the Royal Glamorgan Militia continue to this day in the safe hands of an equally proud Welsh Regiment, The Royal Regiment of Wales.

Lt. Colonel A. Thrale Perkins — Commanding Officer — 1895 to 1902
The Badge on the Field Service Cap is the standard Officers Gilt and
Silver Cap Badge of The Welsh Regiment.
Courtesy of The Welch Regiment Museum.

MAP SHOWING LOCATIONS IN THE CAPE COLONY, ORANGE
FREE STATE AND BRITISH BECHUANALAND WHERE THE 3rd
BATTALION, THE WELSH REGIMENT (MILITIA) WERE ACTIVE
DURING THE BOER WAR, 1899-1902.

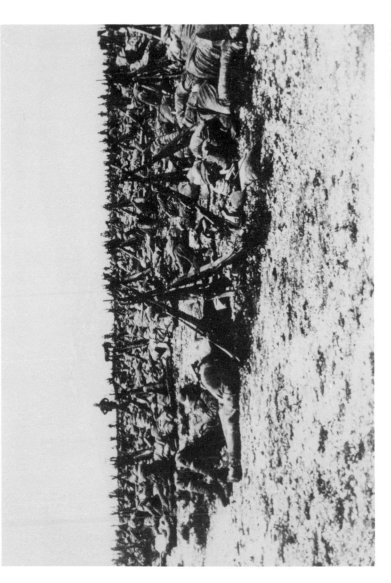

TROOPS (INCLUDING 3rd WELSH) ASLEEP ON THE VELDT  SOUTH AFRICA 1901
Courtesy of The Welch Regiment Museum

THE CAMP AT De AAR JUNCTION  CAPE COLONY, c.1900
*Courtesy. The Welch Regt. Museum*

## TERMS OF SERVICE.

*Enlistment, Re-enlistment, and Re-engagement.*

Every Militia recruit will be enlisted for a period of six years as a Militiaman for the county for which he is raised; he will be appointed to the corps for that county, or for the area comprising the whole or part of that county; and will be posted to the unit in which he is intended to serve.

Where the unit to which a Militiaman is posted forms part of a corps which also includes an unit of the Regular Army, he will not be posted to such unit of the Regular Forces without his consent.

A Militiaman who has been discharged after completing at least one engagement, may re-enlist in the Militia, for a period of four years at any time within three years of discharge if under 45 years of age.

Men who have been discharged from the Army or Army Reserve, Royal Marines or Royal Navy, with not less than three years' service, and with good or fair characters but without pension, may also re-enlist in the Militia within three years of discharge if under 45 years of age.

A Militiaman may re-engage at the termination of the last training of his current engagement, or at any subsequent period prior to the expiration of his engagement, for four years, reckoned from the termination of that engagement, if under 45 years of age.

No Militiaman who has received pay during three months, or during the whole period of preliminary training if less than three months, or during one whole period of annual training, shall be entitled to claim his discharge on the ground of error or illegality in his enlistment or re-engagement.

---

*Militiaman's Name and Description.*

Morgan _____ (Name)

Enlisted for the Militia of the unit of Glamorgan.

and appointed to the _____ Regiment

on the 26/9/00

at Neath

in the County of Glamorgan

at the age of 17 years 8 months.

Born in the Parish of Neath

in or near the Town of Glamorgan

in the County of Glamorgan

Trade or Calling Steelworker

Last Permanent Residence _____

Height 5 Feet 7 ⅞ Inches.

Complexion Fresh

Eyes Blue

Hair Black

Marks _____

Religion Wesleyan

---

PAGES FROM THE PAY BOOK OF PTE. MORGAN DIAMOND OF
NEATH ENLISTED 3rd (MILITIA) BN, THE WELSH REGIMENT, SEPTEMBER, 1900
Courtesy of The Welch Regiment Museum

# THE THIRD WELSH,

## WARM PRAISE AND HONOUR,

### FOR THE

# GALLANT REGIMENT.

*The Regiment where J.ROBERT WOOD:*
*have been Serving, &c.*

The following is a Copy of a cutting from a Vryburg Newspaper; which was send home to Craigcefnparc; Clydach, by a clydach man, serving with the Third Welsh Regiment, in South Affrica. — 'On Thursday last, when the news got about that the 3d Welsh — the regiment which has formed the principal part of the garrison of Vryburg; for 16 months past,—was about to leave: the opinion was expressed on all sides that it would never do to allow such an occasion to pass unnoticed. During the stay of the regiment in Vryburg. the Officers have been most popular, whilst the behaviour of the men has been such as to earn the esteem of all classes of the inhabitants. The regiment has had a share of fighting here, in the relief of Schweizer Reucoke, and in escorting conveys to Kuruman. as well as local skirmishes; and their duties, whether in the field or in garrison; have always been performed in an excellent spirit. — It was resolved by the Townspeople, to subscribe for a piece of plate to be send to the Headquarters of the Regiment as a permanent Memento of Vryburg. and South Africa War. A substantial number of guineas was subscribed for the Presentation. And great many of the Officials gave a very good Testtimonials to the 3d Welsh, before embarking for home.

Several young Clydach men belong to the Regiment: and their return was enthusiasticaly welcomed by the inhabitants of the little town in the Swansea Valley.

Extract from a South African Newspaper
Courtesy of The Welch Regiment Museum

Homecoming
3rd Battalion march up Crwys Road, Cardiff 8th March, 1902
*Courtesy. The Welch Regt. Museum*

3rd (MILITIA) BATTALION
MAINDY BARRACKS SQUARE
1902

3rd BATTALION CAMP
Aldershot 1902

FIELD EXERCISE
3rd Bn, The Welsh Regiment, near Aldershot, 1902

A BATTALION GROUP POSE WITH MUSKETRY TROPHY, c.1905
STANDING (L/R) Lt. J.H.P. Clarkson, Capt. E. Pope, Capt. W.S. Masterman, Sgt. Maj. J.A. Bryant
SEATED (L/R) Colonel W. Watts, CB, Lt. Colonel W. Forrest, DSO

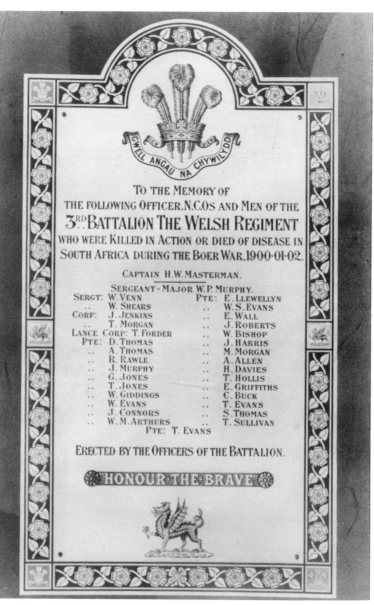

BOER WAR MEMORIAL PLAQUE
3rd BATTALION, THE WELSH REGIMENT
LLANDAFF CATHEDRAL, CARDIFF
*Courtesy. The Welch Regt. Museum*

3rd BATTALION CENTREPIECE

# 3rd Battalion Centrepiece

The Silver Centrepiece presented to the Officers Mess of the 3rd (Militia) Battalion, The Welch Regiment by Officers past and present, takes the form of a solid silver Corinthian Column having the Regimental Colours draped at its base and a figure of 'Victory' at the top. The Column stands on an ebonised pedestal with a silver panel mounted on the front on which is depicted in relief a Boar War Convoy scene, the whole above the commemorative title 'SOUTH AFRICA' in silver letters. On one side is the Dragon of Wales in Silver and on the other the Plumes, Coronet and Motto of The Prince of Wales and the regimental Motto. On the left side is a finely modelled silver figure in the campaign dress worn in South Africa and on the right an Officer in the Full Dress Uniform of the Regiment.

The Centrepiece is now in the care of the Officers Mess of the 3rd (Territorial) Battalion, The Royal Regiment of Wales at Maindy Barracks, the old Depot of The Welch Regiment.

# THE ROYAL GLAMORGAN ARTILLERY MILITIA
# 1854-1908

## The Swansea Bay and Milford Haven Defences

As the primary role of the Artillery Militia was coastal defence, it is necessary to give the reader some idea of the state of those defences in 1854, and to briefly outline their development in Swansea Bay and Milford Haven during the period of the Regiment's involvement.

Defences in Swansea Bay were in 1854 non-existent, and in consequence certain influential gentlemen, not the least amongst which in Swansea, was George Grant Francis, M.P., had for some time being pressing Government and the War Office to rectify the situation. Promises were made, surveys carried out, and steps taken to raise a Regiment of Artillery Militia to man the proposed Works; but the outbreak of War in the Crimea in 1854, followed by the Indian Mutiny crisis of 1857 resulted in the needs of Swansea and other South Wales ports being given a very low priority. The whole matter of Home Defence had been sparked off by a resurgence of French naval and military power and the ambitiousness of Napoleon III. Although an ally during the Crimean War, France was still regarded by many as the traditional enemy and fears were in no way placated when during that costly campaign, the poor organisation of the British Army had been shown up badly in comparison with the efficiency of the French. Later, the demands made on our Army during the great Mutiny in India had stretched its resources to breaking point; so much so, as to create doubts as to its ability to cope with the requirements of Empire whilst still maintaining an ability to protect the British shore.

A Commission of Enquiry found the Home Defence system wanting, and plans were made to improve the situation.

The first Guns to arrive in Swansea were two 18 Pounder Muzzle Loaders on Field Carriages provided for use of the local Artillery Volunteer Corps in March 1860. Meanwhile a proposal to mount a heavy Battery for use of the Artillery Militia on the salient angle of Swansea Pier fell through due to the inability of the structure to take the weight.

In 1859 work commenced on the construction of a Five Gun Battery on the Lighthouse Island off Mumbles Point. The Guns, 68 Pdr Rifled Muzzle Loaders arrived by sea from Woolwich in June 1861, and by mid August had been placed in position by the R.A. A Sergeant and five Gunners of the Coast Artillery Brigade, R.A., were responsible for maintaining the two tier Battery, but its manning was to be the responsibility of the Artillery Militia and the local Corps of Volunteer Artillery.

In the late 1870s at least two of the 68 Pounders were replaced with a pair of 80 Pdr RMLs on traversing slide carriages. An Inspection Team found those

Guns still in use in the Fort in 1882, and proposed that they be replaced with two 10.4" RMLs mounted in a Turret. Financial restrictions prevented that modernisation, and the Fort's armament remained unchanged until the turn of the Century.

In May 1900 a Detachment of Royal Engineers prepared sites at the Fort for the installation of two modern Quick Firing Guns. The old 80 Pounders were removed, and disposed of in pits dug at low tide close to the Island. The new Guns were not installed until several years hence, but Colonel K.W. Maurice Jones, in his Book on the History of Coast Artillery, tells us that there were two 6" Breech Loading Quick Firing Guns mounted in the Fort in 1914.

In 1854 Milford Haven was somewhat better, although inadequately protected. It had 23 guns at Pater Battery built in 1840, Thorn Island which had been fortified in 1852, and if Press reports be correct, a three Gun Battery on the Stack Rock.

Fort Popton was by 1858 armed with eleven 9" RML Guns in Casemates and to which were added by 1872, six 7" RML Guns in Pits and mounted on Montcrieff Disappearing Carriages.

South Hook Fort, also one of the early 1860s developments had in 1871 a combination of 7" and 9" RMLs and Fort Hubberstone by 1872, eight 7" RML Guns in Pits on Montcrieff Disappearing Carriages.

Stack Rock further fortified in 1871 had by the following year, sixteen 10" RMLs in Casemates and seven 7" RMLs, thus providing the Haven with a considerable weight of Armament. Maintenance of the Forts and the Guns was the responsibility of Regulars from the Royal Artillery Coast Brigade, but the manning of the Forts in War was to be shared by the various South Wales Regiments of Milita Artillery, for which in peacetime they provided a valuable training facility.

In 1880, Thorn Island was armed with nine 7" RMLs and by 1881 one or more 10" RMLs on Barbette Mountings were installed at Fort Hubberstone. At South Hook, the late 1890s saw the armament updated with a 9.2" Breech Loader and at least three 12 Pounder Quick Firing Guns, both types of which were still on site in the third decade of the present century.

## The Royal Glamorgan Artillery Militia

Its history commences in 1854 when Mr Talbot of Margam Abbey, Lord Lieutenant of the County, received instructions to raise a Corps of Militia Artillery to man fortifications which it was proposed to erect for the defence of the Glamorganshire Coast and in particular, Swansea Bay. On December 2nd, Captain Evan Morgan, RA (Retd), was appointed Lieutenant Colonel in command of the Corps. Well known in the County as a Deputy Lieutenant and Justice of the Peace, he had considerable military experience, having served with the Rocket Troop, Royal Horse Artillery in the Peninsular War, and also on the Niagara Frontier during the Anglo-American War of 1812-14. Established strength of the Regiment was set at:-

1 Lieutenant Colonel
3 Captains
3 Lieutenants
3 Ensigns
1 Adjutant
1 Surgeon
1 Sergeant Major
9 Sergeants
9 Corporals
3 Trumpeters
286 Gunners

Daily Rates of Pay when embodied for training ranged from £1.2.6 (£1.12½p) for the Lieutenant Colonel down to one Shilling (5p) for a Gunner, but as will be seen, Government was spared that expense for some considerable time after the formation of the Corps was announced. *The Cambrian* on January 12th, 1855, spoke optimistically on future plans for the Corps — "We recently announced the appointment of Captain Evan Morgan, RA, of St. Helens, as Lt Colonel of this new Corps. We are now in a position to state that Swansea has been fixed upon as Headquarters, and Colonel Morgan has nearly completed the necessary Staff arrangements. This being done, the organisation of the Corps will be proceeded with without delay, and we hope to see many of our young Townsmen volunteering into it, so as to obviate the necessity of having recourse to the Ballot." On the subject of defences which the Corps could man, the same Newspaper on the 19th January, 1855, stated — "We are glad to learn that the Government are at last fully alive to the necessity of placing our exposed coast in a state of defence. In addition to some large Guns which will be placed on the Swansea Piers, there will also be a formidable Battery erected forthwith on the Mumbles." The use of the term 'forthwith' proved to be nothing but wishful thinking.

Meanwhile the formation of the Militia Corps continued slowly. On February 9th, George Elliott Ranken, Esq., was appointed Lieutenant, and on March 16th, John Paddon, MD., of the Laurels, Swansea, as Surgeon.

On March 16th also George Grant Francis, MP., announced in the local Press that the Government had on the 12th March confirmed its intention to proceed with the planned fortifications and that money had been allocated for that purpose. The *Times* in April 1855 also confirmed that things were at last on the move, and so they appeared to be judging by the fact that a Regiment was being raised and that public money had been allocated for the construction of defences.

On the 16th April, 1855, the following were appointed Officers in the Corps:-

Captain George Travis Radcliffe
Lieutenant Richard Ilbert Phillips

Lieutenant Josiah Price
and on 20th April,
Captain William Montague Leeds (late 50th Regt) (1)
and 25th April,
Captain John Crymes (late 46th Regt) (2)

Recruiting commenced in about August 1855, *The Cambrian* on September 29th informing us, "In the hill coal and iron districts men are being enrolled for the Glamorgan Artillery as well as the Regulars." Progress was otherwise slow, and by December the Press outlining the sense of frustration, said, "Several months have now elapsed since we announced the various Staff Appointments of this Militia. Since then, several of the Officers have arrived in Swansea, whilst others, after incurring considerable expense and breaking up their establishments, have returned whence they came, seeing no prospect of their services being required. Some of the Officers however, are still engaged in recruiting, but owing to some crochet or other at H.Q., they find it a hopeless task. If we are rightfully informed, they no sooner meet a Recruit panting for the purple reputation at the Cannon's mouth, than they are obliged to relinquish him. We direct this business to the special attention of the Lord Lieutenant and the Hon. Member for Swansea, and if they find that authority procrastinates matters much longer, it is the duty of our representative on the first opportunity to direct the attention of the House of Commons to the subject."

*The Cambrian* repeated the complaint in March 1856 also stating "thanks however to some sapient official, the Men could not be embodied, and thus the whole Staff, in the time of formidable War, has been doomed to a state of inglorious ease — a state, no doubt which has been as repugnant to their own feelings as gallant Soldiers as it has been the subject of general remark in the County." In spite of such strong words it was to be over a year hence before any further move was made in relation to the Regiment.

On August 7th, 1857, the Lord Lieutenant, ignoring the fact that no Guns or defences were available for use by the Corps gave orders to embody the Royal Glamorgan Militia Artillery for training, and in consequence the Corps assembled in Swansea some two years and nine months after the announcement of its formation. No Ballot had been found necessary, as the Men were all Volunteers for Militia service. Their role as described in the *Army and Navy Gazette*, 3rd January, 1857, was to be strictly defence of the coast, and that may account for the fact that the Regiment did not volunteer for any Foreign Service Garrison duty in the years which followed. The training period extended over 28 days and was confined to foot drill and drill under arms. Excellent progress was made and the fine physique and smartness of the men created an excellent impression. In spite of being billeted in Public Houses around the town, their conduct was exemplary throughout, and several Recruits were obtained from the ranks for service with the regular Artillery.

The 1858 training period took place in September/October during which period the Corps was inspected by Colonel Crofton, RA. The smartness of the Men and the manner in which they performed their exercises resulted in an excellent report on their progress.

Annual Training in 1859 took place in August and was still confined to Foot and Carbine Drill. By that date the Regimental Band was formed and were making a name for themselves under the direction of Bandmaster Roberts. Towards the end of the year, the Permanent Staff were in great demand as Instructors for the various Corps of Volunteers then being formed in the County, such as George Grant Francis's Corps of Swansea Volunteer Artillery. This last named Corps was to receive Guns well ahead of the Artillery Militia, but that bitter pill was sweetened by the willingness of the Volunteers to share with them the prized pieces. The arrival of the pair of 18 Pdr Muzzle Loaders for use by the Volunteer Artillery caused great excitement in Swansea, and was the occasion for a grand parade through the town when the Guns were ceremoniously drawn through the streets to prepared positions on the Swansea Embankment where a Royal Salute was fired from them by the Permanent Staff of the Militia Artillery.

Annual Training for the Militia commenced on September 26th, when 120 Gunners — a figure well below the established strength, assembled twice daily in the Square outside the Assembly Rooms. The Regiment trained from 9 a.m. until noon, and from 2 p.m. to 4 p.m. daily, with the exception of Sundays, when headed by the Band they paraded for Church. The annual inspection was carried out by Lord William Powlett in a field at St Helens on the 14th October, the 3rd Glamorgan Rifle Volunteers keeping the ground for the occasion. Gunnery practice in 1860 was carried out on the 18 Pdrs previously mentioned, but by mid 1861, five 68 Pdr RMLs had been installed in the Mumbles Fort and were made use of thereafter during training to fire at floating targets moored off the Island. Annual Training such as has been described continued regularly every year except in 1896. Only the highlights or different locations for that annual event will be mentioned hereafter due to the repetitiveness of the training.

Established strength of the Regiment in 1863 was 325, but the Enrolled Strength amounted to only 189. In 1868, the Regiment consisted of:-

1 Lt Colonel
3 Captains
2 Lieutenants
1 Surgeon
2 Staff Sergeants
12 Sergeants
9 Corporals
3 Trumpeters
151 Gunners

Wanting to complete were 1 Lieutenant and 127 Gunners. In 1869 a Trumpet Major is shown and a Sergeant Major (presumably the two Permanent Staff listed). Two Lieutenants were wanting, but the number of Gunners had increased to 156.

Amongst the Officers at that date were, Captain J. Ballard of 'The Verlands', Cowbridge, Captain Thomas Parry Horsman of Cwm Mawr House, Llanelly, and Lieutenant H. Ford Davies of Abercery, Newcastle Emlyn.

In 1877 the establishment was increased to 414, and the numbers enrolled were returned as 380. From that year up to 1894, the establishment remained unchanged whilst the average numbers enrolled during the period were about 350.

By 1881, Headquarters of the Regiment were located at the Swansea Arsenal where Drill Purpose Guns were installed for training. There on the 17th June during an inspection of Recruits, Colonel Purcell, RA., Inspector of Reserve Forces, watched 80 Non Commissioned Officers and Men exercising Gun and Repository Drill, which drew compliments on their speed and efficiency. On Monday, 20th July, the main body of the Corps assembled for annual training and were inspected by Colonel Purcell on the St Helen's Cricket Ground on July 15th. Present were 320 from an enrolled strength of 350.

The daily routine during training was fairly standard and occupied five hours of each day. The greater part of that time was devoted to Gunnery Theory, Gun and Repository Drills, Instruction in Handling and the care of Charges and Ammunition as also Foot and Carbine instruction. Each battery received an allowance of 90 Cartridges and 45 Projectiles for live firing practice.

General Order No. 72/1882 reorganised the structure of the Royal Artillery. It created amongst other things eleven territorially connected Divisions of Garrison Artillery, ten of which included Regiments of affiliated Militia Artillery. Included in The Welsh Division were four such Regiments, who as a result were required to discontinue the old Militia titles in favour of a more impersonal Brigade designation. Thus the Royal Glamorgan Artillery Militia became known as the 2nd Brigade of the Welsh Division. Locally however such changes were ignored and the regiment was still known as the Glamorgan or Swansea Artillery. The change allowed the Brigade the following Permanent Staff:-

1 Adjutant, 1 Regimental Sergeant Major, 4 Battery Sergeant Majors, 4 Battery Sergeants, 1 Orderly Room Sergeant, 1 Paymaster Sergeant, 1 Sergeant Trumpeter, 1 Sergeant Instructor of Gunnery and 4 Trumpeters. The Staff when not about their Regimental and Recruiting duties were very much an accepted part of the local scene, appearing at Church Parades and any local function involving Volunteer activities. When recruiting they drew in men not only for the Militia, but also for the Regular Artillery, and in pursuance of that task were much in evidence at Fairs, Market days and around Public Houses. Always generous to a likely recruit, they were masters of their trade, and more than ready to pass the Queen's Shilling over to the unwary.

In 1883 the Brigade was inspected by Colonel Cumming, Inspector of The Welsh Division, RA. He expressed great satisfaction with their keeness and progress and was particularly pleased with the accuracy and speed with which they could dismount and mount the heavy Artillery pieces. Apart from live firing practice which took place at the Mumbles Fort, training was concentrated on the Arsenal. That place had a disadvantage in as much that it had no Barrack accommodation which would have done much to improve regimental discipline. In that year as in 1857, the men were still billeted on the Inns and Lodging Houses of Swansea. 346 Militiamen attended annual training in 1884 and were trained and lodged in the locations heretofore described. In 1885, having assembled in April, the Brigade, breaking with past custom proceeded by rail to Devonport and were trained for the usual period in more realistic conditions, namely the Forts defending the approaches to Plymouth and Plymouth Sound. The break from past custom proved popular and gave the majority of the men their first experience of seeing another part of the country outside their native South Wales.

In 1886 the annual training was concentrated upon Swansea, and again in 1887, but with a difference. Due to difficulty in finding accommodation for 400 men in the town over several weeks, the Brigade was placed under canvas at Parc Wern — a move which proved to be a great success. More control was exercised, particularly in off duty hours, discipline was greatly improved and the men were involved in numerous sporting activities. The Camp became a great attraction with the public visiting in large numbers to see the Militiamen under training and at play. Very popular were the Regimental Band Concerts, and the weekly outdoor Church Parade became a magnet when both Regiment and visitors made of it a singing festival, better known in Wales as a 'Gymanfa Ganu'. June 1888 saw the Brigade train for the first time in Pembrokeshire in one of the Haven Forts already described. As at Plymouth, South Hook Fort allowed for training in more realistic defended port conditions, and in the years which followed the Regiment were to become well known annual visitors to that district. The enrolled strength not including the Permanent Staff, was 365.

By Army Order 367/1889, the eleven territorial Divisions of the Royal Artillery were reorganised to form three large Divisions. The change placed the four Welsh Regiments of Militia Artillery into the 3rd or Western Division, RA. Brigade designations were discarded and the Regiment became known as the Glamorgan Royal Garrison Artillery Militia. Training in 1889 and 1890 was concentrated upon Swansea and the four Batteries were commanded respectively by Major Mansfield, Major Morris, Captain Robertson and Captain Stoughton. The 1890 Inspection was carried out by Colonel Tyler, Officer Commanding Auxiliary Artillery, prior to their dismissal from training on July 12th. In 1891 Recruits commenced 56 days training on April 13th and were joined by the main body on 15th June. The Regiment then entrained for Pembrokeshire where it trained at Fort Hubberstone, Milford Haven. Prior to dismissal on July 12th the Regiment was inspected at Swansea. Visits to the Pembrokeshire Forts were now a regular annual event, such as in 1895, when during training at South Hook Fort, the Glamorgan Gunners took part in a large scale defence exercise involving 4,000 troops of all arms. A Smallpox epidemic caused the 1896 training to be cancelled, but additional days were allowed during the following year to make up the lost time. The year 1897 produced the only unfavourable comment found concerning the conduct of the Corps. *The Cambrian,* reporting its departure from Swansea for the Haven Forts states — "It is no exaggeration to say that not one quarter of the men who passed through the principal streets to the Station were sober." The report was vehemently denied by the Officers, but it is likely that there was some truth in the allegation, and that they in part could be blamed. The custom of paying training Bounty to the men on reporting for training was unwise to say the least. It had long been found more sensible to pay it to them at the end of training whilst at the same time ensuring that they were clear of the training centre before being given the opportunity to spend it.

The outbreak of War in South Africa in 1899 resulted in the Regiment being embodied for wartime garrison duty for the first and only time in its comparatively short history. It was first intended that the Regiment garrison the Lavernock Fort of the Severn Defences, but after taking into account the obsolescent nature of its armament Pembroke Dock and the Haven Forts were instead selected. The embodiment extended from May 1st to October 2nd, 1900.

During the next six years several Commissions enquired into the state and organisation of the Land Forces of the Crown and the changes recommended together with plans of his own were set in motion by War Secretary Haldane who took office under the Liberal Government of 1905. The sweeping changes which became Law under the Territorial and Reserve Forces Act of 1907 reduced the three echelons of the Army to two. From Regular troops available in the United Kingdom was created an Expeditionary or Field Force (which on paper at least) was ready in all respects for mobilisation on the outbreak of War. The Volunteer Force (i.e. such of them as were willing to transfer) were to form a second line at home to be known as the Territorial Force, which serving under more stringent terms and with up to date weapons, would in addition to Home Defence and Home Garrison commitments provide Volunteers to expand/reinforce the Expeditionary Force abroad.

The Militia as such was no longer required, but such Regiments of that Force as were selected to survive (mainly Infantry) would become Special Reserve Battalions to the Regular Army Regiments to which in 1881 they had been linked as Militia Battalions.

The changes which took place on April 1st, 1908, had no immediate effect upon the Regiment, and on the 4th July, 1908, it assembled at High Cross Camp, near Newport, Monmouthshire, for training.

There 10 Officers and 230 Other Ranks underwent a period of training different to that which had previously been customary. The accent was on the Field Artillery role and designed by the Regular Staff to prepare those of them who were willing to transfer into the new Army Special Reserve.

On the 27th July, the Regiment became part of the Army Reserve, Royal Garrison Artillery, into which 10 Officers and 188 Other Ranks had agreed to transfer. In September its role was changed from that of Coast Artillery to Royal Field Artillery under the title Glamorgan Royal Field Artillery, Special Reserve. The new role was to be shortlived, as in 1909 came the order for its disbandment. In that year Glamorgan's Militia Artillery disappeared from the Army List, but had given to its Country and County 51 years of loyal and unbroken service.

*Footnotes*

1. West Kent Regiment
2. South Devonshire Regiment

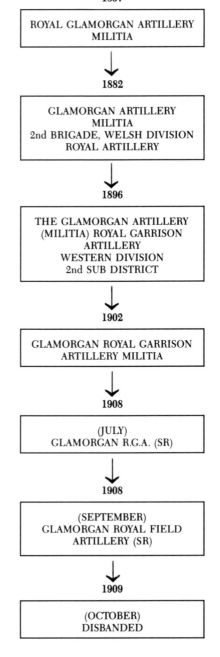

**1857**

ROYAL GLAMORGAN ARTILLERY
MILITIA

↓

**1882**

GLAMORGAN ARTILLERY
MILITIA
2nd BRIGADE, WELSH DIVISION
ROYAL ARTILLERY

↓

**1896**

THE GLAMORGAN ARTILLERY
(MILITIA) ROYAL GARRISON
ARTILLERY
WESTERN DIVISION
2nd SUB DISTRICT

↓

**1902**

GLAMORGAN ROYAL GARRISON
ARTILLERY MILITIA

↓

**1908**

(JULY)
GLAMORGAN R.G.A. (SR)

↓

**1908**

(SEPTEMBER)
GLAMORGAN ROYAL FIELD
ARTILLERY (SR)

↓

**1909**

(OCTOBER)
DISBANDED

*GUNNER. GLAMORGAN ARTILLERY MILITIA. c.1875*
*Courtesy of N. Litchfield*

Glamorgan Artillery Militia and Glamorgan Artillery Volunteers
at Firing Practice, Mumbles Fort, Swansea. c.1880
*Courtesy. The Swansea Museum*

Mr Brian Price of Killay, Swansea,
with the 80 Pdr RML Gun recovered from the sea off Mumbles Fort
*Courtesy of Mr B. Price*

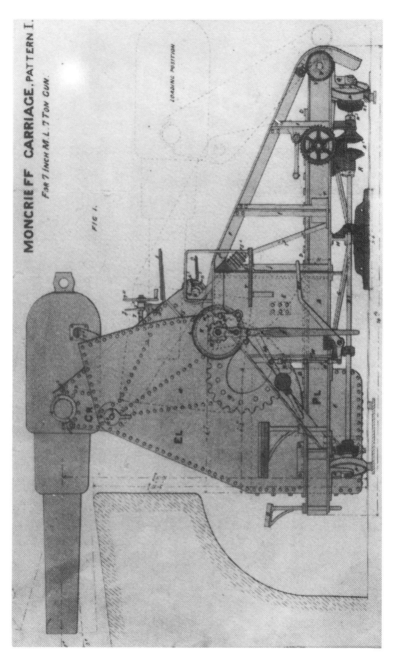

A Seven Ton 7″ RML Gun on a Montcrieff Disappearing Carriage

*Courtesy of The Welch Regt. Museum*

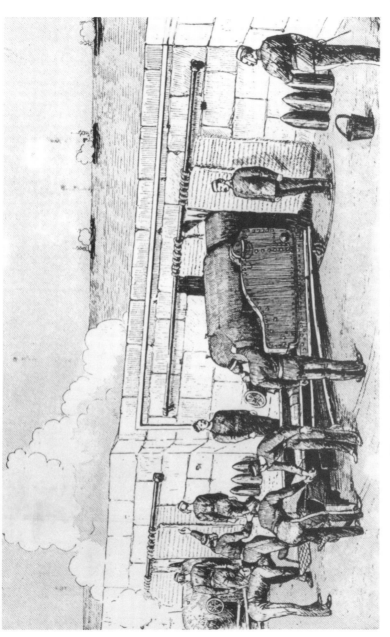

Garrison Artillery at 10" Gun Practice c.1897
*Courtesy. The Welch Regt. Museum*

A Heavy Coast Artillery RML Gun on a travelling Carriage. c.1885
*Courtesy of Major A. Harfield*

Artist's Impression of a night attack during manoevres on a Coastal Fort

*Courtesy of Major A. Harfield*

# APPENDIX 1

# GLAMORGAN MILITIA COLOURS

## COLOURS
As an Infantry Regiment the Glamorgan Militia carried Colours, a Stand being issued to the Regiment on its formation in 1760.

### 1760-1778
*The First or King's Colour*
This consisted of the Great Union Flag which at that time did not carry the Cross of St Patrick.

*The Second, or Regimental Colour*
No description of this Colour has been found, but as the Second Colour usually matched the Regimental Facings, one presumes that it was blue, and carried as motif the Arms of Other Lewis Windsor the Lord Lieutenant.

Both Colours by dimension were 6'2" on the Pole and 6'6" flying. The length of the Pole from butt to spear head was 9'10". From the Pole head of both Colours hung cords and tassels of crimson and gold silk.

### 1778-c.1804
When the regiment assembled in 1778 the Lord Lieutenant was then Lord John Mounstuart. Once again in the absence of any written record or visible proof, one can only assume that his Coat of Arms replaced those of Other Lewis Windsor on the Second Colour. In December 1768 a new regulation reduced the length of the Colours on the Pole to 6'. Presumably the 1778 Colours conformed with that requirement, hence the new Stand would consist of

*A First or King's Colour*
The Great Union as before Six feet Square.

*The Second, or Regimental Colour*
The Arms of Lord John Mountstuart on a Blue Ground, six feet square.

### c.1804-1854/1855
c.1804 a new Stand of Colours was presented to the Regiment and superceded presumably the Stand previously described.

## The First, or King's Colour

A Great Union as in previous years, but on this occasion of updated pattern. The Act of Union with Ireland which had been authorised by an Order in Council, 5th November, 1800, and which took effect January 1st, 1801, required that the Cross of St. Patrick be incorporated in the Flag. The new First Colour included that change. Another difference was the inclusion of the Cipher 'GR' in gold lettering at the centre of the Colour.

No fragment of this Colour has survived through to the present day.

## The Second, or Regimental Colour

This Colour was also of new design as approved by the Inspector of Colours Of Garter Blue Silk. It incorporated in the upper canton nearest to the Pole a small Union. Replacing the Arms of the Lord Lieutenant at the centre and painted onto the silk was a design consisting of a gold edged circle with the title 'ROYAL GLAMORGAN MILITIA' within, in gold letters on a red ground. Inside the circle, the Plumes, Coronet and Motto of the Prince of Wales worked in White, Royal Blue and Gold, the whole so far described enclosed within a Union Wreath of Roses, Thistles and Shamrocks and ensigned with a Crown.

Fortunately, the remnants of this last survived to be restored, framed and displayed in the Welch Regiment Museum, probably due to the fact that when the Stand was replaced c.1854- 55, that both the retiring Colours were retained by the Officers Mess of the Regiment or by the Colonel.

## 1854/55-1870

At a date unrecorded in 1854 or 1855 new Colours of similar dimensions were issued.

## The First or Queen's Colour

The Union Flag having superimposed at its centre along the lines of the Cross of St George, a long scroll of yellow silk ensigned with the Victorian Crown and carrying in black lettering the title 'Royal Glamorgan Militia'.

## The Second, or Regimental Colour

Royal Blue Silk with a small Union in the upper canton nearest the Pole. At the centre, a device similar to that carried on the previous Colour, silk embroidered, and consisting of a gold edged circle carrying the title 'ROYAL GLAMORGAN MILITIA' on a red ground. Inside the circle, the Plumes, Coronet and Motto of the Prince of Wales, the whole within a Union Wreath of Roses, Shamrocks and Thistles and ensigned with the Victorian Crown.

In 1870, this Stand was replaced with new Colours which complied with the current regulations. The old Stand was in due course to pass into the hands of Colonel A. Thrale Perkins and for years lay at his home in Wookey, Somerset.

Following the death of his daughter in law who had inherited the Stand, they were put up for sale and were purchased by a Bristol Antiques Dealer and thence into the hands of Mr J.W. Garland, a private collector. Due to the efforts of Mr T.W. Webster, an ex member of The Welch Regiment, and the generosity of Mr Garland, the Colours were returned to the Regimental Museum, where today, those sections which could be preserved, were restored, framed and put on display to the public.

### 1870-1889

As already stated, in 1870 a new Stand of Colours was issued to the regiment, and presented by Miss Talbot of Margam Abbey at a ceremony held on the Cardiff Arms Field. The Colours, which conformed to the then current regulations were smaller; the dimensions being 4' on the Pole and 4'6" flying. The Colours had additionally silk and gold fringes, and a gilt Lion and Crown on the Pole in place of the old spearhead finial.

In 1889 the Stand was replaced with new Colours representative of the Corps as the 3rd Bn, The Welsh Regiment. The 1870 Stand was then presented to the Marchioness of Bute to be laid up in Cardiff Castle, they being the last to carry the old Glamorgan Militia designation. Sadly, the Stand has not survived, and hence no description of them can be given. One assumes however that the design on both, although of smaller dimensions, was similar in most respects to that carried on the Stand which they had replaced.

### 1889-1908

The Stand issued in 1889 conformed with the revised regulations of 1881. Both Colours were of silk and of dimensions 3" deep on the Pole and 3'9" flying. Each had a fringe about 2" in depth. The Pole including the Royal Crest was 8'7½" long from which hung Cords and Tassles of crimson and gold mixed.

### The Queen's or First Colour

The Great Union having at the centre a circle with the Regimental title on a crimson ground. Inside the circle the Battalion Number in Roman numerals. The whole surmounted by the Imperial Crown.

### The Second or Regimental Colour

This was similar to the Regimental Colour of the two Regular Battalions, namely white silk bearing the Red Cross of St George with the territorial designation and regimental device at the centre surmounted by the Imperial Crown. In the dexter canton the Battalion number in Roman numeral script. A Battle Honour Scroll for South Africa 1900-01 was later added.

What remains of the Stand are now laid up in Llandaff Cathedral, Cardiff.

# APPENDIX 2

# THE GLAMORGAN MILITIA
# BRIEF NOTES ON UNIFORM DRESS, 1760-1908

The Uniform Dress worn by the Regiments of Militia was similar in most respects to that worn by the Line Infantry of each period in their history and matched the designated role, eg, Light Infantry and Rifles. The dress was in consequence subject to similar rules and dress regulations, and changed from time to time in order to keep pace with the Regular Army. Such records as exist suggest that the Officers of Militia kept very much up to date with the changes due to the fact that like their regular contemporaries, they were responsible for purchasing their own outfits. The Permanent Staff also seem to have kept very much in line with the changes, but the situation for Other Ranks was much different. At times, they lagged very much behind, and were in early times often required to wear out ex regular cast offs. Much depended however on the interest, and particularly the influence of individual Commanding Officers, and this appears to have been very much the case in the Glamorgan Regiment of Militia.

In the absence of Colours, the Regiments were identified by their distinct Facings, Lace and Insignia, but only at close quarters. At a distance, one red coat or green clad Rifleman looked much the same as another.

An example of a regiment at its best in regard to up to date dress would be the Glamorgan Regiment, c.1856. At worst, possibly the Carmarthenshire Regiment in 1831, when the Private Men of the Corps were clothed in outdated fatique and undress bits and pieces, due to the fact that the Quartermaster had not one complete set of up to date uniform dress to issue to them. Such had been the run down of Militia organisation since 1825, that it is unlikely that the Carmarthenshires were the one and only exception.

The Glamorganshire Militia, c.1761, very likely wore a Red Coat with blue facings. This was certainly the case in 1780, and is confirmed by the sketches of Lt Colonel John Osborne of the Bedfordshire Milita who describes the dress of the Glamorgan Corps as follows:-
Blue Facings, Bastion Loops, edged lapels, etc. It is therefore somewhat confusing to find that C.C.P. Lawson, who quotes the Militia List 1778 and Inspection Returns, contradicts Osborne's eyewitness account in part by stating that the Facings in 1779 were Black.

"Glamorganshire. 1779. Black velvet Facings. White Waistcoats and Breeches, Half Gaiters, silver embroidery."[1]

In view of the fact that facings at a later date were of a dark blue cloth, almost Navy Blue, I am inclined to support Osborne's description. This opinion draws some support from a description for 1781, given on the same page of Lawson's earlier statement which tells us that the Glamorgan Militia, c.1781, wore "Blue Facings, Gold embroidered Epaulettes and Plain Hats."

In his sketches of Militia Head-dress executed at Warley Camp, c.1778, De Loutherbourg includes a most interesting Head- dress. Worn by the Light Company of the regiment it is described as black leather with peak and white edged false front. It had a red worsted crest and a black plume mounted on the side, and on the false front a white metal badge, viz: The Plumes, Coronet and Motto of the Prince of Wales.

(see illustration).

On the 23rd April 1804, the Glamorgan Militia having received permission to bear the appellations of a Royal Regiment were entitled to wear Royal Blue Facings. It is difficult to state categorically that such shade was immediately adopted, as the visible evidence of an Officers Coat, c.1822, shows dark blue facings (almost black).

The Shako Plate worn by Other Ranks c.1812, was of the Universal Pattern. The officers, however, may well have worn something more distinctive.

On the 26th March, 1812, the Regiment was authorised to be clothed, equipped and exercised as a Corps of Light Infantry. The change does not appear to have resulted in any great alteration to the Uniform worn, except for the use by the whole of Green Feather Plumes or Tufts on their Shakos.

A Regimental Order of November 1812 shows that the Officers of the Corps were well up with the military fashion of the day.

"Blue Pantaloons will be worn on the Morning and Evening Parade from 10th October to the 10th March. White Pantaloons in the morning and Blue Pantaloons in the evening from 10th March to the 10th October."

"White Breeches and Long Gaiters, the Breeches to have Regimental Buttons at the knees, and the Gaiters a flat yellow button."

For Officers, the Regimental Button thus described would be gilt and carrying the motif of the Plumes, Coronet and Motto of the Prince of Wales and the inscription 'Royal Glamorgan'.

The Orders further state — "Officers will wear Grey Overalls whenever the Men are ordered to appear in theirs, and they will be in strict conformity to the pattern given by Lt. Colonel Morgan to the Master Tailor of the Regiment. At Balls and Drawing Rooms, Officers will appear in White Pantaloons and half Boots, with Jacket having the Lapels buttoned back, and the Sash worn over the Dress Waistcoat."

The Jacket referred to would be the long tailed Regimental Coat which with the Lapels buttoned back would allow the Waistcoat and Sash to be worn and displayed in the manner ordered.

By 1812, Overalls of a Grey or Blue Grey material had in Line Regiments almost replaced the White Breeches and knee Length Gaiters as the main netherwear. Not so in the Royal Glamorgan, for the Order Book shows that although in possession of Overalls, the Men more often than not still paraded in the White Breeches with Gaiters.

Hamilton Smith's Militia Charts of 1815 gives the following information on Royal Glamorgan Uniform:-
Red, with Blue Facings, White Breeches, Officers jackets laced in Gold, those of Other Ranks, Blue.

A Warrant of 1830, issued shortly after the Accession of William IV brought about many changes to the Uniform Dress of the Army. It ordered amongst other things that Gold Lace was to be reserved for the Regulars. The Militia, henceforth, was to wear Silver Lace. The wearing of the Gorget, that last vestige (in metal at least) of ancient armour, was also abolished. That change is confirmed in the Orders of the then disembodied Glamorgan Regiment — "Officers of such regiments as were 'Royal' would wear by distinction silver embroidery instead of Lace."

Early in 1855 great changes were authorised in Infantry Uniform. The Royal Glamorgan was on this occasion quick to adopt the new pattern double breasted Tunic, the first two Companies appearing in same in early March. Whether the regiment was as rapid in adopting the new pattern shako and the new single breasted tunic, which last was introduced in 1856, has gone unrecorded.

For Infantry Militia, the Dress Regulations of 1874 state that the Uniform and Horse furniture was to be similar to that of the Infantry of the Line, but with the following exceptions:- "Silver is substituted for gold in the Lace, Braid, Buttons, Plates and Sashes; and gold for silver in the Badges of the Rank. Regiments of Light Infantry were to conform with the style of dress prescribed for such Corps in the regulations. In 1881, the Royal Glamorgan on being redesignated as the 3rd (Militia) Battalion The Welsh Regiment, adopted in 1882, the Scarlet and White Facings of the Territorial Line Regiment. Progressively also, the silver lace and other similar distinctions gave way to gold, the Militia Officers being distinguished by the letter 'M' embroidered below the badges of rank on the Shoulder Cords and Shoulder Straps. Officers were soon to be seen in the new Home Service Blue Cloth Helmet, but the Other Ranks having discarded the last Shako, wore instead a blue Field Service Cap. Not until 1897 did they receive an issue of the Other Ranks pattern of the Home Service Helmet.

In South Africa, 1900-1901, the 3rd Welsh wore the drab khaki campaign dress with khaki cloth covered sun helmet standard to most of the British Regiments involved in the war.

At home in 1902 and 1903 the Bush Hat was worn during annual training, but was later discarded in favour of the blue Field Service cap.

In 1902 a universal khaki serge uniform was adopted by the Army as standard for most forms of dress, and thereafter the old scarlet full dress was reserved for ceremonial occasions.

A photograph taken c.1906 shows 3rd Battalion recruits under training at Maindy Barracks in the new khaki serge and wearing the rather ugly but shortlived Broderick Cap which by 1908 had been replaced by the peaked khaki Forage Cap.

By that date the Other Ranks of the Militia were apart from the absence of a distinguishing cloth shoulder title, dressed similar to their comrades in the Regular Battalions of the Welsh Regiment.

*Footnote*
1. Lawson. C.C.P. *A History of the British Army Vol. III.* Norman Military Publications Ltd. 1961.

# APPENDIX 3

# GLAMORGAN MILITIA BADGES, BUTTONS AND OTHER APPOINTMENTS

*Plate. Cap. Light Company, c.1778*
The Plumes, Coronet and Motto of the Prince of Wales in Silver Plate or White Metal. This Badge is shown in a sketch made by De Loutherbourg when sketching at Warley Camp in 1778[1]

*Plate. Shoulder Belt. Officers pattern, c.1807*
This Plate is described in an Article by Parkyn on the Welsh Militia.[2] A gilt oblong Plate with cut corners having superimposed on its face the Plumes, Coronet and Motto of the Prince of Wales within a Garter Belt inscribed 'ROYAL GLAMORGAN MILITIA'. The Plumes and Garter in silver, the Coronet and Motto Scrolls gilded. The whole on a blue enamelled ground. There exists evidence to suggest that an earlier oval silver plate carried similar devices, but that the Garter Belt on that pattern was gilded.

*Plate. Cap. Belgic Shako, c.1815*
The Universal Shako Plate for the pattern Shako, consisting of a crowned and gilded Plate having as motif a Garter Belt with Motto 'HONI SOIT QUI MAL Y PENSE' enclosing the Cipher 'GR'. A Shako and Plate as worn by the Regiment is preserved in The Welch Regiment Museum.

*Plate. Shako. Officers pattern, c.1830*
This Plate is described by Parkyn in his Article on the Welsh Militia[3] A gilded crowned Star having at its centre a circle inscribed 'ROYAL GLAMORGAN LT. INFY'. Inside the circle on a burnished ground, the Cipher 'VR'. Pendant below the circle, a Light Infantry Bugle Horn without strings.

*Plate. Shako. Officers Pattern, 1844-1855*  (illustrated)
A Gilded Star of eight points, rayed, and surmounted by the Victorian Crown. Superimposed on its centre a silver Bugle Horn of the Light Infantry pattern with the Plumes, Coronet and Motto of the Prince of Wales inset within the strings. Below the motif, a silver scroll inscribed 'ROYAL GLAMORGAN'.
  It is highly likely that this pattern Plate continued in use on the Second Albert Pattern Shako after 1854.

*Note*

Although no Shoulder Belt Plate of the type worn by Officers of the Regiment during the same period has been sighted, a comparison with the 'Royal Monmouth' who wore a similar design of Shako Plate suggests that the Royal Glamorgan Officers wore an Oblong Gilt Shoulder Belt Plate carrying a design on its face similar to that carried on the Shako Plate.

*Badge. Cap. Other Ranks Pattern, c.1855*            *(illustrated)*

A Stringed Light Infantry Pattern Bugle Horn over a semi circular Scroll inscribed 'ROYAL GLAMORGAN'. A two piece Badge in White Metal.

This Badge was worn over several years on the Other Ranks Undress Foraging (or Pork Pie) Cap.

*Clasp. Waist Belt. Officers Pattern, 1855-1878*       *(illustrated)*

A decorative Locket type Waist Belt Clasp in Silver.

The Circle or Female section is inscribed 'ROYAL GLAMORGAN LIGHT INFY' and the Male section or Lock Plate carries the design of the Plumes, Coronet and Motto of the Prince of Wales below a Victorian Crown. Another variation of this Clasp worn from about 1870 onwards displays the Crown and Coronet in Gilded Metal.

*(The Welsh Regiment Museum)*

*Clasp. Belt. Other Ranks Pattern, c.1870*          *(illustrated)*

A Brass Locket Pattern Clasp.

The Female Section or Circle carries the raised inscription 'ROYAL GLAMORGAN LIGHT INFY'. The Male Section or Lock Plate, the Plumes, Coronet and Motto of the Prince of Wales.

*(The Welch Regiment Museum)*

*Plate. Shako. Officers Pattern, 1861-63*          *(illustrated)*

An eight pointed star surmounted by the Victorian Crown. At the centre a raised circle containing the fretted inscription 'ROYAL GLAMORGAN LIGHT INFY'. Inside the Circle the Cipher 'VR' on a burnished ground. The whole in silver Plate.

*(The Welch Regiment Museum)*

*Plate. Shako. Officers Pattern, 1864-69*          *(illustrated)*

A design similar in all respects to the 1863 Pattern, but with a Light Infantry Pattern Bugle Horn without Strings pendant below the Circle. The whole in Silver Plate.

*(The Welch Regiment Museum)*

*Plate. Shako. Officers Pattern, 1869-1878*
A design similar to the 1864 Pattern. The whole Gilded.
One presumes that this Plate was worn at this late stage on the last pattern
Shako, but by being a gilded finish it contravenes the Dress Regulations of
the day which stipulate that Militia were required to wear Silver, White Metal
or Blackened Ornaments.

*(Lewis Collection)*

*Badge. Cap. Officers Undress Forage, c.1875*
The Plumes, Coronet and Motto of the Prince of Wales over a Stringed Light
Infantry Pattern Bugle Horn. A two part Badge in Silver Bullion on a Black
cloth ground.

*(Photographic Evidence)*

*Badge. Cap. Other Ranks Pattern, c.1877*                      *(illustrated)*
The Plumes Coronet and Motto of the Prince of Wales. Pendant below, a
stringed and tasseled Bugle Horn of the Light Infantry Pattern. The whole
in White Metal.

*(The Welch Regiment Museum)*

*Plate. Helmet. Officers Pattern for home service blue cloth helmet, c.1878*
*(illustrated)*
A Crowned Star having at the centre the superimposed design of a Circle
set within an open ended wreath of Laurels, and the circle containing the
cut inscription 'ROYAL GLAMORGAN LIGHT INFY'. Inside the Circle on
a burnished ground the Cipher 'VR'. The whole in silver Plate.
    The fittings on the Helmet on which this is displayed are silver plated.

*(The Welch Regiment Museum)*

*Plate. Helmet. Officers Pattern for home service blue cloth helmet, c.1880*
*(illustrated)*
A Crowned Star Plate similar to the 1878 Pattern but with a Stringed Light
Infantry Pattern Bugle Horn pendant below the circle and superimposed on
the lower point of the Star. The inscription 'ROYAL GLAMORGAN LIGHT
INFY' and the Stringed Bugle Horn in Silver Plate, the remainder Gilded.

*(Park St. Collection)*

*Badge. Officers Pattern for Undress Forage Cap, c.1882*
The Plumes Coronet and Motto of The Prince of Wales in Silver, Gold and
Royal Blue embroidery on a black cloth ground.

*(Photographic Evidence)*

*Badge. Officers and Other Ranks Patt. Glengarry Cap, c.1885*
A two part Badge consisting of the Helmet Plate Centre of The Welsh Regiment as worn on the Other Ranks Home Service Blue Cloth Helmet, with the Victorian Crown above. The Officers Pattern Gilded, the Other Ranks Pattern in Brass.

The Badge was secured on the inside of the Cap by a special cut out plate of Brass and fixing pins.

*(Photographic Evidence)*

*Badge. Officers Pattern for Glengarry Cap, c.1896*
The Plumes, Coronet and Motto of the Prince of Wales approx 53 mm high. Pin fixed or Loops. The whole in Silver Plate.

*(Photographic Evidence)*

*Badge. Cap. Field Service, c.1898*
The authorised Cap Badge of The Welsh Regiment, i.e., The Plumes, Coronet and Motto of the Prince of Wales over the Scroll inscribed 'THE WELSH'.

The Badge was worn by all ranks from c.1898 onwards on a variety of Head-dress ranging from the Blue Field Service (Side Cap), the Bush Hat and Khaki Service Dress Forage Cap.

There is evidence to show that prior to 1902 it was worn by Officers in Silver Plate or Silver Plated Metal, and by Other Ranks in White Metal. During the South African War the Bi-Metal Pattern as worn by the Regular Battalions appears to have ousted the silver and White Metal variety.

*Plate. Helmet. Officers and Other Ranks for Home Service Blue Cloth Pattern Helmet, 1881-1908*
The authorised Helmet Plate of The Welsh Regiment as worn by Officers and Other Ranks of the Regular Battalions were brought into use by the Battalion.

*Button. Officers Coatee, c.1816*
A Gilt, Convex, Open backed Button stamped with the following design. A Circle inscribed 'ROYAL GLAMORGAN MILITIA'. Inside the Circle, the Plumes, Coronet and Motto of the Prince of Wales.

This style of Button was still in use c.1830 and through to 1854. One presumes that the Other Ranks wore a similar Button made of Pewter or White Metal carrying a similar design during the same period.

*Button. Tunic. All Ranks, 1855-1881*                              *(illustrated)*
A slightly convex, closed back Button, die-stamped and carrying a similar design to that used on the Coatee Button.

The Officers Buttons in Silver, or Silver Plated Metal. Other Ranks Buttons in White Metal.

*Button Tunic. Officers. 1881 onwards*
The authorised Regimental pattern Button of The Welsh Regiment was brought into use. At first they were worn in Silver Plate or Silver Plated Metal, but by the late 1890s the Gilded Regular Pattern replaced them.

*Button. Tunic. Other Ranks. 1881 onwards*
For a period the White Metal General Service Pattern was used, but by the late 1890s these were being replaced by the Brass G.S. Pattern.

# REGIMENTAL MEDAL

D. Hastings Irwin in his 'War Medals and Decorations, 1588-1898' (L. Upcott Gill, 1899), describes a Regimental Medal — Award for Merit.

Obverse: A Crown and Bugle Horn with legend 'Royal Glamorgan Militia'
Reverse: Presented by the Marquis of Bute — Reward for Merit, 1827.
The silver Medal one and five eighth inches diameter was c.1898 held in the Day Collection.

*Footnotes*
1. Lawson. C.C.P. — A History of the Uniform of The British Army Vol.III. p.156
2. Article — Welsh Militia 1757-1881 — Journal Society for Army Historical Research. Vol.XXXII, No.130. 1954
3. Article — Welsh Militia 1757-1881 — Journal Society for Army Historical Research. Vol.XXXII, No.130. 1954.

*Centrepiece of the Regimental Colour of The Royal Glamorgan Light
Infantry carried during the Long Embodiment 1803-16
The design is painted onto the Silk.
Preserved in The Welch Regiment Museum, Cardiff Castle.*

*Centrepiece of the Regimental Colour carried c.1857*
*at present preserved in The Welch Regiment Museum*
*Courtesy of The Welch Regiment Museum*

*Centrepiece of the Queen's Colour carried by the Regiment c.1857*
*Courtesy of The Welch Regiment Museum*

*A Light Company Man's Cap*
*Glamorgan Regiment of Militia c.1780*

*Belgic Pattern Shako with Universal Plate of the type worn by the Glamorgan Regiment of Militia, c.1810.*
*Courtesy of The Welsh Folk Museum (N.M.W.)*

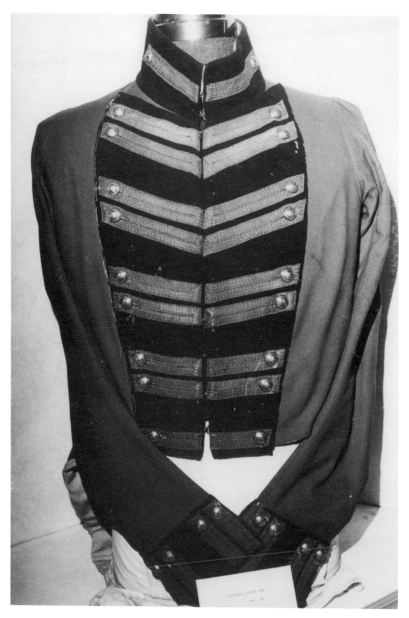

*Officers Regimental Coat of the Light Company, Royal Glamorgan
Light Infantry Militia, c.1822
(The Welch Regiment Museum)*

*Officers Regimental Coat. Royal Glamorgan Light Infantry Militia,*
*c.1822*
*This rear view shows clearly the Light Company Bugle Horns on the*
*Turnbacks of the coat.*
*(The Welch Regiment Museum)*

*Shako. Officers Pattern, c.1868*
*— Royal Glamorgan Light Infantry*
*with Silver Plated Regimental Shako Plate*
*(The Welch Regiment Museum)*

*2/Lt. Charles Morton Hastings — 3rd Battalion — c.1884*
*Of interest here is the large silver Plumes, Coronet and Motto of the*
*Prince of Wales which was worn by Officers as the*
*Glengarry Cap Badge.*
*Courtesy of The Welch Regiment Museum*

*Lieutenant Edward P. Dashwood — 3rd Battalion c.1885*
*A small silver badge consisting of the Plumes, Coronet and Motto of the*
*Prince of Wales is worn in the Field Service Cap.*
*Courtesy of The Welch Regiment Museum*

*Major Phillip Dowson in the Undress Uniform of the 3rd Welsh, c.1896*
*Courtesy of The Welch Regiment Museum*

*Shako Plate*
*Officers Pattern*
*Royal Glamorgan Light Infantry*
*1844-1855*

*Clasp. Waist Belt. Officers Pattern*
*Royal Glamorgan Light Infantry Militia*
*1855-1881*

*Shako Plate. Officers Pattern. Royal Glamorgan Light Infantry,*
*1861-1863*

*Shako Plate. Officers Pattern. Royal Glamorgan Light Infantry.*
*1864-1878*

*Clasp. Waist Belt. Other Ranks Pattern.*
*Royal Glamorgan Light Infantry c.1870*

*c.1856*            *c.1878*

*Cap Badge. Other Ranks. Pattern. Royal Glamorgan Light Infantry.*

*Helmet Plate. Officers Pattern.*
*Royal Glamorgan Light Infantry. c.1880*

*Officers Home Service Blue Cloth Helmet 1878 Pattern Royal*
*Glamorgan Light Infantry Militia*
*The Helmet depicted was worn by Lt. Colonel Lawrence Heyworth.*
*Of dark blue cloth set on a cork body, it has silver plated fittings, silver*
*Chin Chain and a Silver Plated Helmet Plate.*
*(The Welch Regiment Museum)*

*Buttons — Officers Pattern — 1855/1881*
*Convex, Silver, Closed back*
*Buttons worn by Other Ranks were similar but made of White Metal.*

# APPENDIX 4

Roll of Officers. Glamorgan Militia, 1780-1908
Miscellaneous Militia Lists
Regimental Rolls
Appointments of Officers. South Africa, 1900-01
Honours and Awards. South Africa. 1900-02
Roll of Honour

## ROLL OF OFFICERS

### As at November 1780

| | |
|---|---|
| Lt. Colonel Commandant, Viscount Mountstuart | 26 Mar. 1778 |
| Major Robert Jones | 18 Nov. 1767 |
| Captain John Richards | 26 Dec. 1767 |
| Captain Edmund Traherne | 18 Nov. 1769 |
| Captain Thomas Mansell Talbot | 4 June 1777 |
| Captain John Price | 18 May 1778 |
| Captain John Popkin | 25 June 1778 |
| Captain Lieutenant John Llewelyn | 20 July 1778 |
| Lieutenant and Adjutant Samuel Sabine | 1 July 1773 |
| Lieutenant Samuel Hancorne | 4 June 1777 |
| Lieutenant John Bennett Popkin | 20 April 1778 |
| Lieutenant Reinhold Thomas Deere | 25 May 1778 |
| Lieutenant and Quartermaster Phillip Jenkins | 25 June 1778 |
| Lieutenant Lewis Jenkins | 25 June 1778 |
| Lieutenant William Gibbon | 20 July 1778 |
| Ensign Wyndham Lewis | 18 May 1778 |
| Ensign H.J. Stuart | 18 May 1778 |
| Ensign John Lucas | 25 June 1778 |
| Ensign Watkin Jenkins | 25 June 1778 |
| Ensign and Surgeon David Landeg | 25 June 1778 |
| Ensign John Jones | 25 June 1778 |

### Officers serving in May 1781 were:

| | |
|---|---|
| Lieutenant Colonel Sir Humphrey Mackworth, Bt. | 21 July, 1780 |
| Major Lewis Jenkins | 20 Oct. 1780 |
| Captain William Gibbon | 5 June 1780 |
| Captain Thomas Popkin | 20 Oct. 1780 |
| Captain John Williams | 21 Oct. 1780 |

| | |
|---|---|
| Captain Gabriel Powell | 23 Oct. 1780 |
| Capt. Lieutenant Jon Evans | 1 July 1773[4] |
| Lieutenant and Adjutant Samuel Sabine | 1 July 1773 |
| Lieutenant Samuel Hancorne | 5 July 1777 |
| Lieutenant and Quartermaster Phillip Jenkins | 20 July 1778[6] |
| Lieutenant Hon. John Stewart | 20 Feb. 1780 |
| Lieutenant John Perkins | 20 Feb. 1780 |
| Lieutenant William Gough | 20 Feb. 1780 |
| Lieutenant and Surgeon William Craig | 20 Feb. 1780 |
| Ensign Eyre Evans | 18 Mar. 1780 |
| Ensign Watkin Jenkins | 19 Mar. 1780 |
| Ensign Thomas Davies | 20 Oct. 1780 |
| Ensign John Bevan | 21 Oct. 1780 |
| Ensign William Wright | 21 Oct. 1780 |
| Ensign Christopher Hancorne | 21 Oct. 1780 |

## Officers as at February 1793
Colonel, The Viscount Mountstuart
Major Lewis Jenkins
Captain William Gibbon
Captain Gabriel Powell
Captain John Richards
Captain Lieutenant John Quinn
Lieutenant Samuel Sabine (Adjutant)[1]
Lieutenant William Jones
Lieutenant and Quartermaster John Bevan[2]
Lieutenant Thomas B. Tyndale
Lieutenant and Surgeon John Langley
Lieutenant Thomas H. Hughes
Ensign (A/Adjutant) Thomas G. Tyndale

## Officers serving as at February 1800
| | |
|---|---|
| Lieutenant Colonel Richard Aubrey | 21 April 1794 |
| Major Thomas Edmondes | 1 Nov. 1798 |
| Captain Thomas Lewis | 10 July 1796 |
| Captain Richard M. Hansard | 17 March 1796 |
| Captain Nicholas Price | 20 July, 1796 |
| Captain James Sheldon | 1 Nov. 1796 |

### Footnotes
1. Sabine was actually on Sick Leave. He was succeeded as Adjutant by T.B. Tyndale on the 12th April, 1793
2. The holding of more than one appointment by an Officer of a Militia Regiment was not unusual in those days.

| Lieutenant Richard Bates | 22 April 1798 |
| Lieutenant John Syre | 1 June 1798 |
| Lieutenant Thomas Smith | 3 August 1799 |
| Lieutenant John M. Cottle | 23 August 1799 |
| Lieutenant Charles Gearing | 24 August 1799 |
| Lieutenant George Thomas | 7 September 1799 |
| Ensign Hickman Chartres | 10 April 1799 |
| Ensign Richard Morrow | 30 July, 1799 |
| Ensign John Norcott | 1 January 1800 |
| Captain and Adjutant Martin Irving | 24 April 1797 |

The Posts of Quartermaster, Surgeon and two Ensigncies were vacant.

### Officers as at 3rd July, 1815

| Colonel Henry Knight of Tythegston | 30 April 1808 |
| Lt. Colonel Richard Morgan of Llandough Castle | 14 August 1808 |
| Major John Robinson | 16 August 1808 |
| Captain Thomas Smith | 25 July 1803 |
| Captain Richard Turberville Turberville | 5 September 1808 |
| Captain John Nicholas Lucas | 22 March 1813 |
| Captain John Jenkins Jones | 25 March 1814 |
| Captain Edward Henry Jones | 17 June 1815 |
| Captain Lieutenant John Langley (also Paymaster) | 2 May 1798 |
| 1st Lieutenant William Pelham Langley | 26 Nov. 1803 |
| 1st Lieutenant Joseph Brandon | 9 April 1806 |
| 1st Lieutenant John Rees | 8 June 1806 |
| 1st Lieutenant John Davies (also Surgeon's Mate) | 6 May 1811 |
| 1st Lieutenant Thomas Rowe | 28 Sept. 1812 |
| 2nd Lieutenant Gerald Fitzgerald | 30 Oct. 1813 |
| Captain and Adjutant William Ray | 30 April 1814 |
| Quartermaster Archer John Langley | 30 April 1814 |
| Surgeon William Hopkin | 26 August 1803 |

### Officers listed as serving with the disembodied regiment in December 1823 were:

Colonel Henry Knight
Lieutenant Colonel Richard Morgan
Captain John Thomas Smith
Captain John Nicholas Lucas
Captain Edward Henry Jones
Captain Christopher Hancorne
Captain William Groves
Lieutenant and Paymaster John Langley
Lieutenant William Pelham Langley

Lieutenant Joseph Brandon
Lieutenant John Rees
Lieutenant and Surgeon's Mate John Davies
Lieutenant Thomas Rowe
Lieutenant Gerald Fitzgerald
2nd Lieutenant John Hewitt
2nd Lieutenant Tobias Fitzgerald
2nd Lieutenant Thomas Evans Chapman
2nd Lieutenant George Puddicombe
Quartermaster George Frederick Steel
Captain and Adjutant William Ray
Surgeon William Hopkins

**Officers as at December 1826**
Colonel, The Marquis of Bute
Major Thomas Smith
Captain John Nicholas Lucas
Captain Christopher Hancorne
Captain William Robert Groves
Captain, The Lord Dudley Stuart
Captain Robert Savours
Captain Frederick Frederick
Lieutenant and Paymaster John Langley
Lieutenant Joseph Brandon
Lieutenant John Rees
Lieutenant Thomas Rowe
Lieutenant Gerald Fitzgerald
2nd Lieutenant Tobias Fitzgerald
2nd Lieutenant Thomas Evans Chapman
2nd Lieutenant William Ray
2nd Lieutenant and Surgeon's Mate James Bird
Captain and Adjutant William Ray
Quartermaster George Frederick Steel
Surgeon Richard Reece

**Officers as at December 1850**

| | |
|---|---|
| Colonel C.J. Kemeys Tynte | 2 Jan. 1849 |
| Lieutenant Colonel J.N. Lucas | 3 April 1849 |
| Major Sir Charles Morgan | 3 April 1849 |
| Captain F. Frederick | 18 April, 1826 |
| Captain H. Seymour | 5 Jan. 1827 |
| Captain J.J. Wheatley | 18 April 1832 |
| Captain J. Hewitt | 10 Feb. 1846 |
| Captain Henry Lewis | 13 Feb. 1846 |
| Captain Lieutenant and Paymaster John Langley | 2 May 1798 |

| | |
|---|---|
| Lieutenant Thomas Rowe | 28 Sept. 1812 |
| Lieutenant Gerald Fitzgerald | 17 July 1815 |
| Lieutenant Tobias Fitzgerald | 17 Feb. 1846 |
| Lieutenant Thomas Place | 23 Feb. 1846 |
| Lieutenant William Morgan Harries | 25 Feb. 1846 |
| Lieutenant Henry Goldfinch | 27 Feb. 1846 |
| 2nd Lieutenant George Chapman | 17 Feb. 1846 |
| 2nd Lieutenant Webster Austin | 20 Feb. 1846 |
| 2nd Lieutenant William Lewis | 28 Feb. 1846 |
| 2nd Lieutenant William Wyndham Lewis | 21 March 1846 |
| Captain and Adjutant J.H. Armstrong | 21 March 1846 |
| Quartermaster George Steel | 7 July 1822 |
| Surgeon James Bird | 8 Nov. 1850 |
| Asstistent Surgeon H.J. Payne | 8 Nov. 1850 |

### Officers as at October 1859

| | |
|---|---|
| Colonel C.J. Kemeys Tynte | 4 January 1849 |
| Lieutenant Colonel E.R. Wood | 29 October 1858 |
| Major John Popkin Treherne | 29 October 1858 |
| Captain H.A. Goldfinch (late H.E.I.C. Army) | 15 Nov. 1852 |
| Captain C. Deacon (late 9th Lanc. Militia) | 25 April 1853 |
| Captain R.M. Hickson (late 40th Regt) | 19 May 1855 |
| Captain H. Firth | 11 April, 1856 |
| Captain J.W.N.B. Parry (late 41st Regt.) | 3 May, 1856 |
| Captain W.B. Abbot | 7 Feb. 1859 |
| Captain G.R. Gompertz | 2 April 1859 |
| Captain J.F.N. Hewett (late 72nd Regt.) | 18 August 1859 |
| Lieutenant T. Fitzgerald | 17 Feb. 1846 |
| Lieutenant H. Burrowes | 28 Dec. 1855 |
| Lieutenant F.J. Shortis | 22 March 1856 |
| Lieutenant R.F. Evans | 30 Sept. 1858 |
| Lieutenant H.H. Spencer | 30 Sept. 1858 |
| Lieutenant J.B. Kemeys Tynte | 21 July 1859 |
| Ensign F.W. de M. Moleyns | 1 June, 1856 |
| Paymaster M.C. Maher (late R. Veterans Bn) | 14 Dec. 1854 |
| Captain and Adjutant W.H. Bennett (late 42nd Regt.) | 15 May 1856 |
| Surgeon H.J. Paine | 8 Nov. 1852 |
| Assistant Surgeon J. Evans | 8 Nov. 1852 |

### Officers (March 1863)

| | |
|---|---|
| Lieutenant Colonel Edward R. Wood | 29 Oct. 1858 |
| Major John Popkin Treharne (late 39th Foot) | 29 Oct. 1858 |
| Captain H.A. Goldfinch (late H.E.I.C.) | 15 Nov. 1852 |

| | |
|---|---|
| Captain Charles Deacon | 25 April 1853 |
| Captain Henry Firth | 11 April 1856 |
| Captain John F.N. Hewett (late 72nd Foot) | 18 August 1859 |
| Captain Richard F. Evans | 23 May 1862 |
| Lieutenant Tobias Fitzgerald | 17 Feb. 1846 |
| Lieutenant John B. Kemeys Tynte | 21 July 1859 |
| Lieutenant Martin W. Kirwan | 2 March 1861 |
| Lieutenant Bernard Byrne | 2 June 1861 |
| Paymaster Martin C. Maher (late R. Vet. Bn.) | 14 Dec. 1854 |
| Captain and Adjutant M.B. Harrison (late 62nd Foot) | 13 July 1861 |
| Surgeon H.J. Paine | 8 Nov. 1852 |
| Assistant Surgeon Wm. Taylor. MD. | 8 March 1862 |

**Officers (November 1869)**

| | |
|---|---|
| Lieutenant Colonel E.R. Wood | 29 Oct. 1858 |
| Major Charles Deacon | 4 May 1863 |
| Captain Vaughan H. Lee (Late 21st Foot) | 4 Nov. 1865 |
| Captain Robert F. Evans | 23 May 1862 |
| Captain Richard T. Roberts (late R.A.) | 28 March 1866 |
| Captain Herbert C. Gould (late 31st Foot) | 21 May 1866 |
| Captain George R. Gunning | 4 Oct. 1866 |
| Captain John D. Wedgewood (late 61st Foot) | 4 Oct. 1866 |
| Captain Lawrence Heyworth (late Lanc. Militia) | 30 July 1868 |
| Captain Jocelyn B. Fennell (late 65th Foot) | 31 Oct. 1868 |
| Captain George F. Heyworth (late 3. DG) | 7 July 1869 |
| Lieutenant Robert A. Morris | 4 July 1868 |
| Lieutenant Home S. Gordon (late 44th Foot) | 7 July 1869 |
| Lieutenant William C. James (late R. Marines) | 7 Sept. 1869 |
| Captain and Adjutant Herrick A. Palmer | 1 August 1863 |
| (late 62nd Foot) | |
| Quartermaster Francis Goodfellow (late R. Marines) | 30 Jan. 1863 |
| Surgeon H.J. Paine. MD. | 8 Nov. 1852 |
| Assistant Surgeon W. Taylor, MD. | 8 March 1862 |

**Officers (April 1873)**

| | |
|---|---|
| Lieutenant Colonel E.R. Wood | 29 Oct. 1858 |
| Major C. Deacon | 4 May 1863 |
| Major H.C. Gould | 4 May 1872 |
| Captain G.R. Gunning | 4 Oct. 1866 |
| Captain L. Heyworth | 30 July 1868 |
| Captain J.B. Fennell | 31 Oct. 1868 |
| Captain G.F. Heyworth | 7 July 1869 |
| Captain R.A. Morris | 21 June 1870 |
| Captain H.S. Gordon | 21 June 1870 |

| | |
|---|---|
| Captain W.C. James | 13 May 1871 |
| Captain Robert W. Llewellyn (late 1st Dgns.) | 22 May 1872 |
| Lieutenant Alfred T. Crawshay | 24 Dec. 1870 |
| Lieutenant James C.R. Reade (late 14 Huss.) | 1 Feb. 1871 |
| Lieutenant George Williams | 17 May 1871 |
| Lieutenant A.M.P. Kemeys Tynte | 6 March 1872 |
| Lieutenant Wm. A. Manning | 3 August 1872 |
| Lieutenant Edw. A.W.S. Groves (late Cheshire Militia) | 17 July 1872 |
| Captain and Adjutant H.A. Palmer | 1 August 1863 |
| Quartermaster F. Goodfellow | 30 Jan. 1863 |
| Surgeon W. Paine, MD | 8 Nov. 1852 |
| Assistant Surgeon W. Taylor, MD | 8 March 1862 |

## Officers as at November 1880

| | |
|---|---|
| Lieutenant Colonel H.C. Gould (late 31st Regt.) | 24 Feb. 1875 |
| Major L. Heyworth | 15 April 1874 |
| Major J.B. Fennell (late 65th Regt.) | 5 May 1875 |
| Captain G.F. Heyworth (late 5th Dgn. Guards) | 7 July 1869 |
| Captain R.A. Morris | 21 June 1870 |
| Captain J.C.R. Reade (late 14th Hussars) | 30 July 1873 |
| Captain W.H.H. Wilson | 31 Jan. 1877 |
| Captain C.S.C. Crespigny (late 41st Regt.) | 7 March 1877 |
| Captain G.L. Gwatkin (Inst. of Musketry) | 18 July 1877 |
| Captain A.H. Galland | 1 June 1880 |
| Captain R. Harrison | 1 June 1880 |
| Captain E.P. Kemeys Tynte | 26 June 1880 |
| Lieutenant B.A. Bloxsome | 23 Nov. 1878 |
| Lieutenant T. Dwyer | 11 June 1879 |
| Lieutenant P.C.B. Hervey | 11 June 1879 |
| Lieutenant S.F. White | 24 Jan. 1880 |
| Lieutenant P.H. Morris | 24 Jan. 1880 |
| Lieutenant R.T. Triscott | 26 June 1880 |
| 2nd Lieutenant S.J.L. Faddy | 24 March 1880 |
| 2nd Lieutenant H.R.B. Thurston | 12 April 1880 |
| 2nd Lieutenant F.J. Heyworth | 12 April 1880 |
| 2nd Lieutenant L.A. Lindsay | 12 April 1880 |
| 2nd Lieutenant E.H. Gilbert | 9 June 1880 |
| Captain and Adjutant B.N. Anley (41st Regt.) | 15 June 1877 |
| Quartermaster W.D. Wiltshire | 1 April 1877 |
| Medical Officer H.J. Payne, MD | 1 March 1873 |
| Medical Officer W. Taylor, MD | 8 March, 1874 |

**Officers as at September 1881**

Lieutenant Colonel H.c. Gould
Major L. Heyworth
Major J.R. Fennell
Captain G.F. Heyworth
Captain R.A. Morris
Captain J.C.R. Reade
Captain W.H.H. Wilson
Captain C.S.C. Crespigny
Captain G.L. Gwatkin
Captain A.H. Galland
Captain R. Harrison
Captain E.P. Kemeys Tynte
Lieutenant T. Dwyer
Lieutenant P.C.B. Hervey
Lieutenant S.F. White
Lieutenant P.H. Morris
Lieutenant S.J.L. Faddy
Lieutenant H.R.B. Thurston
Lieutenant L.A. Lindsay
Lieutenant F.J. Heyworth
Lieutenant E.H. St. G. Gilbert
Lieutenant E.J. Story
Lieutenant R.E. Benson
Lieutenant R.G. Lewis
Lieutenant R.P. Thomas
Captain and Adjutant B.N. Anley
                    (1st Bn., The Welsh Regiment)
Quartermaster W.D. Wiltshire
Medical Officer W. Taylor, MD


**Officers (December 1896)**

| | |
|---|---|
| Hon. Colonel. Rt. Hon. R.G. Lord Windsor | 26 Feb. 1895 |
| Lieutenant Colonel A.T. Perkins | 15 July 1895 |
| Major W. Watts | 5 May 1894 |
| Major P.S. Dowson | 18 Sept. 1895 |
| Captain E.P. Dashwood | 2 May 1895 |
| Captain S.M. Thomas | 16 March 1889 |
| Captain W. Forrest | 13 July 1891 |
| Captain C.M. Hastings | 17 Feb. 1894 |
| Captain R.W. Taylor | 26 Sept. 1894 |
| Captain H.F.W. Popplewell | 24 Oct. 1894 |
| Captain A.T. Perkins | 13 May 1896 |

| | |
|---|---|
| Captain J. Haywood | 4 Nov. 1896 |
| Lieutenant B.F. Perkins | 14 Nov. 1894 |
| 2nd Lieutenant J.T.L. Davies | 12 Dec. 1894 |
| 2nd Lieutenant A.J. Marten | 13 Feb. 1895 |
| 2nd Lieutenant G.H. Stevenson | 8 July 1895 |
| 2nd Lieutenant C.H. Hill | 22 Jan. 1896 |
| 2nd Lieutenant A.S. Mitchell | 1 Feb. 1896 |
| 2nd Lieutenant W.A. Jacomb | 5 Feb. 1896 |
| 2nd Lieutenant C.B. Benson | 28 Oct. 1896 |
| Captain and Adjutant A.H.U. Tindal (Welsh Regt.) | 15 June 1892 |
| Quartermaster T. Tinnock | 10 May 1893 |

**Officers as at September 1900**

| | |
|---|---|
| Hon. Colonel Rt. Hon. Lord Windsor | 26 Feb. 1896 |
| Lieutenant Colonel A.T. Perkins | 15 July 1895 |
| Major W. Watts | 5 May 1894 |
| Captain R.W. Taylor | 26 Sept. 1894 |
| Captain A.T. Perkins | 13 May 1896 |
| Captain J.W. Aldridge | 27 Oct. 1897 |
| Captain R.D. Stevens | 3 Sept. 1898 |
| Captain H.W. Masterman | 8 March 1899 |
| Captain E.A. Pope | 4 May 1899 |
| Captain W. Elton | 28 Nov. 1899 |
| Captain F.P. Latham | 29 Nov. 1899 |
| Captain H.H. Esplin | 10 Feb. 1900 |
| Captain D. How | 10 April 1900 |
| Captain R.P. Ryder | 24 May 1900 |
| Lieutenant D.W. Panton | 4 Dec. 1899 |
| Lieutenant A.H. Hobbs | 24 Jan. 1900 |
| Lieutenant G.H.S. Williams | 24 Jan. 1900 |
| 2nd Lieutenant E. Barker | 8 Nov. 1899 |
| 2nd Lieutenant E.R. Udal | 29 Nov. 1899 |
| 2nd Lieutenant E.A. Ellis | 4 Dec. 1899 |
| 2nd Lieutenant G. Woodfull | 11 Jan. 1900 |
| 2nd Lieutenant A.K.H. O'Brien | 12 Jan. 1900 |
| 2nd Lieutenant H.E. Berry | 19 Jan. 1900 |
| 2nd Lieutenant P.G.P. Hill | 27 Jan. 1900 |
| 2nd Lieutenant D.L. Campbell | 27 Jan. 1900 |
| 2nd Lieutenant A.K. Budge | 27 Jan. 1900 |
| 2nd Lieutenant M.O. Boyd | 10 Feb. 1900 |
| 2nd Lieutenant K. le H.M. Heath | 27 Feb. 1900 |
| 2nd Lieutenant R.B. Woosnam | 6 March 1900 |
| 2nd Lieutenant C.S. Linton | 10 April 1900 |
| 2nd Lieutenant R. Browning | 9 May 1900 |

| 2nd Lieutenant V.F. Banfield | 24 May 1900 |
|---|---|
| 2nd Lieutenant L.M. Miller | 6 June 1900 |
| Captain and Adjutant H.E. Taylor (Royal Berks Regt.) | 1 Dec. 1899 |
| Hon. Lieutenant and Quartermaster T. Tinnock | 10 May 1893 |

**Officers as at 1903**

| Hon. Colonel Rt. Hon. R.G. Lord Windsor | 26 Feb. 1896 |
|---|---|
| Lieutenant Colonel W. Watts, CB | 4 Feb. 1903 |
| Major W. Forrest, DSO | 6 June 1900 |
| Captain J.W. Aldridge | 18 April 1894 |
| Captain R.W. Taylor | 26 Sept. 1894 |
| Captain A.T. Perkins, DSO | 15 May 1896 |
| Captain R.D. Stevens | 2 Dec. 1896 |
| Captain E.A. Pope | 4 May 1899 |
| Captain W. Elton | 28 Nov. 1899 |
| Captain F.P. Latham | 29 Nov. 1899 |
| Captain H.H. Esplin | 10 Feb. 1900 |
| Captain R.P. Ryder | 6 June 1900 |
| Captain D.W. Panton | 4 Oct. 1900 |
| Captain W.s. Masterman | 3 May 1901 |
| Captain B.F. Perkins | 25 May 1901 |
| Lieutenant E.E. Ruddell | 3 May 1901 |
| Lieutenant M.O. Boyd | 23 August 1901 |
| Lieutenant C.S. Linton | 23 August 1901 |
| Lieutenant R.M. Kelsey | 5 Feb. 1902 |
| Lieutenant P.G. Mandley | 15 Nov. 1902 |
| 2nd Lieutenant H.F. Herd | 20 March 1901 |
| 2nd Lieutenant H. Furber | 17 June, 1901 |
| 2nd Lieutenant G.E. Todd | 5 Sept. 1901 |
| 2nd Lieutenant F.H. Linton | 14 Jan. 1902 |
| Captain and Adjutant H.E. Taylor (Berks Regt.) | 1 Dec. 1899 |
| Hon. Lieutenant and QM T. Tinnock | 10 May 1893 |

**Officers as at February 1908**

| Hon. Colonel Rt. Hon. Earl of Plymouth, CB | 26 Feb. 1896 |
|---|---|
| Lieutenant Colonel W. Watts, CB | 4 Feb. 1903 |
| Major W. Forrest, DSO | 6 June 1900 |
| Major R.W. Taylor | 10 June 1905 |
| Captain E.A. Pope | 4 May 1889 |
| Captain W. Elton | 28 Nov. 1899 |
| Captain F.P. Latham | 29 Nov. 1899 |
| Captain H.H. Esplin | 10 Feb. 1900 |
| Captain D.W. Panton | 4 August 1900 |
| Captain W.S. Masterman | 3 May 1901 |

| | |
|---|---|
| Captain H.F. Herd | 14 May 1904 |
| Captain R.N. Kelsey | 22 April 1905 |
| Captain P.G. Mandley | 22 April 1905 |
| Captain H. Furber | 10 June 1905 |
| Captain N.M. Biggs | 7 Feb. 1906 |
| Captain W.J. Quin | 11 Oct. 1906 |
| Captain A.C. Tucker | 20 August 1907 |
| Lieutenant J.P. Clarson | 30 April 1904 |
| Lieutenant W.H.H.H. Sargeant | 10 June 1905 |
| Lieutenant A.O. Oppenheim | 10 June 1905 |
| Lieutenant H.T. Adams | 24 June 1905 |
| Lieutenant C.F. Rowthorn | 25 August 1906 |
| Lieutenant A.G. Hayman | 25 August 1906 |
| Lieutenant H.R. Radford | 26 Sept. 1906 |
| 2nd Lieutenant A.V. Pope | 26 May 1906 |
| 2nd Lieutenant P.E.M. Richards | 14 Nov. 1906 |
| Lieutenant J.H.P. Clarson (Inst. of Musketry) | 12 May 1906 |
| Captain and Adjutant C.G. Lewes (Essex Regt.) | 11 Feb. 1905 |
| Hon. Captain and Quartermaster J. McDonald | |

# MEN ELIGIBLE FOR SERVICE IN THE GLAMORGAN MILITIA SAMPLE LIST

PARISH OF ABERDARE, CWMDARE HAMLET, (SCHEDULE B) MILITIA LIST MADE PURSUANT TO THE DIRECTIONS OF AN ACT PASSED IN THE FORTY-SECOND YEAR OF THE REIGN OF KING GEORGE THE THIRD. 12th NOVEMBER, 1819.

| NAMES RETURNED | RANK AND OCCUPATION |
|---|---|
| Hugh Jones | Smith |
| Morgan Watkin | Miner |
| Lewis Llewelyn | Hallier |
| Daniel Thomas | Labourer |
| John David | Farmer |
| Howel David | Miner |
| James Rees | Collier |
| James Rees | Collier |
| Thomas Rees | Agent |
| Thomas Jones | Miner |
| Richard Jones | Do |
| Jenkin Jones | Do |
| Phillip David | Collier |
| Thos Prichard | Do |
| Thomas Thomas | Miner |
| Morgan Rees | Do |
| William Jones | Chandler |
| Elias David | Collier |
| Richard Thomas | Farmer |
| David Morgan | Miner |
| Thomas Morgan | Do |
| Rees Williams | Collier |
| David Arnold | Miner |
| William Llewelyn | Do |
| Lodwick Jones | Mason |
| William Jenkin | Labourer |
| Amos Thomas | Miner |
| Jenkin Lewis | Collier |
| Thos Morgan | Shoemaker |
| Evan Morgan | Collier |
| Edmund Jones | Miner |
| Tho Jones | Do |
| John Williams | Smith |

| | |
|---|---|
| David David | Miner |
| David Edwards | Do |
| Thos Edward | Hallier |
| Howel Pilchford | Shoemaker |
| John Davies | Draper |
| John Jones | Weaver |
| Daniel Thomas | Miner |
| Isac Phillips | Do |
| Rees Edwards | Navigator |
| John Morgan | Miner |
| Wm. Llewelyn | Farmer |
| John Greenhouse | Sadler |
| John Thomas | Farmer |
| Henry Thomas | Shoemaker |

## PARISH OF ABERDARE, FORCHAMAN HAMLET
### 12th NOVEMBER, 1819

| **NAMES RETURNED** | **RANK OR OCCUPATION** |
|---|---|
| James James | Farmer |
| Edward David | Do |
| Howell Watkins | Do |
| Lewis Lewis | Cordwainer |
| William Amos | Farmer |
| David Llewelyn | Servant |
| Howele Howele | Farmer |
| David John Jones | Do |
| William Williams | Do |
| Lewis Jenkins | Servant |
| Thomas Edwards | Do |
| Richard Williams | Farmer |

## ABERDARE PARISH, LWYDCOED HAMLET
### 12th NOVEMBER, 1819

| **NAMES RETURNED** | **RANK OR OCCUPATION** |
|---|---|
| Edmund Parry | Farmer |
| William Parry | Do |
| Howell Price | Do |
| Rees Rees | Hallier |
| John Morgan | Farmer |
| Morgan Morgan | Do |

| | |
|---|---|
| Howell Morgan | Do |
| John Watson | Miner |
| John Watson | Miner |
| David Rosser | Do |
| David Rosser | Do |
| Thomas Morgan | ? |
| Richard Richards | Collier |
| David Richards | Collier |
| John Jones | Miner |
| Nicholas John | Blacksmith |
| Thomas Jones | Moulder |
| Benjamin Lewis | Carpenter |
| Rich Daniel | Smith |
| Thomas David | Miner |
| Jacob Edwards | Do |
| Daniel Llewllin | Do |
| Morgan Evans | Do |
| Evans Evans | Do |
| Thomas Harrison | Farmer |
| William Llew!lin | Collier |
| Richard Lewis | Publican |
| William Morgan | Cinderworker |
| William Evan | Smith |
| H? Morgan | Filler |
| R. Howell Parry | Ploughman |
| John Compton | Baker |
| Benjamin Pritchard | Hostler |
| David Lewis | Carpenter |
| Frank Wood | Moulder |
| David James | Labourer |
| Thomas Hathnal | Smith |
| ? Lewis | Farmer |
| Edward Pugh | Miner |
| Adam ?omager | Clerk |
| Watkin Rhys | Surgeon |
| Thomas Lewis | Tyler |
| David Moore | Filler |
| Harry Moore | Do |
| John Reynold | Shoemaker |
| Morgan Morgans | Miner |
| David Thomas | Collier |
| Thomas Edwards | Founder |
| Jenkin Thomas | Miner |
| William Edwards | Cinderworker |

| | |
|---|---|
| William Williams | Shopman |
| Joseph Evans | Smith |
| John Davies | Labourer |
| William Morgan | Shopman |
| William Thomas | Founder |
| Thomas Phillip | Collier |
| David Edwards | Miner |
| Thomas Griffith | Do |
| Richard Griffith | Do |
| David Llewellin | Do |
| William Griffith | Do |
| Rees Rees | Do |
| William Smith | Navigator |
| Richard Phillip | Miner |
| Richard Phillip | Miner |
| William Phillip | Do |
| John Haries | Collier |
| James Finegan | Navigator |
| Jenkin Jenkin | Miner |
| Jenkin Thomas | Collier |
| Thomas Jones | Miner |
| David Lewis | Do |
| Rees Simon | Hallier |
| Jenkin Jenkins | Miner |
| John David | Collier |
| John Jenkins | Do |
| Thomas Mirthy | Agent |
| Thomas Evans | Miner |

# PERMANENT STAFF — 3rd (MILITIA) BATTALION
## 21st JULY, 1896

| | | |
|---|---|---|
| 2417 | Sergeant Major W.P. Murphy | 'B' Coy |
| 1325 | Quarter Master Sgt. T.H. Hill | 'C' Coy |
| 521 | Sgt. Drummer W. Kelly | 'G' Coy |
| 4439 | Clr. Sgt. W.J. Weddell | 'A' Coy |
| 4001 | Clr. Sgt. J. Fidler | 'B' Coy |
| 1404 | Clr. Sgt. W. Compton | 'C' Coy |
| 5223 | Clr. Sgt. W. White | 'D' Coy |
| 2472 | Clr. Sgt. C. Nash | 'E' Coy |
| 601 | Clr. Sgt. J.A. Bryant | 'F' Coy |
| 3234 | Clr. Sgt. F. Priest | 'H' Coy |
| 2286 | Clr. Sgt. J. Kerr | 'I' Coy |
| 2689 | Clr. Sgt. W. Warmington | 'K' Coy |
| 1507 | Clr. Sgt. C. Bradley | 'L' Coy |
| 2263 | Clr. Sgt. W. Howell | 'M' Coy |
| 2739 | Clr. Sgt. W.H. Chattin | 'A' Coy |
| 822 | Sgt. W. Shears | 'B' Coy |
| 2202 | Sgt. J. Landell | 'C' Coy |
| 233 | Sgt. J. Wigley | 'D' Coy |
| 1124 | Sgt. C. Rowley | 'E' Coy |
| 536 | Sgt. W. Lewis | 'F' Coy |
| 504 | Sgt. W. Rees | 'C' Coy |
| 656 | Sgt. H. Williams | 'H' Coy |
| 1156 | Sgt. W. Smith | 'I' Coy |
| 1126 | Sgt. R. Foster | 'K' Coy |
| 677 | Sgt. L.E. Williams | 'L' Coy |
| 1298 | Sgt. Edwin Lewis | 'M' Coy |

**Drummers**

| | | |
|---|---|---|
| 4117 | Dmr. H. Higgs | 'A' Coy |
| 4866 | Dmr. F. Chaplain | 'B' Coy |
| 4938 | Dmr. W. Tucker | 'C' Coy |
| 2271 | Dmr. A. Sutton | 'D' Coy |
| 2275 | Dmr. J. Anderson | 'E' Coy |
| 4127 | Dmr. B. Clear | 'F' Coy |
| 3120 | Dmr. F.H. Shannon | 'G' Coy |
| 2272 | Dmr. E. Hery | 'H' Coy |
| 3181 | Dmr. F. Clare | 'I' Coy |
| 4939 | Dmr. W. Sergeant | 'K' Coy |
| 2507 | Dmr. A.J. Andrews | 'L' Coy |

# ROLL OF OFFICERS AND OTHER RANKS OF THE 3rd (MILITIA) BATTALION THE WELCH REGIMENT WHO PROCEEDED ON SERVICE WITH THE BATTALION TO SOUTH AFRICA ON THE 12th FEBRUARY, 1900, AND MISCELLEANEOUS MATERIAL RELATING TO THE CAMPAIGN.

Lt. Colonel and
  Hon. Colonel A.T. Perkins
Major and
  Hon. Lt. Colonel W. Watts
Captain W. Forrest
Captain R.W. Taylor
Captain A.T. Perkins
Captain I.W. Aldridge
Captain R.D. Stevens
Captain H.W. Masterman
Captain E.A. Pope
Captain W. Elton
Captain F.P. Latham
Lt. H.H. Esplin
Lt. D. How
Lt. R.P. Ryder
Lt. D.W. Panton
Lt. I.H. Nash

Lt. A.H. Hobbs
Lt. G.H.S. Williams
2/Lt. E. Barker
2/Lt. E.R. Udal
2/Lt. E.A. Ellis
2/Lt. G. Woodful
2/Lt. A.K.H. O'Brien
2/Lt. W.R. Carey
2/Lt. H.E. Berry
2/Lt. A.K. Budge
2/Lt. D.L. Campbell
2/Lt. P.G.P. Hill
2/Lt. G.E. Ruddell
Captain and Adjutant H.E. Taylor
Quartermaster
  and Hon. Lt. T. Tinnock
Civil Surgeon M. Smith

## 'A' COMPANY

458 QMS (Armourer) W. Burgess
523 C/Sgt. L.H. Davies
2285 C/Sgt. J. Kerr
2739 Sgt. W.H. Chattin
9278 Sgt. A. Addis
411 Sgt. W.D. Evans
8541 Sgt. D. Evans
9590 Cpl. I. Coombes
9508 Cpl. T. Gallivan
7150 Cpl. G. Mansell
158 Cpl. D.E. Roberts
4117 Drummer H. Higgs
9847 Pte. A. Ashman
9887 Pte. R. Astley
291 Pte. G. Badham
9618 Pte. C. Barrett
9166 Pte. W.I. Barnes
9485 Pte. J. Barwell
4305 Pte. W. Bathnell
6282 Pte. W. Barrett
484 Pte. W. Bevan
7281 Pte. A. Bowen
5560 Pte. D.J. Campbell
9943 Pte. I. Carroll
7596 Pte. G. Cooper
8157 Pte. M. Connolly
9580 Pte. G. Cook
8922 Pte. M. Coclin (Cocklin)
7759 Pte. E.W. Cross
397 Pte. T. Davies
16 Pte. D. Davies
9833 Pte. J. Davies
9570 L/Cpl. D.J. Davies
9782 Pte W. Davies
9542 Pte. M. Donovan
9462 Pte. B. Downes
9229 Pte R. Edwards
299 Pte I. Evans
9401 Pte. C. Edmunds
9650 Pte W. Francis
9313 Pte. T. George
9051 Pte. C. Green

151 Pte. D. Griffiths
9642 Pte. I.W. Griffiths
9840 Pte. I. Hancock
9478 Pte. I. Harris
9246 Pte. T. Harris
9862 Pte. D.I. Hill
140 Pte. H. Howe
9438 Pte. E. Hyde
8995 L/Cpl. E. James
197 Pte. E. James
4137 Pte. W. Jenkins
7553 Pte. I. Johnson
9312 Pte. E. John
9719 Pte. H. Jones
9211 Pte. E. Jones
9457 Pte. W.I. Jones
8510 Pte. P. Keating
5585 Pte. E. Keefe
6248 Pte. W. Knott
28 Pte. C. Markey
1921 Pte. C. Mathews
4321 Pte. T. Mills
7977 Pte. R. Millward
9097 Pte. I. Morgan
245 Pte. S. Morgan
7625 Pte. C. Nash
9402 Pte. R. Nolan
233 Pte. D. Owen
9864 Pte. W. Owen
9466 Pte. D.I. Perry
100 Pte. M. Ryan
178 Pte. E. Roberts
52 Pte. A. Russell
9321 Pte. W. Short
9678 Pte. J.C. Smith
4464 Pte. D. Sullivan
6172 Pte. I. Sullivan
7831 Pte. S. Slee
5781 Pte. D. Thomas
88 Pte. T. Thompson
9665 Pte. T. Trick
122 Pte. A. Watchman

9331 Pte. D. Williams
7431 Pte. H. Williams
3967 Pte. T. Williams*

\* Attached from Depot, The
Welch Regt. as Adjutant's Servant

## 'B' COMPANY

2417 Sgt. Major W.P. Murphy +
4001 C/Sgt. I. Fidler
 822 Sgt. W. Shears
4467 Sgt. A.G. Griffiths
8708 Sgt. T.H. John
9357 Sgt. M. O'Connor
8882 Cpl. E. Hall
  29 Cpl. I. Jenkins
9559 Cpl. T. Morgan
8991 Cpl. W. Williams
4866 Drummer F. Chaplain
8405 Pte. E.I. Branch
 275 Pte. I. Brown
9522 Pte. D. Butler
8708 Pte. E. Carlyon
4425 Pte. L. Cummins
5621 Pte. D. Cotter
9884 Pte. W. Davies
7428 Pte. T. Davies
7428 Pte. T. Davies
9405 Pte. D. Davies
 171 Pte. I. Davies
9566 Pte. G. Davies
  41 Pte. C. Duffy
9902 Pte. E. Evans
  65 Pte. D. Evans
7349 Pte. W. Forrest
  89 Pte. F. Fuller
 179 Pte. I. Gibson
8698 Pte. T. Griffiths
 150 L/Cpl. W.H. Griffiths
9965 Pte. I. Gilbert
7091 Cpl. A. Hunter
  77 Pte. I. Harding
9968 Pte. G. Harris
9304 Pte. G. Isaacs
 190 Pte. A. Isaacs

9138 Pte. M. Jenkins
9607 Pte. H. Jones
8293 L/Cpl. E. Jones
5047 Pte. T. Keeley (Keely)
9468 L/Cpl. T. Kemp
9571 Pte. I. Mahoney
9463 Pte. C. Maloney
8801 Pte. I. McCarthy
 166 Pte. H. Morgan
 168 Pte. D. Morgan
 186 Pte. R. Morgan
  72 Pte. A. Morgan
  84 Pte. E. Parry
9583 Pte. M. Philpott
 113 Pte. H. Phasey
 268 Pte. W. Price
  60 Pte. I. Phillips
 238 Pte. A. Phillis
8689 Pte. S. quantick
8750 Pte. G. Radmore
9974 Pte. R. Robertson
 219 Pte. I. Richards
9643 Pte. I. Samuels
9530 Pte. D. Shea
9305 Pte. I. Smith
9332 Pte. M.S. Sweet
9813 Pte. I. Thomas
6328 Pte. E. Thomas
6077 Pte. S. Thomas
9355 Pte. I. Thomas
 323 Pte. A. Thomas
9655 Pte. W. Todd
 212 Pte. W.H. Townshend
9792 Pte. I Turner
9835 Pte. W. Turner
7063 Pte. I Venn
5464 Pte. E. Williams

7329 Pte. F. Williams
8398 Pte. S. Williams
9280 Pte. R. Williams

246 Pte. W. Williams
9857 Pte. D. Willimas

## 'C' COMPANY

3006 QMS D. Gaughan
573 C/Sgt. W.J. Rawlings
1366 Sgt. G. Paish
9766 Sgt. E.J. Wood
8543 Sgt. W. Rosser
9644 Cpl. T. Hayes
8494 Cpl. W. Huish
9548 Cpl. D. James
9247 Cpl. D. James
9247 Cpl. D. Johns
9591 Cpl. I. Jones
5855 Drummer W. Wheeler
9176 Pte. A.I. Allen
235 Pte. W. Aston
9334 Pte. I. Bennett
9603 Pte. I. Beeke
8756 Pte. T. Barry
9903 Pte. W. Breth
9854 Pte.W. Brice
2157 Pte. I. Bryan
1076 Pte. C. Cadmore
9480 Pte. T. Collins
9397 Pte. T. Collins
8664 Pte. C. Coutanche
9861 Pte. M. Cranston
9560 Pte. E. Davies
9627 Pte. E.I. Davies
231 Pte. I.H. Davies
9786 Pte. A. Donovan
6546 Pte. — Driscolls
8910 Pte. O. Famandril
121 Pte. E. Field
7001 Pte. T. Ford
312 Pte. G. Ford
327 Pte. W. Flemmings
9281 Pte. L. Francis
8755 Pte. F. Francis

9567 L/Cpl. I. Harvey
6270 Pte. I. Hantin
9413 Pte. I. Hickey
7775 Pte. W. Howells
7720 Pte. I. Hughes
9922 Pte. R. Hughes
9651 Pte. H. Hibbard
9620 Pte. I. Iles
9772 Pte. D. James
9579 Pte. I. James
893 Pte. I Jenkins
288 Pte. E.I. Jones
9273 Pte. I. Johnson
7983 Pte. R. Jites
9793 Pte. D. Kennedy
8448 Pte. I. Lewis
9684 Pte. I. Lewis
9608 Pte. S. Lewis
8054 Pte. W. Lewis
4504 Pte. M. Lee
9523 Pte. C. Mathias
66 Pte E.I. Merriman
6270 Pte. D. Miles
8997 Pte. D. Morgan
8824 Pte. W. Nelson
247 Pte. M. O'Donnell
8086 Pte. A. Palmer
9069 Pte. W. Pugsley
90 Pte. T. Rees
114 Pte. I. Regan
42 Pte. D.J. Smith
5407 Pte. W. Smith
6057 Pte. F. Sullivan
2194 Pte. T. Sullivan
8819 Pte. I. Thomas
9632 Pte. E. Williams
7898 Pte. G. Williams

7042 Pte. I. Williams
9936 Pte. R. Williams

124 Pte. I.B. Williams
9584 Pte. G. Wynn

## 'D' COMPANY

1124 C/Sgt. C. Rowley
233 Sgt. J. Wigley
8025 L/Sgt. S. Griffiths
9958 Cpl. I. Howells
9736 Cpl. I. Rees
455 Cpl. C. Robertson
8861 Cpl. T. Watkins
107 L/Cpl. C. Barrel
9739 L/Cpl. T. Burgess
8855 L/Cpl. C. Davies
9337 L/Cpl. T. Thomas
2271 Drummer A. Sutton
4939 Drummer W. Sargeant
134 Pte. C. Burding
9731 Pte. E. Cooke
237 Pte. T. Cunningham
8074 Pte. E. Davies
8330 Pte. E. Davies
9722 Pte. W.G. Davies
7046 Pte. W. Evans
9755 Pte. W. Evans
3635 Pte. I. Green
259 Pte. G. Grey
9335 Pte.S. Griffiths
318 Pte. S. Griffiths
9378 Pte. T. Hawkins
9621 Pte. B. Hood
9609 Pte. C. Hopkins
9585 Pte. B. Howells
5318 Pte. O. Hughes
9679 Pte. M. Jackson
125 Pte. B. James
7369 Pte. T. Jones

8924 Pte. C. Lake
49 Pte. T. Lane
9486 Pte. G. Morgan
9705 Pte. B. Mock
9988 Pte. N. Morris
474 Pte. C. Newman
9230 Pte. R. Newbury
3649 Pte. W. Outley (Oatley)
254 Pte. C. Oatway
6456 Pte. D. O'Connor
192 Pte. R. O'Neil
9854 Pte. D. Parker
9807 Pte. C. Phillips
9370 Pte. R. Raymond
97 Pte. D. Rees
9690 Pte. R. Redden
9395 Pte. C. Roberts
176 Pte. I. Roberts
9447 Pte. I. Russell
9746 Pte. I. Scott
9727 Pte. R. Sheehan
9205 Pte. I. Sullivan
3132 Pte. T. Starr
13 Pte. T. Tarr
9392 Pte. I. Tanner
103 Pte. G. Thomas
9848 Pte. R. Thomas
9891 Pte. C. Thomas
9430 Pte. C. Whiting
9418 Pte. I. Williams
9058 Pte. W. Williams
9386 Pte. D. Williams

## 'E' COMPANY

579 C/Sgt. W. Evans
2150 Sgt. D. Jones
1298 Sgt. E. Lewis

9802 Sgt. F. Holloway
9240 Cpl. G. Hodge
104 Cpl. G. Price

9203 Cpl. W. Mitchell
9871 Cpl. G. Jones
  68 Pte. T. Anderson
9880 Pte. W. Allen
9271 Pte. F. Brooks
9663 Pte. F. Barry
8993 Pte. F. Burrows
9592 Pte. S. Burrows
7645 Pte. B. Callaghan
9059 Pte. W. Court
8596 Pte. A. Crandon
5928 Pte. P. Carr
6905 Pte. S. Cummings
8099 Pte. D. Davies
 325 Pte. W. Davies
 301 Pte. F. Dawson
4980 L/Cpl. D. Denner
2026 Pte. I. Donohue
9259 Pte. I. Edwards
8344 Pte. W. Evans
8700 Pte. W. Evans
  80 Pte. W. Evans
9254 Pte. W. Evans
9556 Pte. T. Evans
9586 Pte. W. Evans
 110 Pte. I. Evans
 283 Pte. W. Griffiths
6644 Pte. I. Harries
8720 Pte. W. Haycock

6217 Pte. I. Higgins
9491 Pte. H. Howells
9748 Pte. D. Jones
9525 Pte. B. Jones
9778 Pte. B. Jones
9482 Pte. A. Lewis
6864 Pte. W. Linchan
5648 Pte. D. Miles
9818 Pte. G. Morgan
5217 Pte. I. Murphy
9860 Pte. P. Murphy
9507 Pte. I. Nagle
9870 Pte. S. Owens
9513 L/Cpl. W. Pugh
 153 Pte. T. Pugh
8281 Pte. I.A. Reed
7751 Pte. H. Rice
7532 Pte. T. Richards
9117 Pte. E. Rogers
9897 Pte. A. Sims
9469 Pte. — Sullivan
5311 Pte. B. Thomas
 162 Pte. S. Thomas
9929 Pte. P. Thomas
  50 Pte. I. Thomas
7624 Pte. I. Tucker
 171 Pte. W. Vines
 238 Pte. W. Wilson
 529 Pte. I. Watkins.

## 'F' COMPANY

 601 Clr/Sgt. I.A. Bryant
1126 Sgt. R. Foster
 677 Sgt. L. Williams
5724 Sgt. — Claringbold
7554 Sgt. C. Venn
7524 Sgt. F. Hill
9360 Cpl. L. Jones
  14 Cpl. W. Phillips
  86 Cpl. D. Richards
2509 Drummer A. Andrews
9658 Pte. A. Ace

4945 Pte. N. Allman
4302 Pte. I. Ballard
9470 Pte. W. Barrett
8230 Pte. D. Barry
 272 Pte. W. Bowen
 163 Pte. C. Bull
8108 Pte. C. Bull
8108 Pte. C. Carey
9828 Pte. F. Collins
9427 Pte. W. Conway
9048 Pte. D. Davies

5262 Pte. C. Deen
9724 Pte. T. Donaghue (Donohue)
7353 Pte. D. Downey
8607 Pte. W. Ellis
9628 Pte. I. Evans
349 Pte. T. Forder
1310 Pte. T. Gray
9508 Pte. I. Gallivan
145 Pte. D. Hogan
8459 Pte. D. Jones
8868 Pte. I. Jones
93 Pte. H. Jones
2 Pte. R. King
8172 Pte. B. Llewellyn
236 L/Cpl. J. Loach
21 Pte. D. Lewis
9789 Pte. W. McCarthy
9794 Pte. J. McCarthy
9981 Pte. T. Meenig
8107 Pte. D. Mordecai
3691 Pte. M. Morgan

9717 Pte. R. Morris
105 Pte. J. Morris
7614 L/Cpl. W. Northam (Nothan)
9111 Pte. T. Osborne
7635 Pte. W. Powell
9514 Pte. M. Reardon
9560 Pte. F. Reynolds
9388 Pte. A. Russell
9544 Pte. W. Roberts
7499 Pte. J. Sheehan
5982 Pte. M. Sullivan
8758 Pte. W. Sullivan
5618 Pte. J. Thomas
7066 L/Cpl. T. Thomas
9118 Pte. J. Thomas
9249 Pte. W. Thomas
9859 Pte. D. Thomas
9260 Pte. T. Williams
7041 Pte. E. Williams
9989 Pte. E. Williams

## 'G' COMPANY

1156 C/Sgt. W. Smith
2063 Sgt. D. Lovering
5559 Sgt. H. Stockry
8614 Sgt. J. Bird
7580 Cpl. R. Bateman
9659 Cpl. D. Lawdwick
8917 Cpl. W. Leonard
9990 Cpl. D. Powell
8231 Cpl. J. Sullivan
9477 L/Cpl. T. Thomas
5025 Drummer J. Cross
8058 Pte. A. Allen (Allan)
9444 Pte. W. Amos
9576 Pte. T. Bond
9540 Pte. T. Bryant
9997 Pte. A. Burgess
8353 Pte. H. Carne
8388 Pte. T. Coleman
2585 Pte. E. Colbert
240 Pte. W. Carroll

7863 Pte. T. Davies
8746 Pte. D. Davies
966 Pte. G. Deverell
8006 Pte. W.J. Evans
173 Pte. H. Evans
278 Pte. H. Fisher
9512 Pte. J. Gallavan (Gulllivan)
34 Pte. J. Gullavan
9286 Pte. H. Harding
8073 Pte. J.H. Haskell
8206 Pte. J. Howells
9931 Pte. J. Hallasey
82 Pte. T. Hughes
251 Pte. E.J. Hopkins
285 Pte. J. Hallasey
9084 Pte. Pte. E. Jenkins
9533 Pte. T. Jones
9961 Pte. A. Jones
10 Pte. J. James
8659 Pte. W. Lewis

8907 Pte. B. Lloyd
75 Pte. D. Lewis
7601 Pte. A. Maddock
9604 Pte. F. Maloney
8885 Pte. R. Mones
8538 Pte. W. Meares (Mears)
7926 Pte. G.H. Mills
9049 Pte. J. Mounce
9437 Pte. D. Murry
118 Pte. D. Morgan
309 Pte. B. Morris
9985 Pte. E. O'Neill
279 Pte. J. O'Connor
9347 Pte. E. Parker
7765 Pte. J. Pearce

8515 Pte. D. Powell
3 Pte. A. Price
9612 Pte. E. Rexworthy
6976 Pte. J. Seymoure
9361 Pte. D. Sheehan
9675 Pte. F. Sloon
4893 Pte. E. Sullivan
9804 Pte. W. Sullivan
106 Pte. W. Smith
321 Pte. J. Stanbury
5895 Pte. W. Woolscott
137 Pte. J. Watson
177 Pte. J. Williams
9624 Pte. E. Williams

## 'H' COMPANY

3778 C/Sgt. J.E. Cadogan
2328 Sgt. E. Fowler
8642 Sgt. H. Anderson
9641 L/Sgt. R. Williams
8621 Cpl. D. Cossley
8891 Cpl. W. Sweet
8590 Cpl. T. Brook
9825 Cpl. P. McCarthy
9867 Cpl. T.M. Hussey
2272 Drummer E. Hoey
9120 Pte. N. Adams
322 Pte. A. Abraham
9781 Pte. D. Brian
9541 Pte. W. Brick
9693 Pte. W. Bunster
9838 Pte. S. Brice
7766 Pte. T. Callaghan
8154 Pte. F. Challenger
7050 Pte. J. Connelly
2175 Pte. P. Coursey
7173 Pte. S. Crowley
87 Pte. C. Cushern
8060 Pte. D. Davies
9577 Pte. H.M. Davies
9062 Pte. D. Driscoll
9686 Pte. P. Daniels

8908 Pte. R. Edwards
7243 Pte. — Fisher
9901 Pte. P. Falby
9735 Pte. G. Garratt
8994 Pte. G. Griffiths
9496 Pte. T. Hayde
9050 Pte. G. Hillier
7646 Pte. T. Hollis
229 Pte. R.J. Hughes
241 Pte. T. Harries
290 Pte. T. Jenkin(s)
7551 Pte. G. Jenkins
138 Pte. C. Jones
526 Pte. G. Jones
9557 Pte. J. Jones
8867 Pte. W. Leighfield
71 Pte. A. Leonard
15 Pte. T. Lewis
9682 Pte. J. McCarthy
35 Pte. E.T. Meadin
9805 Pte. T. Morgan
9823 Pte. J. Miles
5259 Pte. P. O'Brien (O'Brian)
165 Pte. F. Owens
9342 Pte. R. Phillips
9484 Pte. F. Pothecary

9664 L/Cpl. W. Phillips
8794 Pte. J. Reardon
9428 Pte. S. Richards
  83 Pte. D.J. Roberts
7807 Pte. W.M. Rees
 244 Pte. J. Ryan
9747 Pte. E. Sullivan
  95 Pte. B. Sansom
9182 L/Cpl. G. Spacey
8348 Pte. J. Thomas
9601 Pte. N. Thomas
9565 Pte. J. Tobin
 218 Pte. O. Thomas
9440 Pte. J. Teague

8120 Pte. W. Thomas
7489 Pte. J. Walker
7780 Pte. J. Williams
 286 Pte. C. Williams
8509 Pte. R. Williams

+ Denotes — Died on service in S. Africa

Note: As the list was transcribed from a handwritten Document, there is a possibility that the Initial 'I' may have been confused for the initial 'J' in some instances.

# Officers of the 3rd Militia Bn The Welsh Regt. who received Commissions in the Regular Army since the Embodiment of the Battalion on the 4th December, 1899, and during the South Africa Campaign

| | | |
|---|---|---|
| Lieut. A.K. O'Brien | 2nd Dragoon Guards | 12.10.1901 |
| Lieut. H.E. Berry | 3rd Dragoon Guards | 12.10.1901 |
| 2/Lieut. P.G.P. Hill | Worcester Regt. | 4.5.1901 |
| 2/Lt. P.B. Woosnam | Worcester Regt. | 7.7.1901 |
| 2/Lt. C.S. Linton | Worcester Regt. | 14.9.1901 |
| 2/Lt. L.M. Miller | E. Surrey Regt. | 27.7.1901 |
| Captain E.L. Willcox | The Welch Regt. | 9.12.1899 |
| Lt. J.F. Nash | The Welch Regt. | 21.4.1900 |
| Lt. A.H. Hobbs | The Welch Regt. | 5.1.1901 |
| Lt. D.L. Campbell | The Welch Regt. | 5.1.1901 |
| Lt. K.L. Heath | The Welch Regt. | 5.1.1901 |
| Captain G.H. Williams | The Welch Regt. | 4.5.1901 |
| Lt. E.R. Udal | The Welch Regt. | 26.6.1901 |
| Lt. E.A. Ellis | The Welch Regt. | 24.7.1901 |
| Lt. D.F. Banfield | The Welch Regt. | 4.9.1901 |
| Lt. W.R. Carey | Loyal N. Lancs. | |
| Lt. E. Barker | Middlesex Regt. | 14.9.1901 |
| Lt. A.R. Budge | Middlesex Regt. | 14.9.1901 |
| Lt. G. Woodfull | Middlesex Regt. | 14.9.1901 |

# Appointments held by Officers of the 3rd Militia Battalion, The Welsh Regiment during the South African Campaign 1900-02

*Colonel A.T. Perkins*
Officer Commanding the Battalion
Command De Aar to Prieska Convoy April 1900
Commandant Prieska
Commandant Vryburg (4 Occasions)
Commanded Kuruman Convoy Jan 1901
Commanded Takoon Column June 1901
Commanded Kuruman Column August 1901

*Lt. Colonel W. Watts*
Commandant Kenhardt May 1900
Commandant Rondesbosch Jan 1901
Commandant Wynburg May 1901
Commandant Prieska Sept. 1901

*Major W. Forrest*
Temp Commanded N.W. District
Commandant Prieska
Asst. Provost Marshall at Kimberley

*Major W. Elton*
Press Censor Capetown and Kimberley

*Captain and Adjutant H.E. Taylor*
Temp. Staff Officer N.W. District
Station Staff Officer Vryburg August 1900 to Jan 1901
Staff Officer Schweitzer Reneka Column
Staff Officer Kuruman Column

*Captain A.T. Perkins*
D.A.A.G. Transport N.W. District

*Captain J.W. Aldridge*
Commandant Kiaarpan
Railway Staff Officer Vryburg

*Captain R.D. Stevens*
Staff Officer to Colonel Milne. DSO
Kuruman Column April 1901
Garrison W.M. Vryburg

*Captain E.A. Pope*
Asst. Provost Marshall, Vryburg

*Captain H.H. Esplin*
Commandant Willowmore
Commandant Maribogo

*Captain R. Ryder*
D.A.A.G. Transport, Pretoria

*Captain D. Panton*
Staff Officer, N.W. District
Commandant Ceres
Commandant Britstown

*Captain H.W. Masterman*
Garrison Adjutant, Prieska

*Captain W.S. Masterman*
Railway Staff Officer, Vryburg

*Captain B.F. Perkins*
Asst. Provost Marshall, Vryburg

*Lt. and QM T. Tinnock*
Garrison Q.M. Prieska
Garrison Q.M. Vryburg

# HONOURS AND AWARDS FOR SOUTH AFRICA 1900-1902

*Companion of The Bath*
Major W. Watts        Hon. Lt. Colonel        London Gazette 31st Oct., 1902

*Distinguished Service Order*
Major W. Forrest                        London Gazette 27th Sept., 1901
Captain and Hon. Major A.T. Perkins        London Gazette 31st Oct, 1902

*Distinguished Conduct Medal*
RSM A.J. Bryant                        London Gazette 27th Sept., 1901
Sergeant R. Foster                        London Gazette 27th Sept., 1901
Colour Sgt. J. Fidler                        London Gazette 31st Oct., 1902

*Mentioned in Despatches*
            Lord Robert's Despatch 4th Sept., 1901
Lt. Colonel A.T. Perkins
Major W. Watts
Major W. Forrest
Captain H.E. Taylor (R. Berks Attchd.)
Captain R.W. Taylor
Captain A.T. Perkins
Captain R.P. Ryder
RSM J. Bryant
Sergeant R. Foster
Sergeant H. Davies
Sergeant W.H. Chattin
Sergeant F. Hill
Sergeant W. Huish


            Lord Robert's Despatch, 23rd June, 1902


Captain H.H. Esplin
Captain A.T. Perkins
QM and Hon. Lt. T. Tinnock
Colour Sgt. H. Fidler
Private Donoghue

# ROLL OF HONOUR
## SOUTH AFRICA
# 3rd BATTALION, THE WELSH REGIMENT

| NUMBER | NAME | RANK | DATE | PLACE | CAUSE OF DEATH |
|---|---|---|---|---|---|
| | Masterman H.W. | Capt. | 29.11.1900 | Prieska | Enteric |
| 2417 | Murphy W.P. | Sgt. Maj. | 18.3.1900 | De Aar | Dysentry |
| 29 | Jenkins J. | Cpl. | 26.4.1900 | Prieska | Enteric |
| 9968 | Harries J. | Pte. | 20.5.1900 | Prieska | Enteric |
| 9559 | Morgan T. | Cpl. | 24.5.1900 | Prieska | Enteric |
| 3691 | Morgan M. | Pte. | 25.5.1900 | Prieska | Enteric |
| 9176 | Allen A. | Pte. | 2.6.1900 | De Aar | Enteric |
| 8060 | Davies | Pte. | 14.6.1900 | De Aar | Enteric |
| 7554 | Venn. W. | Sgt. | 17.10.1900 | Prieska | Enteric |
| 7646 | Hollis. T. | Pte. | 9.11.1900 | Prieska | Enteric |
| 8638 | Griffiths E. | Pte. | 11.12.1900 | Kimberley | Enteric |
| 822 | Shears W. | Sgt. | 18.12.1900 | Prieska | Heart Disease |
| 735 | Buck C. | Pte. | 27.12.1900 | Kimberley | Enteric |
| 391 | Evans T. | Pte. | 1.2.1901 | Kimberley | Enteric |
| 162 | Thomas L. | Pte. | 10.2.1901 | Prieska | Enteric |
| 349 | Forder T. | L/Cpl. | 1.4.1901 | Vryburg | Syncope |
| 2194 | Sullivan T. | Pte. | 5.5.1901 | Van Ales Vlei | Syncope |
| 299 | Evans T. | Pte. | 30.11.1901 | Capetown | Abcsessed Live |

This Roll does not take into account those Men of the 3rd Battalion (Militia Reserve) who were killed in action or died whilst serving with the 1st Battalion, The Welsh Regiment also on service in South Africa.

# APPENDIX 5
## GLAMORGAN MILITIA

## BIBLIOGRAPHICAL, ARCHIVAL
## AND OTHER REFERENCE SOURCES

## BIBLIOGRAPHICAL SOURCES (Welsh Regiment Museum)

*Index to Military Costume Prints 1500-1914*
Army Museums Ogilby Trust, 1972

*A History of the Uniforms of the British Army, Vol.III.*
by C.C.P. Lawson. Kaye & Ward, London, 1961

*The History of The Welch Regiment* by Major A.C. Whitehorne, OBE
Western Main & Echo Ltd., Cardiff, 1932

*The Manual of Military Law* (various issues) H.M.S.O. Publications

Militia and Army Lists (various)

*The Men of Harlech* — Regimental Journal of The Welch Regiment
(various)

*Record of the Services of The Royal Glamorgan Militia*
compiled by Captain A.H. Tindal, The Welch Regiment

*Notes on the Services of the Royal Glamorgan Militia* by B. Owen
(unpublished)

*General Order Book, Royal Glamorgan Light Infantry, 1805-15*

*Diary.* 3rd Battalion, The Welsh Regiment, 1899-1902

*Order Book of a Brigade* which included The Royal Glamorgan Militia
Canterbury, 1812

# ARCHIVAL SOURCES

**Glamorgan County Records Office**

L.C.1.   Roll of Qualifications of Deputy Lieutenants and Militia Officers 1770-1779

L.C.2.   Roll of Qualifications of Deputy Lieutenants and Militia Officers 1802-1807

L.C.M.1.   Resolutions and Orders of a General Meeting held 25th October, 1804

L.C.M.2.   Lists of Militia Officers and Men 1771-1868

L.C.M.3.   Qualifications of Militia Officers 1780-1861

L.C.M.4.   Militia Commissions 1797-1861

L.C.M.5.   Monthly Return of Effectives 1868-1872

L.C.M.6.   Return of Volunteers for Militia Service in the Royal Glamorgan Light Infantry 1868-72/Royal Glamorgan Militia — Petty Bills, 1868-1878


**Glamorgan County Records Office**

**Bute Papers**

| | |
|---|---|
| D/DA.146 | Men Liable and Exempted from Militia Service Neath Hundred |
| D/DA.147 | Return of Enrolment of Men, 14th February, 1817 Neath Hundred, Parishes of Baglan, Neath Town and Cadoxton. |
| D/DA.148 | Schedule of Men Liable and Exempt Dinas Powis Sub Division. |
| D/DA.149 | Certificate of Men Liable and Exempted Caerphilly Upper Sub Division, Parish of Merthyr Tydfil, 21st November, 1816 |
| Bute XXIV | Return of Officers, 1735, 1782, 1820. (MS 4.1052) |
| Bute XXXIV | Glamorgan Militia Lists 1819-1821 (MS 4.1062) |
| Bute XXXV | Glamorgan Militia — Amended Rolls 1822-23 (MS 4.1063) |
| Bute XX | Chartism and the Militia |
| Bute XXXIII | 1/21. Amended Militia Lists December 1821 |
| | 1/22. Draft Return of Private Militia, August 1822 |
| | 1/23. Militia List 1822 |
| Bute XXXIII.3 | Lists of Men liable to serve 1819-1822 |
| Bute XXXIII.5 | Return of Enrolment 1819-1822 |
| Bute XXXIII.6 | Attestation Sheets 1820 |
| Bute XXXIII.7 | Militia Muster Rolls 1820 |
| | List of Men liable for Service in the Militia Upper Caerphilly Division 1828 |
| Bute XXXIII.1/22 | Militia 1824. Return of Numbers. |

**Glamorgan County Records Office**
*Mathew Collection*
D/DXei.          List of Men Liable for Service in the Militia 1763

*Fonmon Estate Papers*
D/DF. F141-145    Papers relating to the Appointment of Robert Jones in
                  the Glamorgan Militia


Also Documents similar to D/DA 146-149 Bute Papers


*Newspapers*
*The Cambrian* 1804-1915
*The Western Mail*
*The Cardiff and Merthyr Guardian*
*The South Wales Argus*
*The Usk Observer*
*The South Wales Daily News*
*The Hereford Journal*
*The Gloucester Journal*
*The Chester Courant*


## PAINTINGS, PRINTS, DRAWINGS AND PHOTOGRAPHS
Head-dress — Glamorgan Militia, c.1778
Loutherbourg Sketches, Plate 35. Print Room, British Library

Glamorgan Militiaman — a Coloured Print, c.1780
'Anon — The Militiaman', Plate 15.

Glamorgan Militiaman — A Coloured Plate
'A Collection of Coloured Plates — Uniforms of the various Militia Regiments,
c.1780' by John Osborne, Colonel of the Bedfordshire Regiment of Militia.
*See Journal Society for Army Historical Research*, Vol. XXXV, No.108.

The Gordon Album.
Photographs Royal Glamorgan Light Infantry Militia, Cardiff, 23rd May, 1871.
(The Welch Regiment Museum)

Album. 3rd Battalion, The Welsh Regiment.
Officers and Regimental Groups 1881-1900
(The Welch Regiment Museum)

## THE PUBLIC RECORD OFFICE

H.O.50
Home Office Military Papers relating to the Appointments of Officers to Militia Regiments in the 18th and 19th Centuries.

H.O.51
Entry Books relating to the Appointments of Officers to Militia Regiments in the 18th and 19th Centuries.

W.O.23/89-92
Register of Pensions paid to Militia Officers 1868-1892

W.O.13
Muster Books and Pay Lists of the Militia from 1780

E.182
Records of Payment to the Families of Men who served in the emodied Regiments of Militia during the Napoleonic Wars

W.O.96
Attestation Forms of Men who served in the Militia giving Dates of Birth, Place of Birth, Records of Service, 1806-1915, but mainly from the second half of the Century.

W.O.68
Miscellaneous Militia Records, including Order Books, Succession Books, Enrolment Books and Records of Officers Services.

GLAMORGAN ARTILLERY MILITIA

Brief Notes on Uniform Dress
Badges, Buttons and Appointments
Roll of Officers 1854-1908
Reference Sources

# BRIEF NOTES ON UNIFORM DRESS

In 1854, the Dress Regulations for Officers of the Militia Artillery state that "The Uniform of Officers of the Militia Artillery is to be in strict conformity with the Regulaton Patterns for the Royal Artillery, silver lace being substituted for gold lace." The rules applied similarly to the Other Ranks of Militia Artillery, who on their scarlet faced, blue Uniform Dress wore in place of silver lace, white cord or braid as appropriate. These rules appear to have been observed throughout by the Glamorgan Regiment, and in consequence there is little point in repeating here a subject which has already been studied in great depth — hence I can do no better than recommend the reader who requires more detailed information to peruse Major D.A. Cambell's 'The Dress of the Royal Artillery', 'The Militia Artillery 1852-1909' by Norman E.H. Litchfield, and 'The History of the Dress of The Royal Regiment of Artillery, 1625-1897' by Captain R.J. Macdonald, RA.

Supplementary Dress Regulations for Dress of the Officers of the Militia Artillery issued August 1853 describe the Helmet then worn by Officers of such Corps — black leather with silver ornament, white horse hair plume, with curb chain scale.

No evidence has been found to confirm that such head-dress was worn by Officers of the Glamorgan Regiment appointed in 1854 and 1855.

In June 1855, the Busby was ordered as replacement for the Shako worn by the Regular Gunners, which Macdonald tells us was being worn within a year of that date together with a Tunic which had replaced the Coatee.

Litchfield states that the Busby was taken into use by most Militia Artillery Regiments between 1855 and 1860. It was therefore almost certainly the Dress Headgear for the Glamorgan Regiment on being drawn out for its first annual training in 1857.

Other Ranks at that date wore a single breasted tunic of dark blue cloth with red collar, edged all round with white worsted cord and fastened at the front with eight white metal buttons bearing the design of three guns (horizontal, one above the other) below the Victorian Crown. Cuffs were ornamented in white worsted cord culminating in a decorative knot. The leading edge and skirts of the tunic were edged with red piping. Blue cloth shoulder straps also piped in red, carried the white embroidered titles 'Gm' over 'M.A.'

Dark Blue cloth trousers had a 1½″ red stripe down each outside leg and were worn with black boots.

A dark blue Shell Jacket was worn for Drill and Fatigue duties. The headdress in most common use during training was a dark blue round Forage Cap with white headband and white button at the centre of the crown.

Officers confined themselves in the main to Undress Uniform, similar to that of the Regular Artillery with the prescribed Militia distinctions.

Regulations of 1881 reiterated the instruction, "The dress of Officers of the Artillery Militia will conform in all particulars to the Uniform authorised for Officers of the Royal Artillery." They were also ordered to wear "a 'M' in gold metal" below the Badges of Rank on Patrol Jackets and Greatcoats, and an embroidered 'M' below the embroidered Badges of Rank on the gold shoulder straps on tunics and jackets.

By 1886, Busbies had been withdrawn from service and had been replaced by the Blue Cloth Home Service Helmet, Artillery pattern with gilded Plate and Fittings.

A photograph of a Glamorgan Artillery Militia Gunner taken c.1890, shows him wearing a Pill Box Cap with red headband. The embroidered title on the shoulder strap reads 'GLAMn'.

In 1902, Khaki Service Dress was introduced for wear by the Militia Artillery. The Officers were ordered to wear the letter 'M' in gilding metal on the collar and later on the lapels below their bronze Grenade Collar Badges.

## BADGES, BUTTONS AND OTHER APPOINTMENTS

### Busby Plume Holders

As far as is known, no distinctive Busby Plume Holder was worn by the Glamorgan Militia Artillery, the regiment confining itself to the standard silver and white metal patterns.

### Helmet Plates

Evidence from material donated to The Welsh Folk Museum supports the premise that the Other Ranks of the Regiment wore the universal pattern Artillery Militia Helmet Plates on the Blue Home Service Pattern Helmet. During a period of 40 years I have never come across a Blue Cloth Home Service Pattern Helmet, either Officers or Other Ranks to the Glamorgan

Artillery which appeared to genuinely carry an Artillery pattern Helmet Plate carrying the Glamorgan Artillery designation, but that does not prove categorically that such a plate was never worn.

The ornament on the Officers black leather Sabretache is a gilt plate of similar size to a Helmet Plate. The two examples which I have seen carried loops, as opposed to screw fittings, and were secured to the flap by strips of leather. It is my personal opinion that such items, having become separated from the original Sabretache, have quite often been mistakenly offered as Helmet Plates, as apart from perhaps some slight variation in size, and being somewhat flatter at the back than a Helmet Plate, there is little to distinguish between them.

It is my personal opinion that the Helmet Plates worn by all ranks of the Glamorgan Artillery were of a standard pattern, and that the Regimental Officers were identified in Full Dress by the ornamental flap of the Pouch and also by the flap of the Sabretache. In Undress, the gilded badge on the flap of the Undress Sabretache provided identification and in the case of Other Ranks, the embroidered shoulder strap designation.

*Embroidered Shoulder Strap Titles*
From 1882 to 1889, the embroidered title 'WELSH' to signify Welsh Division, R.A., was worn on the Shoulder Strap in gold wire by NCOs and in yellow worsted thread by Other Ranks.

From c.1889 to c.1907, a similarly embroidered Shoulder Strap Title with the wording 'GLAMn'.

*Brass Shoulder Strap Titles*
On Khaki Service Dress c.1907, a two part brass shoulder title consisting of 'R.G.A.' over 'GLAMORGAN' secured with pins and a concealed brass plate.

*Buttons*
From 1857 to 1873, Silver/White Metal Buttons bore the design of a Victorian Crown over three field guns in pale.
From 1873 to 1882, Gilt/Brass Buttons of the familiar Crown over Field Gun pattern with Victorian Crown.
From 1902 to 1909, similar, but with the King's Crown.

*Waist Belt Clasps*
As far as is known the Regiment had no distinctive pattern, but wore the standard Waist and Sword Belt Clasps of the Royal Artillery.

*Full Dress Pouch*
When part of the Welsh Division, R.A., Officers wore a Pouch with gold lace and embroidered flap carrying the Royal Arms and Gun design and with scroll inscribed 'WELSH DIVISION'.

From c.1889 to 1908, Officers in Full Dress wore a Pouch of similar design but with a scroll inscribed 'GLAMORGAN ARTILLERY'.

*Sabretaches*
It is likely that a Full Dress Sabretache was worn which carried 'WELSH DIVISION' and 'GLAMORGAN ARTILLERY' scrolls, but I have never seen an example of either type.

Black leather Undress Sabretaches exist which carry on the flap a gilded badge, similar to a Helmet Plate, the first with scroll 'WELSH DIVISION' and the second type with scroll 'GLAMORGAN ARTILLERY.'

Busby Plume Holder. Officers Pattern
Militia Artillery c.1860
*Courtesy. N. Litchfield*

Busby Plume Holders. Other Ranks General Pattern
Militia Artillery.
*Courtesy. N. Litchfield*

Ornament. Officers Undress Sabretache
Welsh Division, RA. c.1887

Pouch or Cartouche. Officers Full Dress
Welsh Division, RA. c.1887

Pouch or Cartouche. Officers Full Dress
Glamorgan Artillery Militia. c.1880

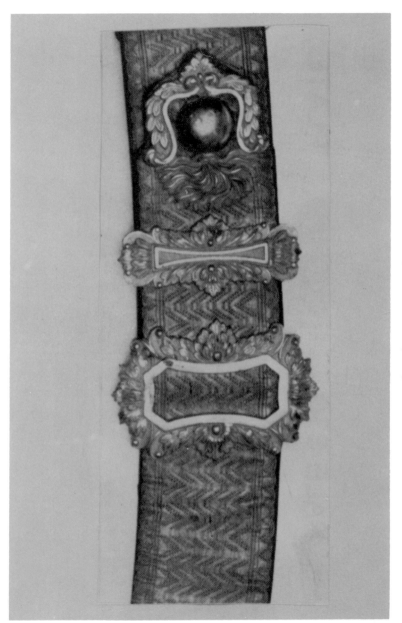

Pouch Belt. Officers Full Dress
Militia Artillery. c.1880

OFFICERS UNDRESS BLACK LEATHER SABRETACHE,
GLAMORGAN ARTILLERY MILITIA WITH GILDED BADGE, c.1896

Ornament. Officers Undress Sabretache
Glamorgan Artillery Militia. c.1896

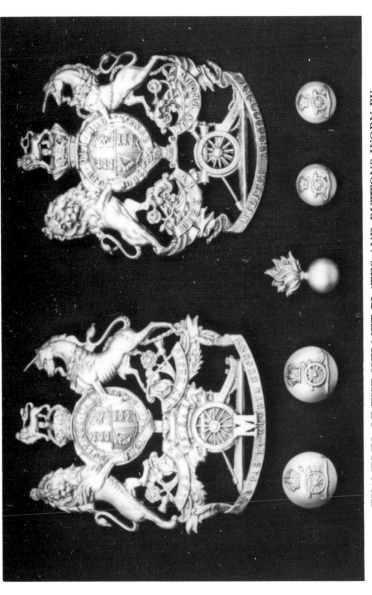

EXAMPLES OF THE HELMET PLATES AND BUTTONS WORN BY
MILITIA ARTILLERY IN THE PERIOD 1878-1908
*Courtesy of The Welsh Folk Museum (N.M.W.)*

Badge Embroidered. Officers Field Service Cap
Glamorgan RGA Militia c.1902
*Courtesy. N. Litchfield*

Shoulder Title. Brass. Other Ranks Patt
Glamorgan RGA Militia c.1907
*Courtesy. N. Litchfield*

## ROLL OF OFFICERS

*1857*

| | |
|---|---|
| Lt. Colonel Evan Morgan | 2 December, 1854 |
| Captain J. Crymes | 25 April, 1855 |
| Captain Josiah Price (late R. Marines) | 20 June, 1857 |
| Captain George Elliot Ranken | 14 October, 1857 |
| 1st Lieutenant Robert William Shortis | 21 June, 1857 |
| 1st Lieutenant Morley Dennis | 21 June, 1857 |
| Captain and Adjutant William Young | 31 January, 1855 |
| Surgeon John Paddon, MD | 9 March, 1855 |

*October 1859*

| | |
|---|---|
| Lieutenant Colonel Evan Morgan | 2 December, 1854 |
| Captain John Crymes | 25 April, 1855 |
| Captain Josiah Price | 20 June, 1857 |
| Captain George Elliot Ranken | 14 October, 1857 |
| 1st Lieutenant R.W. Shortis | 21 June, 1867 |
| 1st Lieutenant Thomas Bateman | 18 May, 1859 |
| 1st Lieutenant James Simpson Ballard | 9 June, 1859 |
| Captain and Adjutant W. Young | 31 January, 1855 |
| Surgeon J. Paddon, MD | 9 March, 1855 |

The Regiment had vacancies for three 2nd Lieutenants and consisted of three Batteries (or Companies)

*March 1863*

| | |
|---|---|
| Lieutenant Colonel Evan Morgan | 2 December, 1854 |
| Captain Josiah Pryce | 20 June, 1857 |
| Captain R.W.A. Shortis | 15 October, 1861 |
| Captain Thomas Bateman | 16 June, 1862 |
| 1st Lieutenant J.S. Ballard | 9 June, 1859 |
| Captain and Adjutant W. Young | 31 January, 1855 |
| Surgeon J. Paddon, MD | 9 March, 1855 |

At full establishment two 1st Lieutenants and three 2nd Lieutenants in addition would be listed, but such appointments were at that date suspended.

*October 1869*

| | |
|---|---|
| Lieutenant Colonel Evan Morgan | 2 December, 1854 |
| Captain J.S. Ballard | 29 April, 1865 |
| Captain John Heyworth | 12 July, 1866 |
| Captain T. Parry Horsman | 7 July, 1868 |

| | |
|---|---|
| 1st Lieutenant T.H. Ford Davies | 31 August, 1865 |
| Captain and Adjutant W. Young | 31 January, 1855 |
| Surgeon J. Paddon, MD | 9 March, 1855 |

### 1873

| | |
|---|---|
| Hon. Colonel Evan Morgan | 19 January, 1870 |
| Major James Simpson Ballard | 21 April, 1871 |
| Captain John Heyworth | 12 July, 1866 |
| Captain William E. Hughes | 30 November, 1871 |
| Captain Lewis T. Lewis | 30 November, 1871 |
| 1st Lieutenant T.H. Ford Davies | 31 August, 1865 |
| 1st Lieutenant Bartholemew P. Bidder | 1 January, 1872 |
| Captain and Adjutant F.R.G. Little, RA | 19 February, 1873 |
| Surgeon John Paddon, MD | 9 March, 1855 |

A vacancy existed for one First Lieutenant.

### November 1880

| | |
|---|---|
| Lieutenant Colonel James Simpson Ballard | 1 January, 1875 |
| Major John Heyworth | 18 April, 1878 |
| Captain William E. Hughes | 30 November, 1871 |
| Captain Robert F. Ballantine | 5 June, 1875 |
| Captain Arthur H. Richardson | 18 April, 1878 |
| Captain Charles B. Mansfield | 24 July, 1878 |
| Lieut. John Morris (Inst. of Arty) | 2 July, 1873 |
| Lieut. Sir Joseph L.E. Spearman, Bt. | 18 June, 1879 |
| 2nd Lieutenant Reginald F.R. Formby | 4 December, 1878 |
| 2nd Lieutenant Robert B. Robertson | 24 April, 1880 |
| 2nd Lieutenant Richard C. Heyworth (Supernumary) | 8 September, 1880 |
| Captain and Adjutant Francis J. Milman, RA | 24 April, 1871 |
| Medical Officer John Paddon, MD | 9 March, 1855 |

The Regiment now consisting of four Batteries had vacancies for two Lieutenants.

### September 1881

As for November 1880 but with the following changes
2nd Lieutenant Formby is no longer listed.
Richard C. Heyworth appointed Lieutenant and no longer Supernumary
Two additional Subaltern Officers are listed, viz:
R.C.E. Marriott and J.C.H.M. Jones.

**OFFICERS (as at October 1885)**
Welsh Division — 2nd Brigade (Royal Glamorgan Artillery Militia)

| | |
|---|---|
| Lieutenant Colonel W.E. Hughes | 22 April, 1882 |
| Major A.H. Richardson | 25 April, 1885 |
| Captain C.B. Mansfield | 24 July, 1878 |
| Captain J. Morris (Inst. of Arty) | 1 May, 1882 |
| Captain R.B. Robertson | 18 July, 1883 |
| Lieutenant J.C.H.M. Jones | 1 July, 1881 |
| Lieutenant C.C.T. Morgan | 22 November, 1884 |
| Lieutenant H. Colquhoun | 2 September, 1885 |
| Captain and Adjutant F.J. Milman | 1 December, 1879 |

*December 1896*
Garrison Artillery, Western Division, Affiliated Militia Artillery

*The Glamorgan Artillery*
Hon. Colonel,

| | |
|---|---|
| The Earl of Dunraven and Mountearl, KP | 17 April, 1895 |
| Lieutenant Colonel J.R. Wright | 28 November, 1894 |
| Major R.B. Robertson | 18 April, 1896 |
| Captain C.C.P. Stoughton | 31 December, 1887 |
| Captain E.J. Evans | 29 August, 1891 |
| Captain L.E.H. Humfrey | 23 October, 1895 |
| Captain S.G.V. Harris | 23 October, 1895 |
| Lieutenant G.W.A. Lloyd | 19 April, 1890 |
| Lieutenant K.L. Bath | 24 October, 1891 |
| Lieutenant R.M. Daniel | 4 June, 1894 |
| Lieutenant W.C. Wright | 1 June, 1890 |
| 2nd Lieutenant C.D. Williams | 18 December, 1895 |
| 2nd Lieutenant D. Burges | 4 March, 1896 |
| Captain and Adjutant E.D.R. Buckley, RA | 2 December, 1891 |

*September 1900*

| | |
|---|---|
| Hon. Colonel Earl of Dunraven and Mountearl, KP | 17 April, 1895 |
| Lieutenant Colonel J.R. Wright | 28 November, 1894 |
| Major S.G.V. Harris | 29 November, 1899 |
| Captain E.J. Harris | 29 August, 1891 |
| Captain L.E.H. Humfrey | 23 October, 1895 |
| Captain W.C. Wright | 28 December, 1898 |
| Captain C.D. Williams | 29 November, 1899 |
| Lieutenant H.W. Boer | 9 July, 1900 |
| Lieutenant C.W.H. Skinner | 9 July, 1900 |
| Lieutenant H.A. Hildebrand | 9 July, 1900 |

Lieutenant E.M. Peel                                    9 July, 1900
2nd Lieutenant P.E. Blackmore                           11 April, 1900
2nd Lieutenant C.G.F. Loder                             29 May, 1900
No Adjutant listed


*1903*
Hon Colonel, The Earl of Dunraven and Mountearl, K.P.17 April, 1895
Lieutenant Colonel John Roper Wright                    28 November, 1894
Major Sampson G.V. Harris                               29 November, 1899
Captain Eliezer Jones Evans                             29 August, 1891
Captain Lorn E.H. Humfrey (late R. Garrison Regt.)      23 October, 1895
Captain Rowland M. Daniel                               6 April, 1898
            (late British S. Africa Police)
Captain William C. Wright                               28 December, 1898
Captain Charles Digby Williams                          29 November, 1899
Captain (Hon. Major) Harry G. Hodgkinson                9 January, 1901
Lieutenant Harold White Beor                            9 July, 1900
Lieutenant Egerton Morton Peel                          9 July, 1900
Lieutenant Phillip E. Blackmore                         25 August, 1900
            (late R. Garrison Regt.)
Lieutenant William Frederick R. Kyngdon                 29 January, 1902
2nd Lieutenant Harold J.B. Heelas                       4 January, 1902
2nd Lieutenant Rhys Penderill Charles                   28 May, 1902
Captain and Adjutant J.A. Fitzgibbon, RA                13 December, 1900


*February 1908*
*Glamorgan Royal Garrison Artillery (Militia)*

Hon. Colonel, Earl of Dunraven and Mountearl, KP        17 April, 1895
Lieutenant Colonel William C. Wright                    1 May, 1907
Captain R.M. Daniel                                     6 April, 1898
Captain C.D. Williams                                   29 November, 1899
Captain E.M. Peel                                       26 May, 1906
Captain E.G.L. Cullum                                   23 June, 1906
Captain S.J. Fowler                                     18 August, 1906
Lieutenant A.H. Peiniger                                23 June, 1906
Lieutenant T.J. Sheild                                  23 June, 1906
2nd Lieutenant C.P.L. Marwood                           24 January, 1906
2nd Lieutenant H.E. de R. Wetherall                     23 February, 1906
2nd Lieutenant R.C. Evans                               12 November, 1906
No Adjutant listed

# GLAMORGAN ARTILLERY MILITIA
## ESTABLISHED STRENGTH AND NUMBERS ENROLLED 1868-1907

| YEAR | ESTABLISHMENT | NUMBERS ENROLLED |
|------|---------------|------------------|
| 1868 | 325 | 189 |
| 1871 | 325 | 250 |
| 1877 | 414 | 380 |
| 1880 | 414 | 404 |
| 1882 | 414 | 387 |
| 1885 | 414 | 366 |
| 1889 | 414 | 365 |
| 1894 | 413 | 406 |
| 1900 | 430 | 396 |
| 1902 | 413 | 419 |
| 1907 | 413 | 397 |

## MILITIA ARTILLERY
**RATES OF PAY** *(extracted from the Militia Regulations 1853)*

**Daily Rates when Training or Embodied**

| | |
|---|---|
| Colonel | £1.2.6. |
| Lt. Colonel | 15.11 |
| Major | 14.1 |
| Captain | 10.6 |
| Lieutenant | 6.6 |
| Ensign | 5.3 |
| Adjutant | 1.0 (additional to disembodied Pay) |
| Quartermaster | 6.6 |
| Surgeon | 11.4 |
| Asst. Surgeon | 5.0 |
| Sergeants | 2.6 |
| Corporals | 1.2 Farthing |
| Gunners | 1.0 |

**Permanent Staff** *(in addition to disembodied Pay)*

| | |
|---|---|
| Sergeant Major | 6d |
| Quartermaster Sergeant | 4d |
| Paymaster Sergeant | 4d |
| Sergeants | 4d |
| Trumpeters | 1d |

## REFERENCE SOURCES

**Public Record Office and Glamorgan County Records**
Such information as exists will be found under the same headings as have been given for the Royal Glamorgan Light Infantry.

**Bibliographical**
Jackson-Hay. *The Constitutional Force*
Lichfield. N. *The Militia Artillery*

*The Army Lists*
Barret. J.H. — *A History of the Maratime Forts in the Bristol Channel 1866-1900.*
Jones. K.W.M. — *History of the Coast Artillery in the British Army* R.A. Inst. 1959.
Campbell. D.A. — *The Dress of The Royal Artillery*
Macdonald. R.J. — *The History of Dress of the Royal Regiment of Artillery 1625-1897*

**Articles**
Pinsent. M. — *The Defences of the Bristol Channel* in the last two Centuries
Misc — *The Journal of the Society for Army Historical Research*
Mics — *The Navy and Army Gazette*

**Newspapers**
As listed under Royal Glamorgan Light Infantry Militia The South Wales Newspapers, *Cambrian* and *Cardiff and Merthyr Guardian* were amongst the most fruitful sources for search on the activities of this Regiment.

# INDEX

269